D0689422

LESSONS FOR INTRODUCING DIVISION

GRADES 3-4

UNIVERSITY of NORTHERN
BRITISH COLUMBIA
LIBRARY
Prince George, B.C.

THE TEACHING ARITHMETIC SERIES

Fall 2001

Lessons for First Grade
Lessons for Addition and Subtraction, Grades 2–3
Lessons for Introducing Multiplication, Grade 3
Lessons for Extending Multiplication, Grades 4–5
Lessons for Introducing Fractions, Grades 4–5

Fall 2002

Lessons for Introducing Place Value, Grade 2
Lessons for Introducing Division, Grades 3–4
Lessons for Decimals and Percents, Grades 5–6

Fall 2003

Lessons for Extending Division, Grades 4–5
Lessons for Extending Fractions, Grades 5–6

Fall 2004

Lessons for Extending Place Value, Grade 3

Teaching ARITHMETIC

LESSONS FOR
INTRODUCING
DIVISION

▲▲▲▲▲

GRADES 3-4

MARYANN WICKETT
SUSAN OHANIAN
MARILYN BURNS

MATH SOLUTIONS PUBLICATIONS
SAUSALITO, CA

Math Solutions Publications
A division of
Marilyn Burns Education Associates
150 Gate 5 Road, Suite 101
Sausalito, CA 94965
www.mathsolutions.com

Copyright © 2002 by Math Solutions Publications

All rights reserved. Limited reproduction permission: The publisher grants permission to individual teachers who have purchased this book to reproduce the Blackline Masters as needed for use with their own students. Reproduction for an entire school or school district, or commercial or any other use, in any form or by any means, electronic or mechanical, including photocopying and recording, or by any information storage and retrieval system, is prohibited without written permission from the publisher, except for the inclusion of brief quotations in a review.

Library of Congress Cataloging-in-Publication Data

CIP is on file with the Library of Congress

Editor: Toby Gordon
Production: Melissa L. Inglis
Cover & interior design: Leslie Bauman
Composition: Cape Cod Compositors, Inc.

Printed in the United States of America on acid-free paper
06 05 04 03 02   ML   1 2 3 4 5

A Message from Marilyn Burns

We at Marilyn Burns Education Associates believe that teaching mathematics well calls for increasing our understanding of the math we teach, seeking greater insight into how children learn mathematics, and refining lessons to best promote children's learning. Math Solutions helps teachers achieve these goals by providing professional development through inservice courses and publications.

Our publications include a wide range of choices, from books in our new Teaching Arithmetic and Lessons for Algebraic Thinking series to resources that link math and literacy; from books to help teachers understand mathematics more deeply to children's books that help students develop an appreciation for math while learning basic concepts.

Our inservice offers five-day courses, one-day workshops, and series of school-year sessions throughout the country, working in partnership with school districts to help implement and sustain long-term improvement in mathematics instruction in all classrooms.

To find a complete listing of our publications and workshops, please visit our Web site at *www.mathsolutions.com*. Or contact us by calling (800) 868-9092 or sending an e-mail to *info@mathsolutions.com*.

We're eager for your feedback and interested in learning about your particular needs. We look forward to hearing from you.

A DIVISION OF MARILYN BURNS EDUCATION ASSOCIATES

CONTENTS

ASSESSMENTS

BLACKLINE MASTERS

INDEX

INTRODUCTION

Originally published in 1995, *Math By All Means: Division, Grades 3–4* was the collaborative success of Marilyn Burns, Joanne Lewin, Susan Ohanian, Bonnie Tank, Leyani von Rotz, Lynne Zolli, and numerous teachers in Tucson, Arizona, and San Francisco, California, who tried the activities in the book with their students and provided feedback. Over the years, we've had time to reflect and explore new ideas. Others have joined the conversation, most key among them Eunice Hendrix–Martin, Carol Scurlock, and Maryann Wickett, who teach in San Marcos, California. And, of course, there are the children. It's both for them and because of them that this book exists. The children in the classes where these lessons have been taught have done their best work, thought hard, and shared their thinking openly and honestly. They have collaborated with us as we have with each other.

As is typically the case, before students begin to study a new topic, I ask them to share what they already know about it. In this case, I asked, "What is division?"

"It's the opposite of multiplication," Seth reported.

Eliza said, "You can divide things in half."

Mason added, "I think things have to be in equal groups, but I'm not sure."

Belinda raised her hand and expressed her anxiety about division being hard and said she didn't know anything about it.

These responses are typical of students just beginning their study of division. Later, after working through the activities in this book, I again asked the students, "What is division?" This time I asked children to write.

Belinda, who had expressed her anxiety about division in the beginning, wrote:

Division is something you could divide in equal groups (or parts). Division sometimes have remainders but not always. Division and multiplication are kind of the same because they are backwards and forwards. For example, 4 × 2 = 8, 8 ÷ 2 = 4. If they have 8 cookies then each person gets 4 cookies.

Belinda had moved from uncertainty to grasping several important concepts about division.

Mason wrote:

Division is dividing the first number into groups of the second number for example If you had 6 bugs and 6 bug cages and you want to make it even so all of the cages got the same amount of bugs how many bugs would each cage get? each cage would get one bug.

Mason demonstrated he understood that division involves equal groups and he could apply this knowledge when writing a story problem.

Eliza wrote:

Division is or can be a backwards multiplication problem (7 × 2 = 14, 14 ÷ 2 = 7). In division you try to divied things equaly but you can have remainders (7 ÷ 6 = 1 R1). You can write division 3 different ways ($8\overline{)7}^{\,1R1}$ $\frac{8}{7}$ = 1 R1 or 8 ÷ 7 = 1 R1). You can also use fractions in division.

While Eliza made an error in her first representation, reversing the dividend and divisor, the rest of her paper indicated strong understanding of the basic concepts of division. She understood the link between multiplication and division and realized that division involves equal groups and can have remainders.

These are a few examples of the kind of growth that can occur when students collaborate and engage in mathematical activities that are meaningful and interesting to them.

Goals for Division Instruction

Division is an important focus of third- and fourth-grade mathematics instruction. Instruction continues into the fifth grade, but the third and fourth grades are key for establishing a firm foundation of understanding and skills. Students with a firm foundation in division should be able to

▲ explain that division involves equal groups;
▲ recognize the two types of division problems—sharing, or partitioning, and grouping—and be able to think flexibly about both;
▲ represent remainders in different ways, choosing a representation that is appropriate within the context of the problem being solved;
▲ represent division problems symbolically in three ways—12 ÷ 2 = 6, $2\overline{)12}^{\,6}$, and $\frac{12}{2}$ = 6;
▲ calculate quotients up to 144 ÷ 12;
▲ interpret division in real-world situations;
▲ solve problems that involve division; and
▲ explain how division relates to multiplication.

Traditionally, instruction in division has focused on two objectives: learning the division facts and developing computational fluency. These are important goals, and reaching them calls for developing in children firm understanding of the concept of division and how division relates to the other operations. Time spent on laying the foundation of understanding is critical for children's later proficiency. Also, students should be able to compute mentally as well as with paper and pencil. They should know when an answer is reasonable and be able to make sense of remainders. The lessons in this book address these broader goals and support students' growth toward proficiency based on understanding.

Two Models of Division

Children informally use division long before they receive any formal instruction. Their early experiences are with two different types, or models, of division. One model of division calls for sharing, such as dividing twenty marbles among four friends and seeing that each person gets five marbles; the second model of division calls for dividing a number into equal-size groups, such as cutting out twenty paper petals, gluing four petals to a flower, and seeing how many flowers there are.

For the first type of division, known as *sharing* or *partitioning*, children typically divide objects by doling them out, one by one, until there aren't any more or there aren't enough for another round. For example, if they want to share twenty marbles among four children, they can give them out, one to a child, until each child has five marbles. Similarly, when organizing a class of twenty-eight students into two teams, children usually assign players one at a time, first to one team, and then to the other, ultimately dividing the class into two groups with fourteen children in each. In sharing situations, the *size of the total amount* and the *number of shares* are known; what's unknown is the *size of each share*. In a real situation, the children can solve the problem concretely. Solving the problem numerically, however, calls for an understanding of multiplication that allows children to answer the question "Four times what number equals twenty?" or "Two times what number equals twenty-eight?"

The other interpretation of division, called *grouping*, calls for splitting a number into equal-size groups. For example, using twenty paper petals to make flowers with four petals on each calls for gluing the petals in groups of four. Organizing a class of twenty-eight students into pairs involves forming groups of two until all children have been accounted for. As in sharing situations, in a grouping problem, the *size of the total amount* is known. However, also known is the *size of each group* and the unknown is the *number of groups*.

Although sharing and grouping problems call for different interpretations, the word *division* is used for both, and they can be represented the same way numerically. For example, assigning twenty-eight players to two teams or organizing twenty-eight students into pairs can both be recorded thus:

$$28 \div 2 = 14 \ or \ \ 2\overline{)28}^{\,14} \ or \ \tfrac{28}{2} = 14$$

In the sharing situation, the fourteen is the result of "twenty-eight students divided into *two groups*"; in the grouping situation, the fourteen is the result of "twenty-eight students divided into *groups of two*."

Children should have many experiences with both types of division. Their power with division increases when they begin to understand the connection between sharing and grouping and they are able to connect both types of division with the other operations of addition, subtraction, and multiplication.

Concentrating instruction on teaching children the algorithm for calculating answers to all division problems is not only a narrow approach to division instruction but also runs the risk of having students misinterpret division as an operation with a unilateral interpretation. Classroom instruction should focus on giving children a variety of division problems of both types to solve, with and without remainders, helping them both to relate sharing to grouping and to use their knowledge of the other operations to explore both types of division. The goal of instruction is to uncover the idea of division in its full complexity, not to cover the idea merely from a view toward algorithmic proficiency.

About Representing Division Symbolically

The lessons in this book include three ways to represent division symbolically. Children see division represented with the use of the familiar division symbols, $\div$ and $\overline{)}$, in addition to seeing division represented using fractional notation. Using fractional notation helps children understand there's an important relationship between fractions and division.

You'll notice in this book that a remainder of zero is often represented by R0. This is not conventional notation, nor is it essential. However, it's helpful for some children as they are developing understanding. The choice to use it or not should be made by you based on what makes sense for your students.

Division by Zero

Division with zero is undefined and complicated for children to understand. There are several ways to think about what happens when you divide a number by zero. For example, think about a simple division statement, such as $12 \div 3 = 4$. Because division is the inverse of multiplication, we can multiply to verify the answer: $4 \times 3 = 12$. If you multiply the answer to the division problem (the quotient) by the divisor, you should get the number you started with (the dividend). Here are some examples:

$12 \div 12 = 1$ $1 \times 12 = 12$

$12 \div 6 = 2$ $2 \times 6 = 12$

$12 \div 4 = 3$ $3 \times 4 = 12$

$12 \div 3 = 4$ $4 \times 3 = 12$

$12 \div 2 = 6$ $6 \times 2 = 12$

$12 \div 1 = 12$ $12 \times 1 = 12$

Now suppose you were trying to solve $12 \div 0$. Typically, children think the answer should be zero, but it doesn't check!

$12 \div 0 = 0$ $0 \times 0 = 0$

Actually, no matter what answer you get, if you try to check it by multiplying, you run into difficulty, because zero times any other number gives zero. Nothing will work. Here are some examples:

$12 \div 0 = 1$ $1 \times 0 = 0$ No

$12 \div 0 = 2$ $2 \times 0 = 0$ No

$12 \div 0 = 3$ $3 \times 0 = 0$ No

$12 \div 0 = 4$ $4 \times 0 = 0$ No

$12 \div 0 = 6$ $6 \times 0 = 0$ No

$12 \div 0 = 12$ $12 \times 0 = 0$ No

Here's another way to try to understand the difficulty of dividing by zero. In the examples showing twelve divided by different numbers listed in the first set of problems, twelve was divided by a smaller number each time, and the resulting answers got larger. This makes sense because dividing a number into fewer parts will produce more in each part. Continuing the pattern of dividing twelve by smaller and smaller numbers requires thinking about fractional divisors. Still, the pattern of increasing answers continues:

$$12 \div 12 = 1$$
$$12 \div 6 = 2$$
$$12 \div 4 = 3$$
$$12 \div 3 = 4$$
$$12 \div 2 = 6$$
$$12 \div 1 = 12$$
$$12 \div \tfrac{1}{2} = 24$$
$$12 \div \tfrac{1}{3} = 36$$
$$12 \div \tfrac{1}{4} = 48$$
$$12 \div \tfrac{1}{6} = 72$$
$$12 \div \tfrac{1}{12} = 144$$
$$12 \div \tfrac{1}{100} = 1,200$$
$$12 \div \tfrac{1}{1,000} = 12,000$$
$$12 \div \tfrac{1}{1,000,000} = 12,000,000$$

Dividing by one-one millionth is an example of dividing by a very small divisor. It's not as small as zero, of course, but it's closer to zero than the others on the list. Looking at the list of those division examples reveals several patterns:

1. The dividend is constant; it is always 12.
2. The divisors get smaller and smaller, getting closer and closer to zero.
3. The closer the divisor gets to zero, the larger the answer gets.
4. If the divisor reached zero, the answer would probably be enormous.

This leads to the conclusion that as the divisor approaches zero, the answer approaches infinity. This discovery isn't particularly helpful or useful, however, since no matter how large the answer is, it still won't check when you multiply it by the divisor of zero. Mathematicians have agreed that division by zero is "undefined," which means the division has no answer that makes any sense, so we can't do it.

Investigating $0 \div 0$, however, seems to present a different situation. Just as no number works for an answer to $12 \div 0$ (or any number divided by zero), it seems that it's possible to solve $0 \div 0$ and check it:

$$0 \div 0 = 0 \qquad\qquad 0 \times 0 = 0$$

However, that system of checking division by multiplying makes any answer to $0 \div 0$ correct!

$0 \div 0 = 0$	$0 \times 0 = 0$
$0 \div 0 = 1$	$1 \times 0 = 0$
$0 \div 0 = 2$	$2 \times 0 = 0$
$0 \div 0 = 50$	$50 \times 0 = 0$
$0 \div 0 = 600$	$600 \times 0 = 0$
$0 \div 0 = 1,000$	$1,000 \times 0 = 0$

Having any answer work is as problematic as having no answer work. So you just can't divide by zero.

Explaining this to elementary school children can be tough. Some students may be fascinated by this sort of thinking; some will be confused; others will be completely disinterested. If you decide to offer an explanation, be sure to do so with a light touch. Quit if students' eyes seem to glaze over and offer to continue with only those who are interested.

About Calculator Use

We assume that calculators are available to students along with paper, pencils, rulers, and other general classroom supplies. In our experience, we've found that while some children find calculators interesting and are fascinated by them, many other children tend to ignore them. However, even though we like children to regard calculators as tools to help them solve mathematics problems, there are times when we ask students not to use a calculator but instead to find a way to solve a particular problem on their own.

Most of the division problems in this book are within the grasp of students to solve without the assistance of a calculator, but students may encounter a few that are beyond their grasp, most often problems the children write themselves. In those instances, using a calculator allows access and further exploration of a problem. One of our goals is to help students recognize when they can solve a problem themselves and when a calculator can give them greater access and understanding.

For students to use calculators appropriately and efficiently, they must correctly interpret what the problem is asking. This means they must be able to determine which numbers to use and the required operation or operations. In addition, they must be able to determine if the calculator answer makes sense numerically and if the solution makes sense in the context of the situation. For example, a calculator answer of 2.5 makes sense when talking about cookies, but not when talking about marbles. An answer of 2.6723421 doesn't make sense for either cookies or marbles.

Many students find the problems in this book appropriately challenging and enjoy solving them with just the materials and paper and pencil. To ask these students to use a calculator would be imposing a tool on them when they have other means of solving the problem. It's important that students make their own choices when determining the tools needed, including calculators, to solve problems.

We routinely ask students to interpret and make sense of their answers whether or not they used a calculator. If the student can't explain an answer, that child must find another way to solve the problem so that he or she can explain the answer in a way that shows understanding.

What's in This Book?

The inspiration for this book was the Math By All Means unit *Division, Grades 3–4*, published in 1995. Since then we've learned much about teaching division, from our individual teaching experiences, from our collaboration in revisiting the lessons from the original unit and working on the new lessons in this book, and from feedback from teachers who have used the initial unit in their classrooms. The changes reflect what we've learned.

This book includes practically all of the lessons and assessments from the initial unit, some reorganized and others with additions and edits. Four completely new lessons are included in this book, in addition to four new assessments. One new children's book has been included.

The Structure of the Lessons

In order to help you with planning and teaching the lessons in this book, each is organized into the following sections:

Overview To help you decide if the lesson is appropriate for your students, this is a nutshell description of the mathematical goal of the lesson and what the students will be doing.

Materials This section lists the special materials needed along with quantities. Not included in the list are regular classroom supplies such as pencils and paper. Worksheets that need to be duplicated are included in the Blackline Masters section at the back of the book.

Time Generally, the number of class periods is provided, sometimes with a range allowing for different-length periods. It's also indicated for some activities that they're meant to be repeated from time to time.

Teaching Directions The directions are presented in a step-by-step lesson plan.

Teaching Notes This section addresses the mathematics underlying the lesson and at times provides information about the prior experiences or knowledge students need.

The Lesson This is a vignette that describes what actually occurred when the lesson was taught to one or more classes. While the vignette mirrors the plan described in the teaching directions, it elaborates with details that are valuable for preparing and teaching the lesson. Samples of student work are included.

Extensions This section is included for some of the lessons and offers follow-up suggestions.

Questions and Discussion Presented in a question-and-answer format, this section addresses issues that came up during the lesson and/or have been posed by other teachers.

Although they are organized similarly, the lessons presented here vary in several ways. Some span one class period, others take longer, and some are suitable to repeat over and over, giving students a chance to revisit ideas and extend their learning. Some use manipulative materials, others ask students to draw pictures, and others ask students to rely on mental reasoning. And while some lessons seem to be more suited for beginning experiences, at times it's beneficial for more experienced students to engage with them as well. An activity that seems simple can reinforce students' understanding or give them a fresh way to look at a familiar concept. Also, a lesson that initially seems too difficult or advanced can be ideal for introducing students to thinking in a new way.

How to Use This Book

Teaching the lessons described in the fifteen chapters requires at least twenty-three days of instruction, not including time for repeat experiences, as recommended in some lessons, or for the ideas for extensions suggested at the end of most lessons, or for the assessment ideas suggested at the end of the book. While it's possible to spend a continuous stretch of five or more weeks on these lessons, we don't think that's the best decision. In our experience, children require time to absorb concepts, and we would rather spend a three-week period and then wait two months or so before returning for another three-week period, or arrange for three chunks of time, each two weeks or so, spaced throughout the year. When students return to ideas after a break, they bring not only the learning they've done in other areas but also a fresh look that some distance can provide.

The three introductory lessons in the book build the foundation for developing understanding, and we suggest that you not skip these lessons. The other lessons are categorized into different aspects of division. Experiences in each of the categories are beneficial for students, but no particular sequence of categories is best. However, the chapters within each category are placed in an order that reflects our experience teaching these lessons in several classes. A section on assessments at the end of the book will help you think about making assessment an integral part of division instruction.

Throughout the lessons, we ask children to work with a partner. There are many ways to assign partners. Some teachers have children change partners every day, while others have their students keep the same partner throughout a unit of study. In some classrooms, children choose their own partners, while in others, partners may be assigned randomly, by drawing names as an example, or the teacher may assign children to be partners. Some teachers simply have students work with the person sitting beside or across from them. There are a variety of ways to do this and what works best with one group of children may not be the best way for another group.

Because student participation is key to learning, we expect students to share their thinking throughout the lessons in this book. Students present their ideas in whole-class discussions, complete individual writing assignments, and talk in small groups, often preceded with a form of pair sharing called dyads. The use of dyads is based on the work of Dr. Julian Weissglass, a mathematics professor at the University of California at Santa Barbara. A dyad is an opportunity for all children to be listened to by another and for all children to listen. The following are the basic guidelines for using dyads:

▲ Each person is given equal time to share and listen.
▲ The listener doesn't interrupt the person who is talking. The listener also doesn't give advice, analyze, or break in with personal comments.
▲ The listener doesn't share what the talker has said with anyone else. This confidentiality allows children to more fully explore their ideas without fear of being ridiculed or having their mistakes shared publicly.

It has been our experience that using these rules has given shy, less verbal children more opportunity to voice their ideas. In many cases, as these students gain confidence by sharing in a safe environment, they share more in class discussions, which often results in deeper thinking and understanding of the mathematics along with increased confidence. Using dyads frequently also helps keep more students engaged in the learning process.

Some children are more willing to share ideas than others. It's important, however, that all students learn to participate fully in our math classes. To facilitate this, we do the following:

▲ We make it a part of the classroom culture and our expectations that all students are capable and can think. They are expected to think and always do their best. Anything less in not acceptable.

▲ We support students by using our behavior as a model. We're constantly thinking and exploring ideas with them. We don't expect them to believe that we know everything—we don't!

▲ To support students' thinking and development of strategies to use, we pose a question and then give students a few moments of quiet "think time," when all students are expected to focus their attention.

▲ After students have a few moments to form their own thoughts, we often use a form of pair sharing called dyads, as described previously.

▲ Class discussions play a big role in our teaching. Before beginning a class discussion, we provide students the opportunity to think about the topic at hand, through think time, a written assignment, or a dyad. When students come to a class discussion prepared, the discussion is more lively and interesting and provides more opportunity for both the students and us to learn.

▲ In class discussions, students usually share strategies that they have used. We record these strategies on the chalkboard or some other highly visible place in the classroom, giving students a reference list of ideas.

As effective as this last strategy is, occasionally a student will still get stuck. In this instance, it often helps to ask a question such as the following:

"How might you begin?"

"What do you think the problem is asking you to do?"

"What would happen if . . . ?"

"Can you draw a picture that represents the problem or find a pattern?"

"Can you think of a smaller, similar problem?"

Our role as teachers is to be supportive and encouraging of all students. Listening carefully with a curious attitude about what children have to say is one way. Writing their responses on the board or a chart during a class discussion is another way. Responding to their thinking with probing questions is another way still. When teachers demonstrate these behaviors, students know that they and their thinking are being valued. Sometimes this means putting aside any preconceived ideas and expectations of hoped-for responses. Being listened to and respected is highly motivating and longer lasting than quick words of praise. Quick words of praise can limit children and actually cause them not to try new ideas for fear of loss of praise or of disappointing the teacher. The focus should be on children expressing their thinking and reasoning processes, not just giving correct answers.

It's likely you'll choose to use these lessons along with other instructional materials or learning activities. It's important, however, to be consistent so that in all lessons you encourage students to make sense of ideas, communicate about their reasoning both orally and in writing, and apply their learning to problem-solving situations.

CHAPTER ONE
EVERYBODY WINS

Overview

The book *Everybody Wins!*, by Sheila Bruce, provides the context for this lesson. Friends in the story figure how to share pizzas, baseball tickets, bubble gum, and more. Students solve and discuss eleven real-world division problems and learn how to represent each division situation mathematically. Students then figure out all the ways to share twelve items so there are no leftovers. The lesson gives students experience with the sharing or partitioning model of division.

Materials

▲ *Everybody Wins!*, by Sheila Bruce (New York: Kane Press, 2001)

Time

▲ one class period

Teaching Directions

1. Read aloud the story *Everybody Wins!*, by Sheila Bruce.

2. As you read the story, present each problem, stopping before the answer is given. Ask students how to solve the problem and how to write a division equation for the problem. Record students' ideas on the board.

3. Continue until the end of the book.

4. Brainstorm with the students things they'd like to win. List their ideas on the board.

5. To model the assignment for the students, choose one item from the list and ask, "If I won twelve items, among how many people could I share them equally so there wouldn't be any leftovers?" Record solutions on the board.

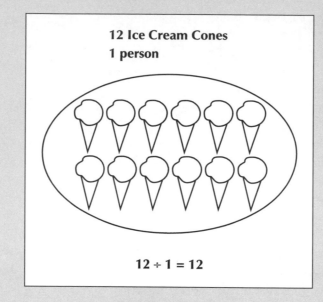

12 Ice Cream Cones
1 person

$12 \div 1 = 12$

6. Have students show all the ways twelve people could share equally with no leftovers.

7. Have students share their work.

Teaching Notes

Everybody Wins!, by Sheila Bruce, is a story about Oscar, Emmy, Hugo, and Tony as they enter several contests. Along the way they share marshmallows, bubble gum, tickets for a baseball game, baseball cards, and finally a forty-dollar second prize from a local pet store. The story provides students the opportunity to share equally the various prizes and other items in the story. Use a sticky note to cover the division sentences provided in the book. The note can be flipped up to show the students the division notation underneath.

This lesson engages students with the sharing or partitioning model of division. It makes a good introductory lesson for students with little or no experience with division and also provides a useful review for students who are more experienced.

The Lesson

▲▲

I gathered the students on the floor near the board. After they settled, I showed them the book *Everybody Wins!* and asked that they sit so they could easily see it. "It's a story that includes some division problems," I said.

"I don't know how to do division at all," Maya said with a worried expression.

"I think the story will help you learn some things about division," I replied.

I began to read the story aloud, stopping at the end of page five. I asked, "What is Oscar's problem?"

"He needs two box tops and he's only got one and the contest is over the next day," Kylie explained.

"What's one way Oscar could solve his problem?" I asked. Several students were eager to share.

"He could look in the cupboard for another box," Clare suggested.

"Maybe a neighbor would have a box top," Hannah said.

"He could go to the store and get one more box," Tony offered.

When the students finished sharing their ideas, I continued, stopping again near the top of page seven. "The prize is one hundred pizzas. If Emmy and Oscar divide them, how many will each get?" I asked. Hands flew into the air. "Tell me in a whisper voice," I said.

"Fifty!" the class said.

"Who would like to explain why the answer is fifty?" I asked.

Kylie said, "I know that fifty plus fifty is one hundred. And adding two fifties is like multiplying fifty by two, and that's one hundred."

I wrote on the board:

$50 + 50 = 100$

$50 \times 2 = 100$

Mark said, "I thought of money. One hundred pennies equals one dollar. If you divide one dollar in half, it's fifty cents."

I recorded Mark's idea on the board:

$100 \text{ pennies} = \$1.00$

$\$1.00 \div \text{in half} = \$.50$

$\$1.00 \div 2 = \$.50$

To introduce the notation for division, I said, "Mark said to divide the dollar in half. Dividing in half is like dividing by two.

That's why I wrote the last line of Mark's thinking with 'divided by two.' There are three ways to record division problems. Here they are." I wrote the following on the board:

$100 \div 2 = 50$

$\frac{100}{2} = 50$

$2\overline{)100}$ with 50 above

"All three are ways to show how to record dividing one hundred pizzas between two people," I explained. Many students nodded and a few looked puzzled. I decided to continue, thinking that the context of the lesson would help those who were still confused.

The next problem for students to solve comes when twenty-four bags of marshmallows arrive. Oscar and Emmy first decide to share between themselves, then change their minds and decide to share the twenty-four bags with their classmates at a weekend campout. There are twenty-four students in the class, including Oscar and Emmy. Four students don't show up, which means they have to share twenty-four bags among twenty people, resulting in four bags left over, a remainder of four. Maya raised her hand.

She said, "I get why twenty-four people would get one bag of marshmallows if there were twenty-four bags, but I don't get the leftovers."

To help Maya and the others understand, I gathered twenty-four cubes and said, "Suppose these cubes were bags of marshmallows. I have to share the unopened bags among twenty people." I started to put the cubes into twenty piles of one along the chalkboard tray. When I finished I said, "There are twenty bags of marshmallows, one for each of twenty people. I still have four bags left. Remembering that I'm not going to open the bags, do I have enough bags to give every person another bag?" The students shook their heads. I continued, "That means one bag per person with four left over, or remainder four."

"But you could open them and split up the marshmallows inside," Tony insisted.

"That's possible if these were real bags of marshmallows," I said, "but the story leads us to believe that the bags weren't opened."

"So the R my sister uses means 'remainder'?" Becky asked. I nodded.

I recorded on the board:

$$24 \div 20 = 1\,R4 \qquad 20\,\overline{)24}^{\,1\,R4}$$

"I think I'm getting this," Maya said. "Is there another problem?" I nodded and continued in this way until we completed the book.

"I liked that story," Jacob said.

"Which of the birds is the new one?" Corinne wondered aloud, referring to the last illustration in the story.

INTRODUCING THE ACTIVITY

"What are some things you'd like to win twelve of that you could share with others?" I asked.

"A house," Nolan piped up.

"One house?" I asked. Nolan nodded. "How would you share it?" I asked.

"Well, everyone could have one room," Nolan explained.

Hannah had a different idea. "Maybe you could win twelve boxes of Girl Scout cookies."

"Yum!" several students responded.

"I like Thin Mints," Corinne said as she rubbed her tummy.

I began a list on the board:

Things We'd Like to Win

houses

cookies

"Maybe we could win twelve puppies," Tony suggested with a giggle.

"How about ice cream sundaes?" Clare said.

I added these ideas to the list and continued adding ideas until all students who had ideas to share had done so.

I chose ice cream cones from the list to use as an example to show the students how to do the assignment. I wrote on the board: *12 Ice Cream Cones.* "If I won twelve ice cream cones, among how many people could I share them equally so there wouldn't be any leftovers?" I paused to give the students time to think. I called on Kylie.

Kylie explained, "You could keep them all to yourself!" The students giggled.

"How would I write a division sentence to show your idea?" I asked.

Kylie came to the board and wrote: $1\overline{)12}$.

"Put your thumb up if you agree with Kylie, put your thumb down if you disagree, and put your thumb sideways if you're not sure," I said. The students indicated their agreement with thumbs up.

"If I kept them all to myself, how many would I get?" I asked.

"Twelve," the students chorused.

I said as I drew on the board, "Here's how I can record on my paper."

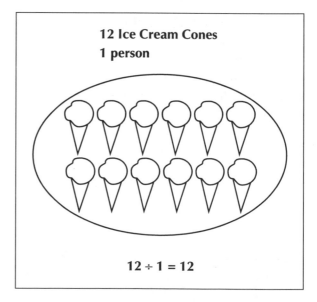

12 Ice Cream Cones
1 person

$12 \div 1 = 12$

"What if I wanted to divide my twelve ice cream cones between two people?" I asked. "Could I do that and have no leftovers?" Hands shot into the air. "Share with your neighbor," I said. "First one of you talks for thirty seconds while the other listens without interruption, then the first talker gets to be the listener and the first listener gets to be the talker." I timed the students for thirty seconds, then gave them the signal to switch roles and timed for another thirty seconds. Then I asked for the students' attention.

"Show me with your fingers how many ice cream cones two people will get if I share twelve between them," I said. Most students put up six fingers. "How could I show this on the board?" I asked.

Becky explained, "Draw twelve ice cream cones and then circle one group of six and then circle the other six." I did as Becky suggested.

"What division sentence could I write?" I asked.

Mark volunteered, "Write it like a fraction. Put the twelve on top and the two on the bottom and then make an equals sign and write six." I followed Mark's directions.

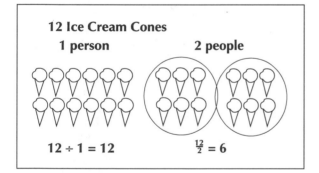

I continued, "What are some other ways I can divide twelve ice cream cones into equal groups with no remainders?"

As the students listed the numbers, I recorded them on the board:

Ways to Divide 12

12 ÷ 1 = 12

12 ÷ 2 = 6

12 ÷ 3 = 4

12 ÷ 4 = 3

12 ÷ 6 = 6

12 ÷ 12 = 1

I said, "I notice five isn't on the list. How come?"

Jamison explained, "You could divide by five, but you'd have leftovers and you said to use numbers that won't make leftovers." Several students nodded.

"Are there other numbers that we can't use, like five?" I asked. Many hands went up.

"You can't use seven," Hannah said. "It would be one ice cream cone for seven people with five left."

Maya added, "Eight and nine won't work either, unless you can have leftovers. Eight has a remainder of four and nine would have a remainder of . . . three."

"Eleven and ten have the same problem," Tony noted.

I returned to explaining the activity. "You need to choose a prize—something you won twelve of. Then show all the ways you can share your twelve prizes equally with no leftovers. Show your work and record the division for each."

Jamison asked, "Couldn't twenty-four people share twelve ice cream cones with no leftovers? They'd each get one-half."

Jamison had a good point. I responded, "I agree that you could divide the twelve ice cream cones in half and then you could share the twenty-four halves with twenty-four people. Half of an ice cream cone would be very messy, I think. Let's agree not to split ice cream cones like that this time." Jamison nodded, satisfied. To give the students a visual reference for the directions, I wrote on the board:

1. *Decide on a prize. Remember there will be twelve of them to share.*

2. *Show all the ways to share your twelve prizes equally with no leftovers.*

3. *On your paper, show how you divided and record the division for each way.*

Becky raised her hand. "Do we work by ourselves?" I nodded.

There were no additional questions. I

handed each student a sheet of paper as they returned to their seats.

OBSERVING THE STUDENTS

The students worked quietly after sharing with their neighbors what their prize would be. Maya chose twelve pens as her prize. Becky chose lunch boxes, Tony chose eggs, and Nolan chose Chinese coins.

Juan became confused when trying to figure the number of surfboards each person would get if there were three people. He already had written the equation, drawn the picture, and figured out how to divide the surfboards among four people. However, he hadn't drawn the picture for twelve divided by three and I suggested he do so. This cleared up his confusion. (See Figure 1–1.)

Madison worked very slowly and carefully, talking to herself as she worked. She was dividing gift certificates to PetCo. Her illustrations showed her understanding of the number of groups and the number in each group. She also recorded the division correctly. (See Figure 1–2.)

When most of the students were finished, I gave a one-minute warning to those still working to finish their work. I gathered the students on the floor so they could share their work.

▲▲▲▲▲▲Figure 1–2 *Madison showed her understanding of the number of groups and the number in each group. She was able to represent division symbolically.*

Clare went first. She had drawn twelve tickets on her paper and, using her hands, she pointed out each of the ways she had divided the twelve tickets. She explained, "I didn't draw on my paper to show all the groups because I thought it would be too messy and confusing. So I just explained how I did it." Her explanation was clear and accurate. (See Figure 1–3.)

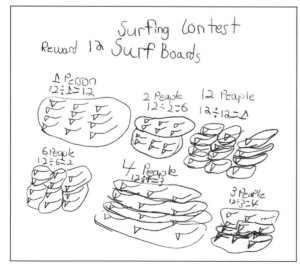

▲▲▲▲▲▲Figure 1–1 *Drawing a picture helped Juan clarify his thinking.*

▲▲▲▲▲▲Figure 1–3 *Clare used her picture and a verbal explanation to show her understanding.*

Maya was next. She explained, "I started with pens as my prize. I did twelve pens divided by twelve people is one pen each. Then I did twelve pens divided by two people and got six pens each. I checked it with multiplication by doing six times two is twelve. Then I did repeated addition. Six plus six is twelve. And then I wrote a division sentence. It was 'Twelve divided by two is six.' I got bored with pens, so I switched to marshmallows and cookies." (See Figure 1–4.)

All who wanted to do so shared their work. Then I collected their papers and posted them on the wall for everyone to admire. Figure 1–5 shows how one other student worked on this activity.

EXTENSION

This activity can be repeated throughout the year as students investigate ways to divide other numbers without having remainders.

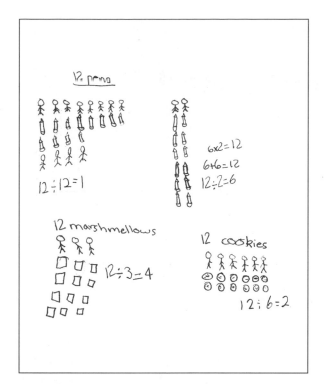

▲▲▲▲▲▲**Figure 1–4** *Maya switched from pens to marshmallows and cookies to show her understanding.*

▲▲▲▲▲▲**Figure 1–5** *Hannah had little trouble with the assignment and was able to make sense of all the ways of dividing by twelve.*

Questions and Discussion

▲▲

▲ *Solving eleven division problems in an introductory lesson seems a lot. What's another way to present the book?*

Another way to present the book and the eleven problems is to read one or two problems per day, discuss students' strategies for solving those problems, write division equations to represent the problems, and then go on to something else. After some experience, it may be appropriate to have students show their solutions on their own paper, using words, pictures, and numbers.

CHAPTER 2
SHARING MONEY

Overview

Sharing Money provides students with a real-world, problem-solving situation involving the sharing or partitioning model of division. Students work in fours to figure first how to divide five dollars equally among themselves, then how to do the same with fifty cents.

Materials

▲ play money, if needed

Time

▲ one class period

Teaching Directions

1. Present students with this situation: On the way to school one morning, four students find a five-dollar bill. They give the money to the principal when they arrive at school. The principal explains that if no one has claimed the five dollars in one week, the students may have the money. The students return one week later to claim the money. The principal gives them the money on the condition that they divide it equally among themselves.

2. Explain to the students that their task is to work in groups of four to determine how they would divide five dollars equally among themselves. (If some groups have only three students, have them pretend that there are four in the group.) Show and explain to students how to represent the problem with a division equation: $\$5.00 \div 4 = \square$, $4\overline{)\$5.00}^{\square}$, $\frac{\$5.00}{4} = \square$.

3. When students have solved this problem, ask them to figure out how to divide fifty cents among four people.

4. Lead a discussion for students to share their solutions.

Teaching Notes

Because of students' familiarity with money, this lesson is suitable as an introductory lesson about the concept of and the symbolism for division. The symbolism is a convention of mathematics; therefore, it's something that teachers need to show and explain to students. The problem in this lesson can be represented as $\$5.00 \div 4 = \square$, $4\overline{)\$5.00}^{\square}$, and $\frac{\$5.00}{4} = \square$.

There are two types of division problems: the grouping model and the sharing model. The difference between the two models is what's known and what's unknown. In the grouping model, you know the *total amount* and the *size* of the groups; unknown is the number of groups. In the sharing or partitioning model, you know the *total amount* and the *number* of groups; unknown is the number in each group. (See the Introduction for further discussion of the two types of division problems.)

Sharing Money gives children experience with the sharing or partitioning model of division. The children know the total amount (five dollars) and the number of groups (dividing among four children means dividing into four groups). They must figure out the amount of money in each group; that is, students share or partition the money into four equal groups.

Critical to students' learning is to recognize when a situation translates to a division problem. In this lesson, we want students to know that the *Sharing Money* problem is a division situation because it calls for sharing an amount into equal groups. Also, we want students to know how to represent a division situation like this symbolically with a number sentence: $\$5.00 \div 4 = ?$. However, when figuring out the answer to a division problem, it's appropriate for students to use a combination of operations, and you'll see different approaches in the samples of student work shown on the following pages.

Some teachers worry that children aren't really "dividing" when they use addition or a combination of addition and multiplication, for example, to solve a division problem. However, keep in mind that even the standard long division algorithm makes use of multiplying and subtracting along with division!

Thinking about equal groups is essential to both multiplication and division. Because of this relationship between multiplication and division and students' familiarity with multiplication, when appropriate, encourage students to use what they know about multiplication to help them solve division problems. One way to do this is as you monitor the students working, ask questions that link the division they're doing with multiplication. For example: "How can you use multiplication to show that your solution makes sense?"

Most students this age have a basic understanding of money and enough experience that they can handle thinking about small amounts abstractly. They know that four quarters make a dollar and can proceed from that knowledge without having money in front of them. However, for some children it is helpful to have a concrete reference, and you may want to make play money available for these students.

The Lesson

▲▲

I began the lesson by gathering the students at the front of the room and telling the following story: "Four children walking to school together found a five-dollar bill. They brought it to the principal, and she told them, 'I'll keep it for a week to see if anyone comes to claim it. At the end of the week, if no one has claimed it, it's yours.' At the end of the week, no one claimed the five-dollar bill, so the principal told the children they could have it. 'But you have to do one thing,' she said. 'You must share the five dollars equally among the four of you.'"

"That makes sense," David commented about the story.

"I think it's good that they turned the money in," Zoe added, "and I like that the person who lost it had a week to find it at the principal's and then the kids got it."

"I think I know how much each kid gets," Afton said.

I replied, "I'd like you to keep your thought in your brain for just a few more moments, Afton. First, I want to show you the three ways to write a math sentence for this problem." I wrote on the board:

$$\$5.00 \div 4 = \square, \quad 4\overline{)\$5.00}, \quad \frac{\$5.00}{4} = \square.$$

"The five dollars is the total amount shared. The four tells how many people will share the money. Our job is to figure how much money each person will get. That's what goes in the box."

Next, I explained the activity. "You'll be working together in groups of four, and since you sit in table groups with four people, you'll work with your table group. The first thing you'll need to do is discuss how the four of you could share five dollars equally. Since you're going to collaborate on your answer, your group needs only one paper. Your explanation should use words, numbers, and, if you like, pictures to describe what each of you would get and how you solved the problem."

Anticipating that groups would finish the problem at different times, I added, "As soon as you're finished, your whole group should come and talk to me. The *whole* group must come. I'll talk with you and then give you another problem." The second problem was to find out how four children could share fifty cents equally. I knew that this problem would be more difficult for the children because the solution wasn't as visual and, when fifty cents were divided, money would be left over.

OBSERVING THE CHILDREN

The room buzzed with discussion as the students got to work. I circulated through the class, handing each group a sheet of paper and answering an occasional question. I observed Afton's table group for a moment, as I knew Afton was eager to show he knew the answer. I wanted Afton to have the opportunity to share, but not before the other members of the group had had a chance to discuss and do some thinking on their own. Afton was waiting patiently as his group started to discuss the question.

"I know how we could start," Afton said. "Everybody should draw a kid and then we can draw the five-dollar bill and show how much each kid gets." His group nodded and Afton began to draw while his partners watched. In order to keep all the members of the group involved and to get the problem done in a reasonable amount of time, I suggested that all four work on their drawings at once. Elijah, Keilani, and Karina liked this idea, and soon the four were drawing at the same time. The group produced a visual representation of how to split the five-dollar bill four ways.

At his table, David immediately announced, "Well, it's a dollar twenty-five." No one paid any attention, but the other students in the group quickly came up with the same answer—also in their heads. The students each decided to record on their own paper how they thought of the problem.

When David, Becca, Catalina, and Emmi showed their answer to me, they were especially proud that after they solved the problem, they checked it in several ways. Becca began, "Here's the division way we did the problem. I explained to the group that we could exchange a five-dollar bill for five ones. That would mean each of us could have a one-dollar bill. That's four dollars and that leaves one. We can trade the dollar in for four quarters. Four kids, four quarters, that's a quarter for each kid. We each get one dollar and one quarter."

David continued, "I knew I could add a dollar twenty-five four times and it would equal five dollars. So we checked it by adding up each person's part. Then we thought that we could multiply one dollar and twenty-five cents by four and that would be five dollars, too."

Emmi added, "You could also check it by starting with five dollars and subtracting one dollar and twenty-five cents four times and you should end up with zero." (See Figure 2–1.)

"I have a new problem for you to solve," I said after listening to their explanation. "How would you four share fifty cents?"

"I think we get fifteen cents each," Catalina said.

Becca wrote: *Each person gets $.15 if there are four people.* The others told her

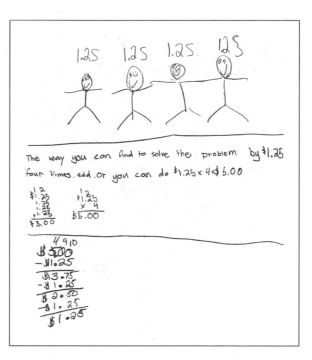

▲▲▲▲▲▲Figure 2–1 *Becca, Catalina, David, and Emmi showed their different approaches to sharing five dollars among four people.*

what else to write: *We think this because 15 + 15 + 15 + 15 equlals 50. So you exchange the 50¢ piece for, four 10¢ and for, four 5¢ pieces.* However, before she was finished, the others realized that the answer wasn't correct.

"It's too much," Emmi said. "That's sixty cents."

"Uh oh," David added. "What do we do?"

As Catalina, Emmi, and David talked, Becca kept writing. She added: *Opssie* [Oopsie] *wrong one Whoops thats 60¢.* David found some play money, and the group figured out the answer. Becca finally wrote: *Each person gets 12¢. In order to get twelve cents for each person you have to have 4, 10¢ pieces and 8 1¢ pieces.* They ignored the remainder. (See Figure 2–2.)

Scott, Carlos, and Luke were a group of three, and they decided to change the problem to dividing $5.00 evenly among three people. First Scott tried adding $1.25 + $1.25 + $1.25 and got $3.75. The boys talked over that answer. "We need a lot

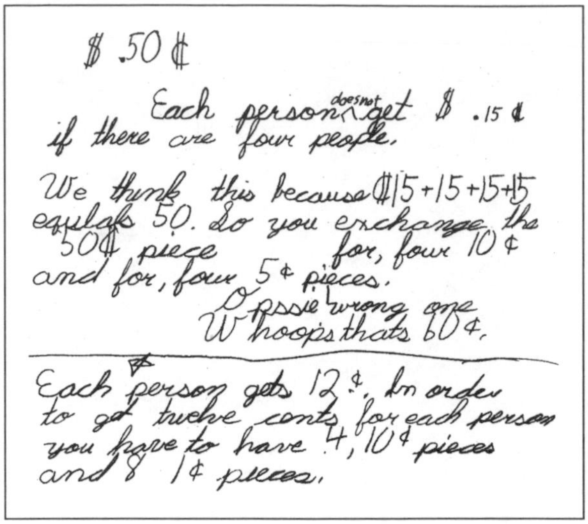

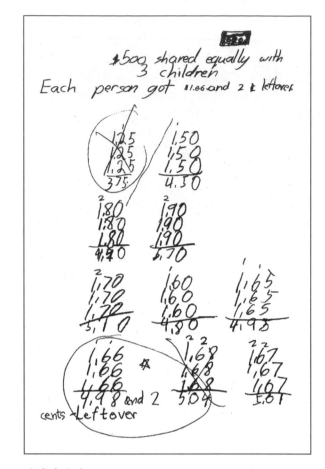

▲▲▲▲▲▲**Figure 2–2** *Becca, Catalina, David, and Emmi made a false start before finally figuring out how to share fifty cents.*

more," they agreed. So Scott tried adding $1.50 three times and got $4.50. "More!" Luke urged. Scott added $1.80 three times, made a calculation error, and wrote the answer as $4.40, still not right. Using $1.90 gave them $5.70, so they tried $1.70. Still too high. Next came $1.60, then $1.65. With $1.66 + $1.66 + $1.66, they got a total of $4.98. So they tried $1.68. That total was $5.04, so they tried $1.67. That total of $5.01 was still too high, so they returned to $1.66 + $1.66 + $1.66, deciding that they would have two cents left over.

They had completed all the addition using paper and pencil, but now Scott decided to check the results with the calculator. They were pleased to see that their total agreed with the calculator total and were proud to show their work to me. (See Figure 2–3.)

The boys then tackled the problem of sharing fifty cents. Totally immersed in the problem, this group remained working when the other children later gathered at the front of the room to discuss their results.

As I walked by, I overheard Seth explaining his idea to his group. He said, "If

▲▲▲▲▲▲**Figure 2–3** *Scott, Carlos, and Luke used trial and error to figure out how to share five dollars among the three of them.*

we had five dollars and there were two of us who had to share it, we'd each get two dollars and fifty cents. Five split in two equal parts is two and one-half, so five dollars split in two halves is two fifty. Then because there are four of us, we could split each of the two fifties into half."

"I don't get it," Silas said.

Seth looked a bit flustered as he thought about how to further explain his idea. "Half of five dollars is two dollars and fifty cents," he began and Silas nodded his head.

"I get that part," Silas said. "I don't get what you did with the two fifty."

"Well," Seth continued to explain, "you can have two dollar bills and two quarters to make two fifty. You have to split it equally between two people. For example, you and me. I get one dollar and you get one dollar, then I get one quarter and you get one quarter. We each get one dollar and one quarter."

"I think I see now," Silas said.

"Is there another way you could prove that your answer of one dollar and twenty-five cents makes sense?" I asked Seth.

"There are four people with one twenty-five," Seth said. "If you add it up, it should come out to be five dollars. Each person has one dollar, so that's four dollars, and then each person has a quarter. Four quarters make a dollar. Four dollars and the dollar from the quarters would make five dollars."

"How could you use multiplication to either help you solve the problem or help show your answer is correct?" I asked. I hoped the students would see multiplication as another way of explaining Seth's solution. I also hoped that my question would help them think about the relationship between multiplication and division. The students were quiet for a moment. Then Silas spoke up.

"I think you can multiply one twenty-five times four instead of adding it," Silas said. "That should show that the answer is correct, but I don't know how to use multiplication to solve the problem."

"I have an idea," Kayla said. "There are four of us and each of us is like a group. So that's four groups. We know there's five dollars and that's like the total amount of money altogether. We don't know how much we get. It's like if we use multiplication, there's a piece missing, like four groups of some amount of money equals five dollars. We have to figure the amount."

To make sense of Kayla's idea, Seth restated it in his own words. "Oh! I get what Kayla means. It's four times something will equal five dollars. We had to figure out the something!"

"But we still had to divide to find the missing piece of the multiplication problem," Silas said.

Kayla responded, "But you can think four times one dollar is four dollars, and I know I need another dollar, and four times twenty-five cents is a dollar, and four dollars and one dollar is five dollars." Silas and the others paused, thought quietly, and nodded.

I gave the group the new problem and they eagerly got to work. "It's a dividing problem because we have to share the money equally, but let's see if we can solve it with multiplication," Seth and Kayla suggested.

"You can think of fifty cents as four dimes and ten pennies," Silas added. I left the group to solve the problem.

Cami, Carol, Kareem, and Gib were working on sharing five dollars. Gib said, "I'd go to the store and get all quarters. There are four quarters in one dollar."

"There are eight quarters in two dollars," Cami offered. Gib glowered at her. He wrote an *8* on the paper, crossed it out, and turned his back on the group.

Cami and Carol started working together, and Kareem and Gib began to talk together about the problem. When she began writing, Cami wrote all four students' names on the paper when, in reality, only she and Carol were working together.

Meanwhile, Gib decided that since he and Kareem were now a group of two, the problem must change. "How would we share five dollars between us equally?" he asked. Gib decided to illustrate the problem. "Here's the principal," he told Kareem. He drew several interactions between the principal and children. Gib got frustrated when he couldn't come up with a mathematical solution to the problem and finally depicted the principal saying, "Go away." (See Figure 2–4.)

Kareem decided to draw as well, and his drawing showed that he had solved the original problem, giving one dollar plus twenty-five cents to each of four people. Kareem seemed to enjoy Gib's company and didn't mention that he had solved the problem.

Gib and Kareem then asked me for another problem. I gave them the fifty-cent problem, asking Gib how he would share fifty cents with another person. I nudged a little, asking, "How many quarters are in fifty cents?" Gib repeated the question, then started counting by ones. He reached thirty-three and said, "Oops! I went too far." He tried adding several doubles—twenty plus twenty, twenty-five plus twenty-five, and so on. Then he and Kareem wrote the solution, with Gib writing the first sentence and Kareem the second. (See Figure 2–5.)

I knew it was important for me to talk with Gib about his understanding of money. Because he was working well with Kareem and seemed engaged in the activity, I decided to wait until a later time to do this.

Jael, Becca, Kelsey, and Jenny were working on the problem of sharing fifty cents. They wrote: *Each person gets 12 cents*

because *50 ÷ 4 = 12 r. 2 and we give 2¢ to the principle for letting us keep the 50¢.* They also drew a picture showing that each person received a dime and two pennies. (See Figure 2–6.)

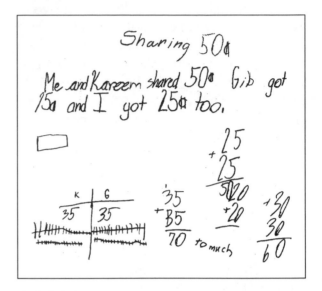

▲▲▲▲▲▲Figure 2–5 *Gib and Kareem worked on splitting fifty cents between the two of them.*

▲▲▲▲▲▲Figure 2–4 *Gib wasn't able to solve the problem.*

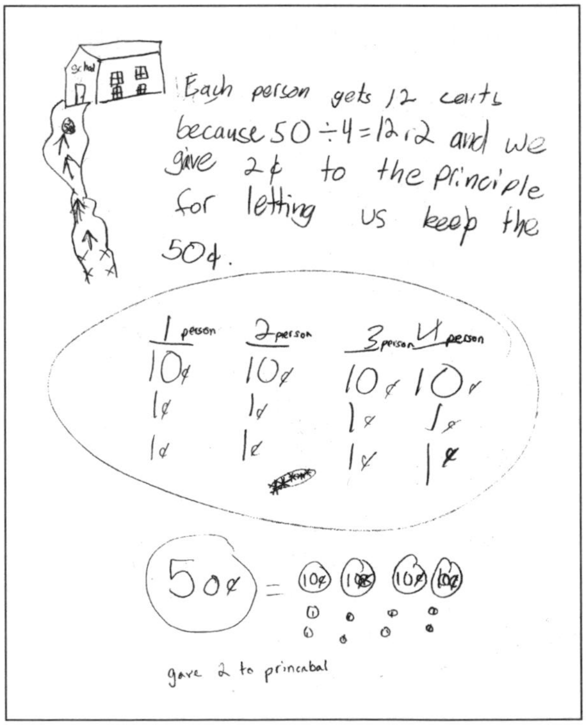

▲▲▲▲▲▲Figure 2–6 *Jael, Becca, Kelsey, and Jenny showed how to share fifty cents among four people.*

Adam, Katie, Kenny, and Garry had been working on the fifty-cents problem together when I had checked on them earlier. I noticed that now Garry was working by himself on a different idea than the rest of the group. Garry explained he couldn't understand what the others were doing, so he decided to do the problem in a way that made sense to him. He drew fifty pennies, distributing them among four groups as he drew the pennies. He found that two groups had twelve pennies and the other two groups had thirteen. "The groups aren't equal and they're supposed to be, right?" Garry asked.

"The groups should be equal," I responded.

"But then there are two pennies left," Garry said with frustration.

"That's correct," I said. "Is there any way you could split the pennies among the four groups?"

"I don't think so," Garry said. "I don't think it would be helpful to saw them all in half. What should I do with the extras?"

"That's up to you," I said.

"I'll take them to Mexico and change two pennies into four pesos," Garry said. "Then each person could get twelve cents and one peso." I didn't know what the current monetary exchange rate was for pesos, but I appreciated Garry's creative thinking.

Seth, Silas, Kayla, and Lindsey called me over. "We were finished with sharing fifty cents among four people, so we decided to do ten dollars with four people," Kayla explained. "Can we share with the class?"

"We'll be gathering on the rug in just a few moments and you may share then," I said as I gave the rest of the students a two-minute warning, indicating they needed to complete what they were doing.

A CLASS DISCUSSION

Near the end of the period I gathered the children on the floor at the front of the room and asked each group to report its findings. "If you solved more than one problem," I said, "choose one to report. Listen carefully to one another to see if you understand how each group got its answer."

Kayla reported how she, Lindsey, Seth, and Silas shared five dollars. "There are four kids and four dollars," she said. "Then we took a dollar away and got four quarters. So each kid gets one quarter and one dollar." (See Figure 2–7.)

Vicki, Len, Jenny, and Caleb also reported how they shared five dollars. They had drawn the five-dollar bill and then shown with pictures how they exchanged it for four dollar bills, two quarters, four dimes, and two nickels.

"You didn't have to use dimes and nickels," Afton commented.

"But it worked," Jenny said, defending their work.

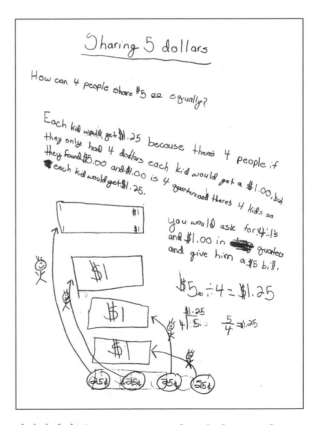

▲▲▲▲▲▲Figure 2–7 *Kayla, Lindsey, Seth, and Silas clearly explained how they shared five dollars.*

"We used nickels," Katie said. "Everybody would get twenty nickels 'cause twenty nickels is the same as one dollar; five times twenty is one hundred. That would leave one dollar left, so exchange it for four quarters. Four quarters, each kid gets one. Twenty nickels and one quarter is one dollar and twenty-five cents." (See Figure 2–8.)

I commented to the class about the legitimacy of different methods of reporting mathematical investigations. "There's more than one way to solve the problem," I said. "Some groups explained with pictures and others with words. Some exchanged just for quarters and others for dimes and nickels as well."

Addie then reported on her group's trial-and-error method for dividing fifty cents. "We tried a bunch of ways. We did fifteen cents, but it was too much because it was sixty cents. Then we tried eighteen cents and it was even bigger. Then we thought we were going the wrong way and tried a smaller number. We tried eleven and then twelve and then thirteen. Eleven and twelve were less than fifty cents, but thirteen was too much. We discovered you could get leftovers. We decided to just throw them out. So we think it's twelve

cents each because that's the closest you can get to fifty cents in four equal groups and there's two left."

Kristen, Karina, Elijah, and Afton shared their solution for sharing fifty cents. Karina began by explaining that her group started by giving each person one dime and then splitting ten pennies so each would get two cents with two cents leftover. She finished by reading from the group's paper. "Each person gets twelve cents and then you need to split the remainder two cents in half. Then everyone gets twelve and one-half cents. But nobody would take a half cent, so you could just give the two cents to the teacher." I appreciated that the students used the context of the problem to make sense of the remainder. (See Figure 2–9.)

Scott, Carlos, and Luke then joined the discussion. I explained to the class, "Scott, Carlos, and Luke solved the problem of dividing five dollars among three people.

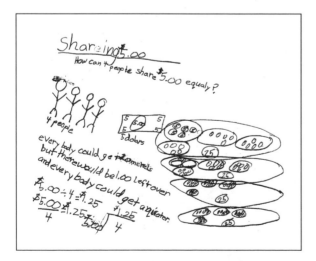

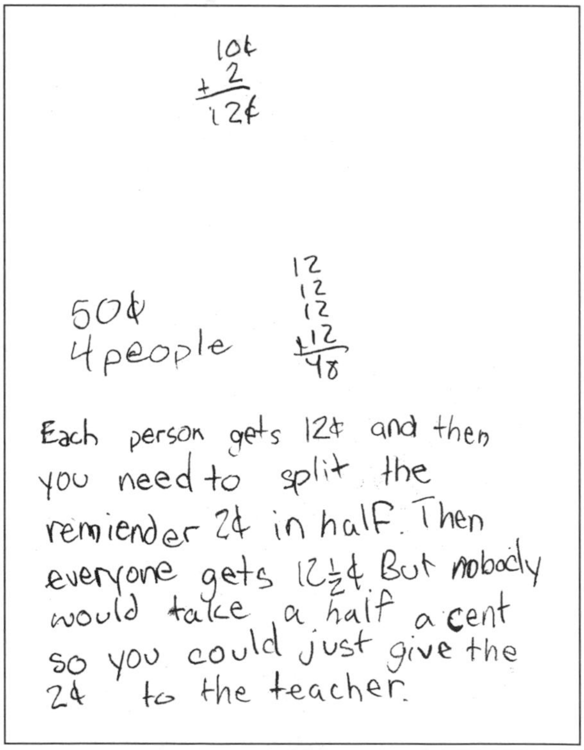

▲▲▲▲▲▲Figure 2–8 *Katie showed how to share five dollars with nickels and quarters.*

▲▲▲▲▲▲Figure 2–9 *Karina, Kristen, Elijah, and Afton solved the problem of splitting two pennies among four people by giving the pennies to the teacher.*

Just think: If you were in a group of three, how would you do it?" I wrote on the board:

$$\$5.00 \div 3 = \square$$

Two other students in the class quickly became engrossed in this new problem. Jenny said, "I'd give one dollar to each person. That uses up three of the dollars." As she spoke, I recorded her explanation numerically on the board:

$$\$3.00 = \$1.00 + \$1.00 + \$1.00$$

Then Jenny explained, "I'd change the two dollars left for quarters. That's eight quarters." I wrote:

$$\$2.00 = .25 + .25 + .25 + .25 + .25 + .25 + .25 + .25$$

Jenny continued, "Each person would get two quarters; that leaves two quarters left over. I'd change those quarters to dimes and give everybody a dime. Now there's twenty cents left over . . ."

"Nickels!" Elijah shouted. "Everybody gets a nickel and you have five cents left over. Five cents remainder."

"No, it's two cents remainder," Luke interrupted. "Can I write on the board?" I nodded.

"Each person gets a dollar sixty-six, and there are two cents left over," Luke explained, and wrote:

$$
\begin{array}{r}
1.66 \\
1.66 \\
\underline{1.66} \\
4.98 \ R2
\end{array}
$$

Jenny and Elijah applauded. "They got it down farther than we did!"

To change the direction of the conversation, I said, "We all seem to agree that when four people share five dollars, each gets a dollar twenty-five. Is there a way to use multiplication to show that the answer of one twenty-five makes sense?" I asked the question to encourage students to consider the connection between multiplication and division. When several hands were up, I called on Adam.

Adam explained, "You could use multiplication by multiplying one dollar times four because there are four kids. Four times one is four. Then you could multiply twenty-five cents times four and that's one hundred cents, which is like a dollar. Four dollars and one dollar are five dollars." Many students nodded their agreement while others sat quietly thinking.

I recorded:

$$\$1.00 \times 4 = \$4.00$$
$$\$.25 \times 4 = \$1.00$$
$$\$4.00 + \$1.00 = \$5.00$$

"I think I know another way," Brittany said. "I think you could write four times something equals five dollars." I wrote on the board:

$$4 \times \square = \$5.00$$

"Is this what you mean?" I asked Brittany to be sure I understood and to give the rest of the class a visual way of thinking about Brittany's idea. She nodded.

"The four is for the number of kids and the kids are like groups, I think," Brittany continued. "There's five dollars in all and you have to figure out how much each kid gets."

"Oh, wow!" James blurted out. "I think I get it. They are, like, all the same, it just depends on what you're trying to figure out!" I chose not to spend too much time on this point as I planned to discuss the relationship between multiplication and division throughout the year.

I asked, "With the fifty-cent problem there were two cents left over. What's something you have to do when you're sharing money and things don't come out equally? What do you do with leftovers?"

Scott answered, "You can buy something you can all share."

"Throw it in the sea and make a wish," Jianna suggested.

"Take it to Mexico and change two cents for four pesos or some other kind of money and then divide," Garry said.

"I think it would be good to donate it to foster children," Afton said.

"Kayla, Silas, Lindsey, and Seth decided to investigate another problem," I said. "They want to tell what they found out about four people sharing ten dollars."

Silas began, "Well, each person would get two dollars and fifty cents. Two dollars times four people is eight dollars. Too small. Three dollars times four people is twelve dollars. Too big. We decided to give each person two dollars and then there were two dollars left over. One dollar divided by four people is twenty-five cents. Two dollars is twice as much as one dollar, so each person would get twice as much, or fifty cents. That's two dollars and fifty cents."

I recorded Silas's idea as follows:

$2.00 \times 4 = \$8.00$

$3.00 \times 4 = \$12.00$

$10.00 - \$8.00 = \$2.00$

$1.00 \div 4 = \$.25$

$2.00 = \$1.00 \times 2$

$.25 \times 2 = \$.50$

$2.00 + .50 = \$2.50$

$10.00 \div 4 = \$2.50$

Seth continued, "I did it differently than Silas, but we still came out with the same answer. I knew ten dollars was twice as much as five dollars. I also knew that each person would get one dollar and twenty-five cents for five dollars, so I just doubled one twenty-five which is two fifty."

I recorded on the board:

$10.00 = 2 \times \$5.00$

$5.00 \div 4 = \$1.25$

$1.25 \times 2 = \$2.50$

$10.00 \div 4 = \$2.50$

Having students explain their thinking strategies is valuable, not only for the students who report but also for those who listen. It also helps me more clearly understand what my students are thinking.

Questions and Discussion

▲ **When children share an answer, is it necessary for them to always explain their reasoning?**

I think this is important for several reasons. In order for children to explain their reasoning, they must think more deeply about what they are doing. This increases the depth of understanding and learning. When children explain, they often make connections they may not have otherwise made. Those children listening to the explanation are given other ways of thinking about a problem, deepening their understanding. For me as the teacher, listening to children carefully gives me insight into potential misconceptions that may go unnoticed when they only give a quick answer. The process also gives children a clear message that I value thinking and reasoning.

▲ **It seems that many of the solutions offered by the students involved operations other than division. How do you know the students knew this was a division problem?**

The methods the students used to solve the problems included repeated addition, multiplication, and repeated subtraction. I was confident the students recognized the problem as a division problem because they showed clearly how they shared five dollars. They indicated understanding of the total amount of money involved and that the money had to be shared equally among four groups, in this case four children.

▲ *It seemed to me that the students weren't really dividing, but finding the answer by using other operations. Don't we want them to learn to divide?*

There are several goals for this activity. One is for students to see a problem as a division situation, that is, to realize that they must share the money so that each child receives the same amount. Another goal is for students to be able to represent the problem symbolically using division; for example, $\$5.00 \div 4 = \$1.25$. A third goal is for students to be able to figure out the correct answer. Your question is about the third goal. In this lesson I let the children make sense of the problem in their own ways and use whatever operations they chose to solve it. Then in a class discussion, students shared their methods. It's beneficial to children to see different approaches. This reinforces for them that there's more than one way to solve a problem and that division is connected to the other operations they've already learned. The purpose here is to build understanding. Efficiency in computation when dividing is a later goal, not appropriate for a beginning experience.

CHAPTER THREE
THE DOORBELL RANG

Overview

The Doorbell Rang, by Pat Hutchins, introduces the lesson and provides the context for teaching students to connect standard division notation with problem situations. The lesson also helps children learn about remainders and how to record them and see how division and fractions are connected. After hearing the story, students retell it with division sentences and draw pictures to show their understanding of the notation. Also, each child invents a sharing problem and writes a one-event sequel to the story.

Materials

▲ *The Doorbell Rang*, by Pat Hutchins (New York: Greenwillow Books, 1986)
▲ 12-by-18-inch drawing paper, 1 per student

Time

▲ three class periods, plus one additional class period for the extension

Teaching Directions

1. Read aloud *The Doorbell Rang*, by Pat Hutchins. Some students might already be familiar with this book. However, tell them that when they hear it this time, they should think about the mathematics in the story.

2. After reading the story, introduce the symbolism for division by reviewing the story and recording the following division sentences on the board to represent each part:

$$12 \div 2 = 6 \qquad 2\overline{)12}^{\,6} \qquad \tfrac{12}{2} = 6$$

$$12 \div 4 = 3 \qquad 4\overline{)12}\,^{3} \qquad \tfrac{12}{4} = 3$$

$$12 \div 6 = 2 \qquad 6\overline{)12}\,^{2} \qquad \tfrac{12}{6} = 2$$

$$12 \div 12 = 1 \qquad 12\overline{)12}\,^{1} \qquad \tfrac{12}{12} = 1$$

3. Have the students figure out the number of cookies on the new tray that Grandma delivers.

4. Pose another problem. Say: "Suppose that Grandma had only eighteen cookies on the new tray. How many cookies would there then be altogether?" After the children figure out that there would be thirty cookies, add another equation to the list on the board:

$$30 \div 12 = \qquad 12\overline{)30} \qquad \tfrac{30}{12} =$$

5. Explain to the students that they'll retell the story with mathematical equations and illustrations, find the answer to thirty divided by twelve, and finally invent an additional episode for the story for which they write all three division sentences and find the answer.

6. Show students how to fold a sheet of 12-by-18-inch paper into eight sections like this:

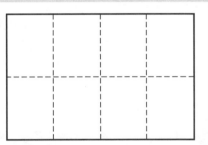

7. Explain that in the first box, students should write *The Doorbell Rang* and their own name. In the next five boxes, they retell the story, writing the five sets of mathematical equations listed on the board. In the remaining two boxes, the children make up a final part of the story.

8. After students have completed the assignment, hold a class discussion, asking students to share their stories and explain how they illustrated the mathematics.

Teaching Notes

In the book *The Doorbell Rang*, by Pat Hutchins, Ma baked enough cookies for two children to share, each getting six cookies. But then two friends arrive and are invited to share the cookies. The doorbell rings twice more, and additional friends enter to share the cookies. When there are twelve cookies and twelve children, the doorbell rings again, and the children are relieved to see Grandma enter with a tray full of cookies.

The story presents children with a context involving the sharing model of division. The total number of cookies is known, twelve. The number of groups, or children in this case, is always known, even though the total number of children changes. Each time more children arrive at the door, the students figure out the number of cookies each child will receive.

It is important that children recognize and be comfortable with the three ways of writing a division problem. Most students recognize $\overline{)}$ and ÷ as symbols indicating division. However, many children don't realize that division can also be represented as a fraction. Introducing the fractional notation along with the other two representations helps children become familiar with it.

In the following vignette, some students chose to use calculators, a tool generally available for student use. While many students ignore them, a few are intrigued and use them. The goals of this lesson include encouraging the development of children's number sense and facility with reasoning numerically. This includes helping children see the relationships among the operations and make use of what they know about multiplication and, perhaps, the other operations, to solve a division problem. The problems in this lesson are within the children's grasp to solve without the assistance of a calculator. If, however, children choose numbers that are out of their grasp to extend their story, it's good learning for them to realize this. Calculators are useful in this situation. Also, it's important that when children use calculators, they be able to interpret and make sense of the answer.

It's important that the use of calculators and discussing the decimal remainders not take precedence over the emphasis on introducing division and encouraging children to use what they already know to solve problems within their grasp.

The Lesson

▲▲▲

DAY 1

I asked the students to sit quietly on the floor so they could easily see the book I was holding. Many students recognized an old friend in *The Doorbell Rang*.

I said, "I could tell from your conversations as you sat down that this is a book many of you have heard or read before. What do you remember about it?"

"There were cookies," Jiana said.

"More people kept coming," Afton added.

"Were there more cookies?" I asked.

"Nooo! Just more kids!" several students responded.

"So what did they have to do?"

"Divide them up again each time some new kids came," Keilani said.

I continued, "As I read the story aloud to you, we'll talk together about the math." I stopped after reading the first page, when Ma tells her two children to share the cookies she made. "How many cookies did Sam and Victoria each get?" I asked. The students tried to count the cookies in the illustration but found it difficult. I asked Lindsey, who was sitting close by, to carefully count the cookies. She counted twelve.

"They both had six," Andy volunteered.

"Tell us more about how you know they

each got six," I replied to Andy to encourage him to share his thinking for the benefit of the other students and to help me more clearly understand his thinking.

"I could tell from the picture that there were twelve cookies on the plate," Andy explained. "I know I have to divide them so each person gets the same amount. There are two kids, and I know six plus six is twelve, so each kid got six cookies."

"How could you use multiplication as another way of saying Andy's idea?" I asked the class. I wanted the students to use their knowledge of multiplication as a tool whenever appropriate.

"There were two groups of six, which is two times six," Brenna explained. "Two times six is another way of thinking about six plus six."

"Another way could be six times two," Karina said.

"How would that relate to the problem?" I asked.

"It would mean six cookies two times," Karina said. While the students were used to interpreting 6 × 2 as "six groups of two," Karina's interpretation of 6 × 2 as "six two times" is also mathematically acceptable. I didn't comment on this to the class.

Luke said, "I have another way. The kids could just take the twelve cookies and give one to one kid, then one to the other kid, like that until all the cookies were gone and each person had the same amount."

"Yeah," several students said, while others nodded their agreement with Luke.

"What division sentence represents the problem?" I asked. I waited until over half the students had a hand up. I called on Seth.

"Twelve divided by two," Seth said. "Twelve is for the cookies and the two tells how many kids shared the cookies. The answer would be six cookies for each kid."

I continued reading the story, pausing each time new guests arrived to let the children figure out how many cookies each person would get. Then I asked the children to state a mathematical sentence for the cookie distribution and gave several a chance. Some used addition, some multiplication, and some division.

When I finished the story, I asked, "Did the book ever say how many cookies there were?"

"No," the children chorused.

"But we counted and it was twelve," Joaquin said.

"The next page after said that the two children got six cookies each," Carlos said. "We could figure it out from that."

"I agree," I responded. "I'd like you to tell me what happened each time new guests arrived, and I'll show you three ways to write mathematically what happened. So, what happened in the first part of the story?"

Natalia raised her hand. "The mother made twelve cookies and divided them by two. And twelve divided by two is six," she said. I wrote on the board:

$12 \div 2 = 6$

I pointed to the division symbol and said, "This is the division sign and we read it as 'divided by.' The equation says, 'Twelve divided by two equals six.'"

"You can also write twelve divided by two equals six like this," I continued. Next to the first representation, I wrote:

$$2 \overline{)12}^{6}$$

"There's a third way to write twelve divided by two equals six," I continued as I wrote:

$\frac{12}{2} = 6$

"What does the twelve stand for?" I asked, pointing to the 12s in all three of the mathematical recordings.

"Cookies," Addie responded.

"What does the two mean?" I pointed to the 2s.

"Two people," Kelsey said.

"And the six is how many cookies each person got," I concluded. "OK, what was the next part of the story?" As students gave answers and talked about them, I wrote the equations on the board. Finally, I had recorded:

$$12 \div 2 = 6 \qquad 2\overline{)12}^{\,6} \qquad \tfrac{12}{2} = 6$$

$$12 \div 4 = 3 \qquad 4\overline{)12}^{\,3} \qquad \tfrac{12}{4} = 3$$

$$12 \div 6 = 2 \qquad 6\overline{)12}^{\,2} \qquad \tfrac{12}{6} = 2$$

$$12 \div 12 = 1 \qquad 12\overline{)12}^{\,1} \qquad \tfrac{12}{12} = 1$$

"These tell mathematically what happened in the story," I said, pointing to the board. "What happened the next time the doorbell rang?"

The children responded enthusiastically. "Grandma came!" "She baked more cookies." "She brought lots more."

"Let's figure out how many more cookies Grandma brought," I said. "She has them in rows." I showed the class the page from the book, and the children counted along with me. When they found out that there were twelve rows with six cookies in each, Karina ran to get a calculator. But Afton, proud of knowing his multiplication facts, called out the answer. "It's seventy-two cookies!" I asked Karina to confirm Afton's answer on the calculator.

"But seventy-two cookies makes a tough problem for the story," I commented and continued. "Let's change it and pretend that Grandma brought eighteen more cookies. How many cookies would then be on the plate altogether? How much is eighteen plus twelve?" The children figured out that thirty cookies would be on the plate, and I wrote on the board:

$$30 \div 12 = \qquad 12\overline{)30} \qquad \tfrac{30}{12} =$$

I then held up a sheet of 12-by-18-inch drawing paper. I said, "Each of you will get a sheet of paper like this and fold it into eight parts, like this." I folded the paper as the students watched.

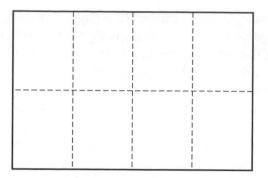

I continued, "On this paper, you'll retell the story, recording mathematically and drawing pictures to illustrate the division. In the first box of your paper, write the title of the story, *The Doorbell Rang*, and your name." I modeled for the students what to do by writing the title and my name in the first box.

"Use the next four boxes for what happened in the story. In each box, write the equations that tell what happened as I did on the board." I pointed to the equations on the board. "Then, in each box, draw a picture to show how you would divide the cookies in the story." To illustrate what I meant, I drew in the second box a sketch of two children with six cookies each and wrote the three mathematical sentences.

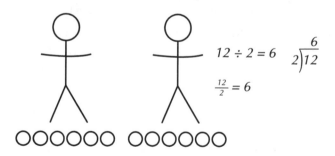

"Do we have to write all three ways?" Kenny asked.

I nodded and continued, "That leaves three more boxes on the paper. Use the next box for the problem of sharing thirty cookies among twelve children." I pointed to the three equations I had written on the board for this problem and added, "Find the answer and draw a picture to show

how you would divide thirty cookies among twelve children. In the last two boxes, you finish the story. Pretend the doorbell rings again. Then you decide: Did more people arrive, or more cookies, or both? It's up to you."

I instructed each table to designate someone to get the sheets of drawing paper for his or her group. I posted on the board the paper I'd used as an example for student reference during the work time.

Observing the Children

Most of the students quickly folded their papers into eight parts. Other students helped those few who were having difficulty. As I observed the students I reminded them to check the board for what should go in each box on their sheet of paper. Scott was uncertain about the idea of picturing twelve divided by two. He asked for my help, and I talked with him, referring him to what I'd drawn on my paper as an example.

Becca started with drawing a picture and then solving thirty divided by twelve. "Look, I figured it out," she said, pointing proudly to her work. "Each kid gets two whole cookies and a half of a cookie. For my new problem, nineteen more cookies are coming, so that's forty-nine cookies, and there will still be twelve kids." I left Becca to solve her new problem, making a note to check back. The numbers she had chosen were challenging.

As I walked toward Breanna's desk, Breanna said, "I know! I'm just going to have eighteen more people come to the door and then each gets one cookie." Then she changed her mind. "No, I'm going to have eight more people come."

"So there will be twenty people now," I commented.

"Yeah, so each person gets one . . . one and a half cookies." Breanna wrote *30 ÷ 20 = 1.5*, displaying her understanding of the decimal notation for one-half.

Afton, sitting next to Breanna, thought

aloud, "Twelve divided by four is . . . four? Am I right? Eight? . . . Every answer is eight, right?"

"No," replied Karina, who was sitting across the table from Afton. "They're all different."

"I don't get it," Afton complained. "What am I supposed to do? I don't get it." After a few minutes of insisting he didn't understand the problem, Afton drew twelve cookies and wrote *12 ÷ 2 = 6* in the first box. Then he drew twelve cookies again and wrote *12 ÷ 4 = 3* in the next box. He brought his paper to me.

"This is a good beginning," I said, "but your drawings aren't complete. They show the twelve cookies but not how many people there were to share them."

"I don't know what to do," Afton said.

"How many people were there in this box?" I asked, pointing to the box in which Afton had written *12 ÷ 4 = 3*.

"Four," he answered easily.

"I have an idea that might help," I said. "May I write on your paper?" Afton nodded. I wrote in the twelve circles he drew: *1, 2, 3, 4, 1, 2, 3, 4, 1, 2, 3, 4.*

"This shows one way to divide the cookies among four people," I said.

"Oh, I get it," Afton said, and returned to his seat. I decided to wait until later to ask Afton also to record the other equations on his paper. Afton used this method and worked independently on boxes three and four. He struggled to represent thirty divided by twelve. The method he used to distribute the cookies worked, but Afton was confused by the leftover cookies. Like many students this age, he thought division problems should come out with equal groups and nothing left over.

David, a careful, methodical worker,

persisted and came up with the answer to thirty divided by twelve: two each with six left over.

"What are you going to do with the six leftover cookies?" I asked.

He paused a moment then asked, "Can I break the cookies into two parts? If I have six cookies and break them into halves, that would be twelve halves, and everyone could get two whole cookies and one-half of a cookie."

"You may break them into halves," I replied.

"Or, I could give them to Grandma and Mom," David said, pleased with himself. "Grandma gets three and Mom gets three!"

Andy was very interested in the idea of each person getting some whole cookies and one-half of a cookie. He added two new problems to end the story. He explained, "Eight kids heard their moms calling and had to go home. That left four

kids and thirty cookies. So, thirty divided by four is seven and one-half each. I know because seven times four is twenty-eight. And four half cookies make two whole cookies. Twenty-eight and two is thirty. It works!" He had difficulty using correct mathematical notation to express the answer to his last problem. He wanted to divide seven cookies among three kids. His picture indicated that each child received two whole cookies and one-third of another cookie. His notation indicated each child received two and one-half cookies. (See Figure 3–1.)

Joaquin was also interested in dealing with leftover cookies. Like Andy, he finished the story with two new problems. The first showed thirty cookies shared by fourteen children. Joaquin explained, "That was two cookies for each kid. Fourteen and fourteen is twenty-eight. Two are left over. To split them, just cut each one into seven parts.

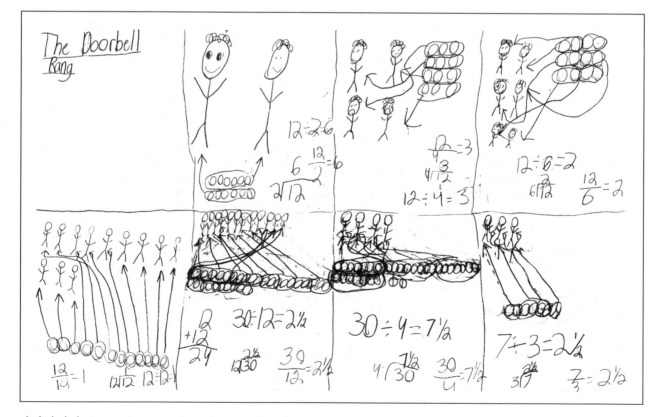

▲▲▲▲▲▲Figure 3–1   *Andy enjoyed using fractions but had difficulty expressing his answer in the last box using standard fractional notation.*

Two cookies times seven pieces in each cookie equals fourteen pieces. Each kid gets two whole cookies and one of the little pieces, and that's one-seventh of a cookie."

I checked back with Becca, who was trying to divide forty-nine cookies among twelve children. Her picture showed each child receiving four cookies with one cookie left over. She incorrectly wrote: $\frac{12}{49} = 4\frac{1}{2}$. However, Becca's drawing indicated her understanding of the concept of division. She drew twelve equal groups of cookies and showed the leftover cookie. Becca needed additional opportunities to learn how to represent division problems numerically, including how to show remainders. (See Figure 3–2.)

At the end of the period, most of the children hadn't completed the assignment, so I collected their work to return to them the next day.

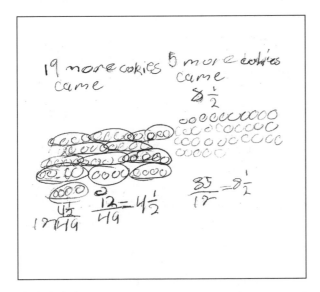

▲▲▲▲▲**Figure 3–2** *Becca's drawing showed a correct solution for forty-nine cookies shared among twelve children. She had difficulty writing the division as a fraction, and she showed the remainder as $\frac{1}{2}$ rather than 1.*

DAY 2

For the benefit of all students, particularly those who were absent the previous day, I gathered the students on the floor to review what we'd done the day before, both the mathematics and the assignment. "Let's look again mathematically at what happened first in the story," I said. I wrote on the board to reinforce for the children the mathematical symbolization:

$$12 \div 2 \qquad 2\overline{)12} \qquad \tfrac{12}{2}$$

"What does the twelve represent?" I asked, not taking anything for granted and wanting to help students who were having difficulty keeping track of which number represented cookies and which represented children and where to write these numbers. We also talked about what the 2 in each equation represented.

I continued in this way to summarize the story, recording mathematically on the board:

$$12 \div 4 \qquad 4\overline{)12} \qquad \tfrac{12}{4}$$
$$12 \div 6 \qquad 6\overline{)12} \qquad \tfrac{12}{6}$$

Some children thought they saw a pattern of counting by twos, offering twelve divided by eight as the next equation.

I suggested, "Let's look in the book. After there were six children, then two more children came and brought their four cousins. How many is that?"

"Six more," Katie said, "and six plus six equals twelve."

I nodded my agreement and wrote on the board:

$$12 \div 12 \qquad 12\overline{)12} \qquad \tfrac{12}{12}$$

"After you write these equations in the boxes, you still have three boxes left," I said. "Who remembers what goes in the next box?"

Amber raised her hand. "Next you do thirty divided by twelve," she said.

"And you have to figure it out and draw a picture," Nicki added.

"But then you still have more room on your paper," I said. "There are two more boxes, and you have to think about what might come next. What could happen if the doorbell rings again? What could you add?"

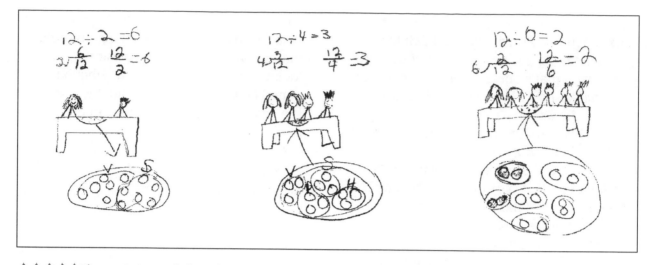

▲▲▲▲▲**Figure 3–3** *Jael drew her cookies on a plate and circled each person's portion.*

"The cookie monster came and ate them all," Breanna suggested with a giggle.

"Maybe the father could come," Jenny said. "He could bring more cookies. Or maybe he doesn't bring any cookies, but he also wants to eat cookies."

"If the father wants to eat cookies, how would that change the problem?" I asked the class.

"Oh, I know," Kelsey said. "That would make thirty cookies divided by thirteen people instead of thirty divided by twelve."

Emmi had another idea. "Grandma could eat cookies."

"Grandpa could come," Addie said.

"More kids could come," Mark offered.

"You can change the number of cookies, the number of people, or both to finish the story," I said.

"I already did all that," Ethan said. "Can I write another problem?"

"When you finish, you may write additional problems," I said.

Before the children returned to work, I asked if anyone would like to share his or her work in progress with the class. "As you listen to each other share," I reminded the students, "think about the different ideas you hear." I wanted the students to see that there are different ways to solve a problem.

"Who would like to show us how you're representing the cookies and the children?" I asked.

Jael volunteered, showing how she drew the cookies on plates and used circles to divide them among the correct number of children. (See Figure 3–3.)

"Who did it a different way?" I asked.

David had drawn arrows to show how many cookies each person received. (See Figure 3–4.)

"Notice the different ways people have done this," I said. "Remember, there's no one right way to do it. There are many ways to solve a problem."

Observing the Children

Soon after the children started working, Kelsey indicated that she was finished. In each box, she had drawn a person and the cookies nearby with arrows showing the person who received them. For thirty divided by twelve, she showed two and one-half cookies for each child. (See Figure 3–5 on page 30.)

On her paper, Kayla showed that she knew something about conventional notation, although sometimes she got it backward. This is typical for children as they are learning something new. (See Figure 3–6 on page 30.)

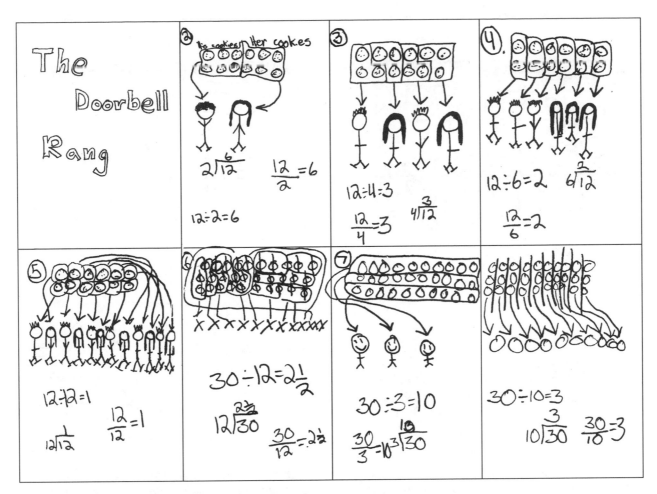

▲▲▲▲▲▲**Figure 3–4** *David used arrows to indicate the cookies for each person.*

Children tried various ways to write the notation for $2\frac{1}{2}$:

Scott: $2 + 1\frac{1}{2}$

Catalina: 2 in a half

Karina: $2\frac{2}{1}$

Carlos used a calculator and wrote the equation $30 \div 12 = 2.5$. He also wrote *2 and a half* to indicate he knew what the equation meant.

Annie used a calculator, but she didn't notice the decimal point and wrote *25*. Emily, sitting next to Annie, also wrote *25*.

"I don't think that's possible," I said to the girls. "If there were thirty cookies altogether, how could each person get twenty-five?"

The girls looked at each other. "We used the calculator," Annie said in defense.

"It's fine to use the calculator," I said, "but you also have to think about the answer and be sure it makes sense. Show me what you did on the calculator."

Emily punched in $30 \div 12$ as Annie and I watched.

"See that little dot between the two and the five?" I asked the girls. They nodded. "It's called a decimal point, and it's very important," I continued. "It means that the answer is two and then some; 'two point five' is more than two but less than three. The 'point five' means one-half."

"What do we do?" Annie asked, confused.

"If you want to use the calculator, then you have to write down exactly what the answer is, with the decimal point," I continued. "But you also need to find some other

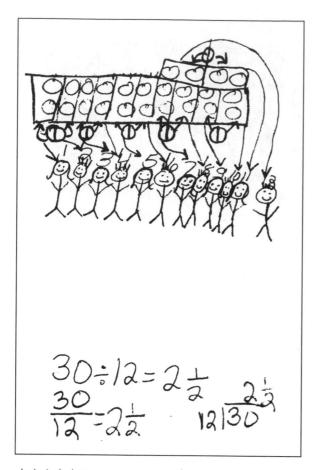

$$30 \div 12 = 2\frac{1}{2}$$
$$\frac{30}{12} = 2\frac{1}{2} \qquad 12\overline{)30}^{\,2\frac{1}{2}}$$

▲▲▲▲▲Figure 3–5 *Kelsey split the leftover cookies in half, drawing arrows to show where each half went.*

$$4\overline{)12}^{\,3} \qquad 4 \div 12 = 3$$
$$\frac{12}{4} = 3$$

▲▲▲▲▲Figure 3–6 *Kayla used conventional division notation but became confused when she wrote 4 ÷ 12 = 3 rather than 12 ÷ 4 = 3.*

way to solve the problem." I left the girls to decide what to do.

Students had different ideas for their own episodes. In describing her own problem for one more ring of the doorbell, Amber wrote the equation *15 ÷ 5 = 3*. However, when I questioned her, it became apparent she had lost track of the meaning of the numbers.

"Which number tells the number of people?" I asked. Amber shrugged.

Pointing to the 15 in the equation she wrote, I asked, "What does the fifteen tell us?"

Amber paused, then replied, "I think they're people. No, maybe it means kids." I could see Amber's frustration growing.

"Let's go back one box to the part where Grandma brought some cookies," I said as I pointed to the equation 30 ÷ 12 = 2½. "What does the thirty tell us?"

"There were thirty cookies," Amber replied. "Oh, I think I get it now. There were thirty cookies and the twelve tells how many kids and the two and one-half means how many cookies each kid got." I nodded to indicate my agreement.

"Let's go back to the equation you wrote," I said. "What does the fifteen tell you?"

"That's the number of cookies," Amber explained with a smile, "and there were five kids, so that's what the five means, and each kid got three cookies." Again I nodded my agreement.

"I notice you haven't drawn a picture to go with your equation," I commented. "Now that you understand better, please include a picture."

Amber nodded and got to work. She easily created one last problem independently. (See Figure 3–7.)

I noticed Addie working intently on her paper and decided to check on her next. She looked up and proudly showed me what she was doing. Addie explained, "There was a huge wind and all but six of the cookies blew away. None of the twelve kids blew away. Now twelve kids have to share six cookies. The math sentence is 'Six divided by twelve equals one-half.' And I proved it with a picture." Addie had not written her story on her paper, but she correctly wrote the division using all three ways. Also, she drew a picture to accurately represent the story she told.

Derek was using interlocking cubes to figure out thirty divided by twelve. He counted out thirty cubes and then put them into ten piles of three each.

"I see that you have ten piles of threes there," I said. "Don't you want to divide the cookies for twelve people?"

He nodded and said, "So what do I do?"

"How many piles do you think you should have if you want to divide thirty cookies among twelve people?"

"Twelve?" he asked.

"Try that and see if it makes sense to you."

Derek came to get me when he had finished. He had twelve piles with two in each and six extras. "What are you going to do with the leftover cookies?" I asked.

"I don't know," he responded

"Can you split a cookie in half?" I asked.

"Yes," Derek said.

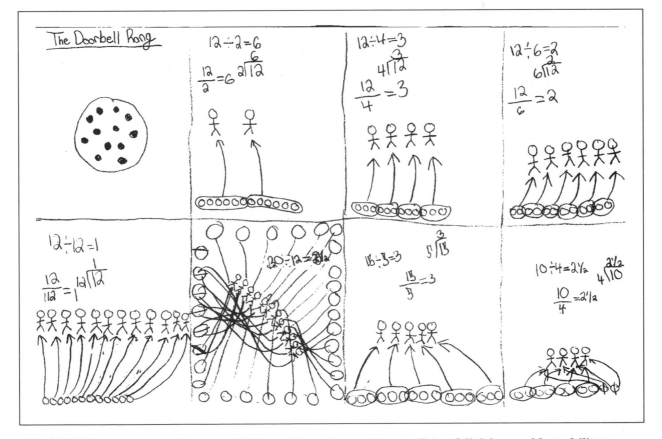

▲▲▲▲▲▲Figure 3–7 *Amber's work showed her clear understanding of division and her ability to use correct division notation.*

"So if you cut the six leftovers in half, how many halves would you have?"

Derek thought for a moment and said, "Twelve. Oh, I know." He drew two boxes and a half circle next to each face on his paper. He recorded: $30 \div 12 = 2\frac{1}{2}$.

Breanna was involved with the idea of sharing thirty cookies. "Look," she explained, "with two people, you get fifteen, and with three people you get ten."

"How did you figure that out?" I asked.

"I just knew," Breanna responded.

"Could you figure out how to share thirty cookies among four people?" I asked.

"Ooooh, I think so," Breanna said. Taking advantage of Breanna's interest, I recorded on her paper:

> 2 people—15
>
> 3 people—10
>
> 4 people—

A few minutes later, Breanna called me over. "It doesn't come out even. There are two extras." I showed her how to record the answer as 7 R2. Breanna was pleased and, on her own, continued the list up to twelve, figuring out how to share thirty cookies among each number of people. (See Figure 3–8.)

Jenny started out drawing two people and twelve cookies. Then she circled every two cookies. What she did made sense for solving twelve divided by two abstractly, but not in this context; instead of making groups of two, Jenny needed to divide the cookies into two groups. Jenny became frustrated. I asked her what the 12 represented and what the 2 meant and then asked her what question she was trying to answer. This clarification was enough for Jenny to solve the problem successfully.

DAY 3

The next day, I initiated a class discussion by inviting the students to present the events they had added to the story. Kirk

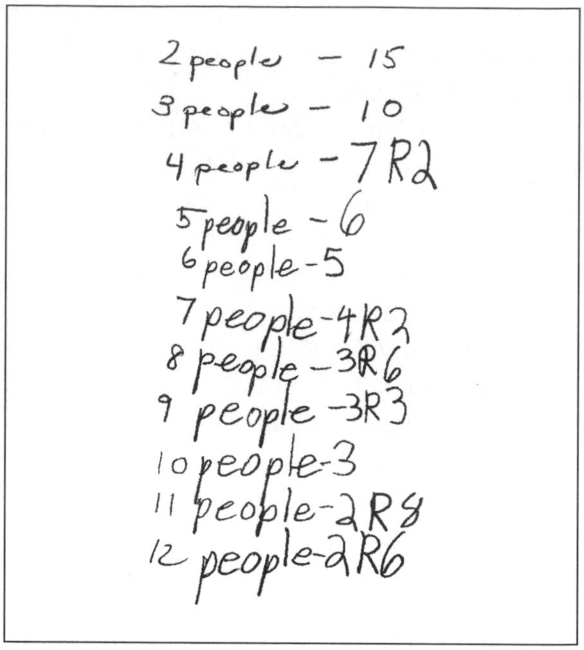

▲▲▲▲▲Figure 3–8 *Breanna figured out how to share thirty cookies among two through twelve people.*

went first. He used the idea of leftovers: *30 ÷ 12 = 2 each and 6 leftover*. Then he found people to eat the leftovers: *Mom 3 and Grandma 3*. In the last box, when the doorbell rang again, *It was Arnold Schwarsanager. He brought 50 more cookies. 80 ÷ 15 = 5 each with 5 left over*. Kirk decided the leftovers should be given to Arnold. "Nobody argues with Arnold," he insisted.

Katie shared next. For her sequel, she wrote: *Cookie Monster came and ate 5 cookies so there is only 25 cookies and 1 more kid came so there is 13 kids and the kid had 1 cookie so there are 26 cookies. How manny cookies would each kid get? Every kid would get 2 cookies.* "I know I'm right because thirteen times two is twenty-six," Katie explained, making an important connection between multiplication and division. (See Figure 3–9.)

For his sequel, Afton wrote: *Then grandpa came in with a giant cookie. And he splits the cookie into 12 pieces. So each kid*

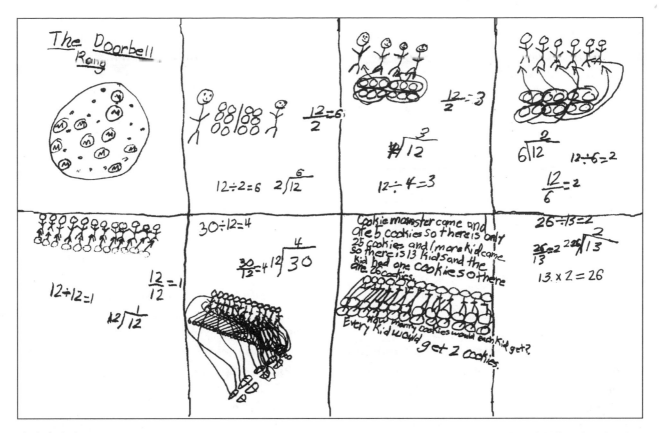

▲▲▲▲▲▲**Figure 3–9** *Katie made an important connection between division and multiplication in the last box, although she wrote one division problem incorrectly.*

got 2½ cookies and a triangle. "He cut it like a pizza," he explained.

Emmi decided that when the doorbell rang, one person was there, wanting cookies. She was stumped at first by the problem of thirty divided by thirteen, and she explained to the class what she had done. "I took counters and made double-deckers by putting one on top of another," she said. "But then there were four extras. So I made three-decker cookies. That didn't work. Then I found out I could have leftovers, so I did double-deckers with four cookies left over."

I then raised the issue of using calculators. "I noticed when some of you used the calculator, you got strange numbers," I said. "For example, when you divide thirty by fourteen, you get two point one four two eight five seven one." I wrote *2.1428571* on the board. "Now that is a very strange number," I continued. "We

don't talk about cookies with this number. So for this problem, the calculator answer doesn't make sense. But when you do thirty divided by twelve, you get two and five tenths." I wrote that on the board.

"Some of you remembered from before that point five, or five-tenths, equals one-half, so you can make sense of the calculator answer," I said. "But I'd solve thirty cookies divided among fourteen people a different way. I'd figure it out by myself. Do you think everyone will get one cookie?" I quickly drew thirty circles on the board. The children nodded.

"Can everyone get two cookies?" I then asked. The students figured out that if everyone got two cookies, there would be two left over. I showed them how to record this mathematically:

$$30 \div 14 = 2\ R2 \qquad\qquad 14\overline{)30}^{\,2\ R2}$$

I continued, "Let's do thirty divided by twelve this way. Talk to your neighbor about how many cookies each person would get and how many would be left over."

After a few minutes, I asked what they had found out. Kayla reported that everyone got two cookies, with six extras. I wrote on the board:

$$30 \div 12 = 2 \, R6 \qquad 12 \overline{)30}^{\,2 \, R6}$$

A number of students insisted that the answer was two and one-half; they were eager to show that they had the "right" answer and didn't want to hear about the remainder.

I explained, "You can write remainders two ways, as leftovers or as fractions. You have to consider the problem to know whether it makes better sense to write the remainder as a leftover or as a fraction. Sometimes either way makes sense. For example, if you are making two teams to play a game at recess and you have five kids, it would make better sense to say

there were two kids on each team with one leftover. To say there were two and one-half kids on each team doesn't make much sense. But if you had two kids and five cookies, you could either write the remainder as a leftover or a fraction. You could give each kid two and one-half cookies or you could give each kid two cookies with one leftover."

EXTENSION

At a later time, have students work individually or in pairs to write their own stories about things that are shared each time the doorbell rings. Remind students how to fold the paper into eight sections as they did before. Then explain that they are to write in each panel what happens each time the doorbell rings. Before students begin their work, it's helpful to generate a list of topics that can be shared each time the doorbell rings. Figures 3–10 and 3–11 show how two students worked on this activity.

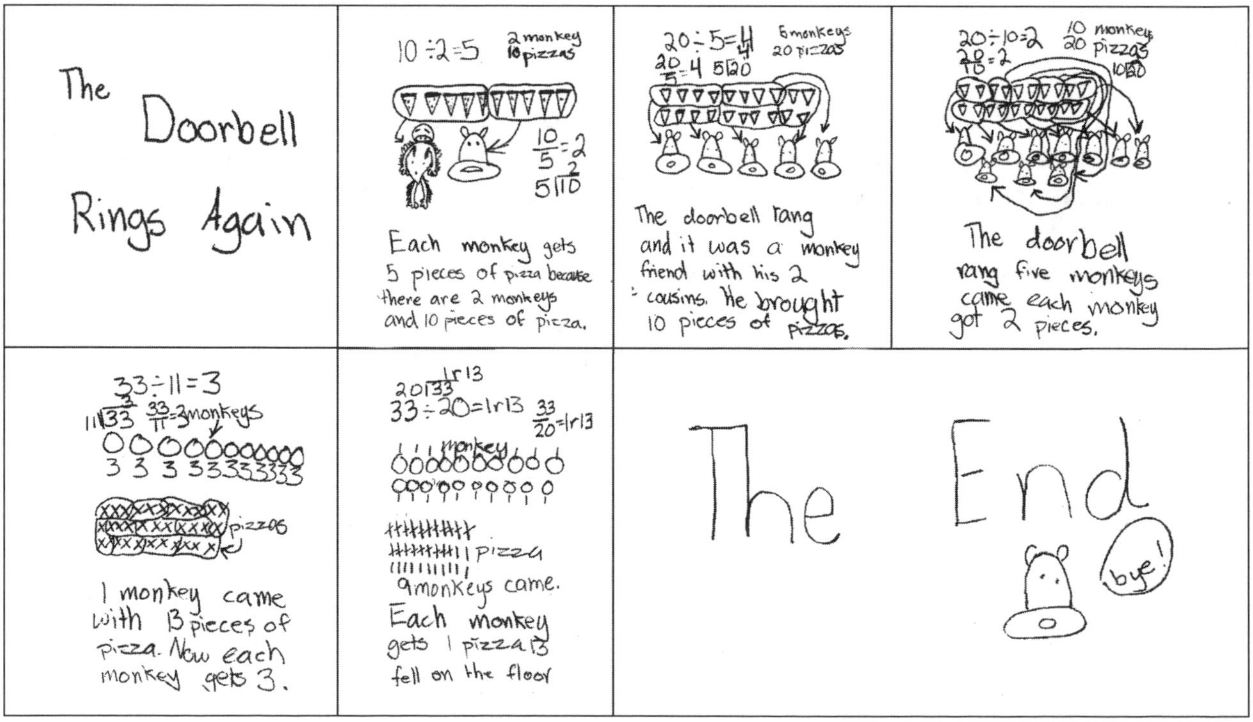

▲▲▲▲▲▲Figure 3–10 *David's work showed strong conceptual understanding of division and his ability to use division notation to represent a problem.*

▲▲▲▲▲▲**Figure 3–11** *Kelsey made an error in the division sentence in the second box. However, her understanding was strong, as her drawings indicate. She made strong connections among operations when she used repeated addition and multiplication to verify her division.*

Questions and Discussion

▲▲▲

▲ *How do you handle careless errors, for example, if a student miscounts the cookies in the drawings?*

As I circulate through the class as students work, I look over shoulders and monitor what they're doing. If I notice an error, I ask the child about it. When the child sees the error, I ask him or her to correct it, giving help if needed. If I notice errors later, I ask students to explain their thinking so that I can better understand their thinking and use the information to plan follow-up instruction.

▲ *Some children became confused when trying to figure out what to draw or what the problem was asking. Why didn't you just tell them?*

To simply tell a child something that he or she can figure out with guidance is to take away an opportunity to discover something independently. Also, telling a child something that has a logical underpinning runs the risk that the student will do what we say but won't understand. When children make sense of something for themselves, their learning is deeper and that builds confidence. With time, the children see themselves as problem solvers capable of thinking independently and understanding.

▲ *When students use calculators, how do you know they understand what they're doing?*

For students to use a calculator, they must understand what the problem is asking them to do. This means they must know what numbers to use and be able to determine correctly the operation or operations required.

In this lesson, as with all others, I asked the students to explain the meaning of their answers. For example, 30 divided by 12 is 2.5. I asked the students to interpret the "point five." If they couldn't, they were instructed to use another way to solve the problem that made sense to them. Even when students correctly interpret the decimal remainder, or find answers using ways other than calculators, I often ask them to verify their answer by finding it a second way.

▲ *Don't children use calculators because it's easier than thinking for themselves?*

This hasn't been the case in my experience. More often, students will become engrossed in the problem, ignoring calculators altogether. Many children enjoy the challenge of figuring out problems on their own. However, it's useful for children to know when the numbers are out of their grasp and to know that a calculator can give them access in these situations.

CHAPTER FOUR
DIVIDING COOKIES

Overview

Dividing Cookies gives children experience with the sharing model of division while also engaging them with fractions and providing the geometric challenge of dividing circles into equal parts. Children must think spatially as they divide various numbers of circles ("cookies") into four equal shares. Asking children to report how much each child gets provides the opportunity to introduce the class to the symbolism of fractions and helps children learn how to use fractions to represent remainders in the answers to division problems.

Materials

▲ *Cookies* worksheet, duplicated on colored paper, at least 2 per group (see Blackline Masters)
▲ *Dividing Cookies* recording sheet, 5 per group (see Blackline Masters)

Time

▲ one class period

Teaching Directions

1. Cut out a few paper cookies to show the class.

2. Tell the children that they will be sharing paper cookies. Show them the ones you cut out and the duplicated worksheets of cookie patterns. Explain that they will have to cut out the cookies they'll use.

3. To introduce fractional notation, draw a circle on the board, divide it into fourths, and shade three of the four parts. Ask students: "How much is shaded?"

Explain to students that the three indicates the number of parts shaded while the four tells the total parts needed to make one whole. Ask a student to write three-fourths on the board as a fraction. Explain to students that we always say the top number first and the bottom number second. Repeat for $\frac{1}{2}$ and $1\frac{1}{2}$.

4. To help students think about dividing cookies into equal shares, ask: "Suppose a group of four had four cookies. How many would each person get if they shared the cookies equally?" The answer will be obvious to the children, but this is a good opportunity to discuss the concept of "sharing equally."

5. Explain that they'll work in groups of four and solve several problems, first sharing six cookies, then five cookies, three cookies, two cookies, and one cookie. Show students the *Dividing Cookies* recording sheet and explain that they should first write each student's name at the top and fill in the number of cookies they are sharing. Then they take the number of paper cookies they need, divide them up, and paste each person's share in one box on the worksheet. Finally, they answer the question at the bottom of the worksheet: How much did each person get?

6. Explain that after solving the first problem of sharing six cookies, the group should check with you before continuing. Once you've checked the group's first solution, the group can continue with the other problems of sharing five cookies, three cookies, two cookies, and one cookie. Remind students that they should use a new recording sheet for each new problem.

7. Organize the class into groups with four students in each. If there are any groups with two or three students, tell them they should solve the problems as if there were four children, so they'll be able to compare their solutions with the others in the class.

8. After the students have solved all the problems, initiate a class discussion. Have students share their solutions for several problems. If you think it's needed or appropriate, take this opportunity to do some instruction about standard fractional notation.

Teaching Notes

Dividing Cookies provides students with a sharing experience in division. Students know the total number of cookies and they also know the number of children, or groups. When they solve the problems, they are finding the number of cookies in each group.

Focusing children's attention on what the numbers in the problem mean will increase and deepen their understanding of division. Ask children questions such as How many cookies did you have when you started? Where is the number of cookies you started with shown in the number sentence? What does the four mean? What are you trying to figure out?

Students encounter fractions in this lesson. Spending a few minutes to model how to write fractions and to explain what the numerator and denominator represent is useful. When fractions are used to represent a remainder, the numerator tells the number left over while the denominator indicates the number needed to make a complete group. For example, a remainder of three-fourths means that there are three left over. The four tells us that if there were four left, there would be enough for each group to have one more.

The Lesson

▲▲

Before class I cut out several paper circles from a *Cookies* worksheet (see Blackline Masters). To begin the lesson I said, "The good news is that today we're going to share cookies. The bad news is that these are the cookies." I held up several two-inch paper circles I'd cut out, and the children groaned.

I then held up a sheet of green copier paper covered with two-inch-diameter circles. "We're going to cut out a lot of these circles and use them to figure out answers to some problems," I said. (The color of the paper doesn't matter; what matters is the contrast, so that when children cut and paste their cookies onto white paper, the fractional parts will stand out.)

Next, I drew a circle on the board, divided it into fourths, and shaded three-quarters of it. I asked, "Who can tell me how much of the circle is shaded?"

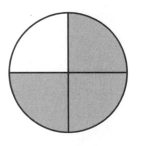

About a half dozen children raised a hand, and I called on Afton.

"It's three-fourths," he said.

"That's right," I confirmed. "I divided the circle into four parts and each part is called 'one-fourth.' Then I shaded in three of the four parts, so the part I shaded is called 'three-fourths.' It's also OK to say 'three-quarters.'"

The children remained quiet, making it difficult to tell who understood, but I continued. "Does anyone know how to write 'three-fourths' or 'three-quarters'?" I asked.

Ling came to the board and wrote:

$\frac{4}{3}$

"You've used the right two numbers," I said, "but you need to switch them. When there are three out of four parts, three-fourths, the first number goes on top and the second number on the bottom."

Ling rewrote the fraction correctly:

$\frac{3}{4}$

"We always say the top number first. It's three out of four," I emphasized, "so three-fourths of the circle is shaded."

Next I drew a half circle on the board.

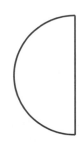

"How much is this?" I asked the class. About half of the students raised a hand.

"It's half," William answered.

"Yes, it is," I confirmed. "Can anyone tell how to write the number for 'one-half'?"

Cindy knew and came to the board and confidently wrote:

$\frac{1}{2}$

Some of the other children nodded their agreement; many just watched.

I drew the rest of the circle using a dotted line.

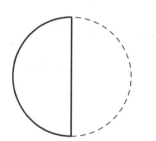

I explained, "What I drew to start with is one of two equal-size pieces, so each is one-half. You write that with a one over a two, just as Cindy did." Next, I drew a circle and a half circle.

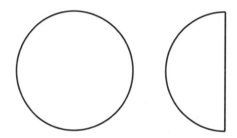

"This is one whole circle and one-half of a circle," I said, writing on the board as I spoke:

$1 + \frac{1}{2}$

"I can also write this another way, without the plus sign." I wrote:

$1\frac{1}{2}$

I pointed out, "I write the whole number larger than the numbers in the fraction."

I wasn't sure what the children knew about fractions or the conventions of fractional notation, since I hadn't done any formal instruction with fractions as yet this year. Although I knew this brief introduction wouldn't be of much use to children who had had no experience with the sym-

bolism of fractions, I hoped that it would serve as a help or reminder to children who did have some prior experience.

I returned to explaining the cookie-sharing activity. "In this activity, you're going to share cookies in groups of four," I began. "Suppose your group has four cookies to share; how many will each person get if you make sure to *share equally*?" I emphasized "share equally," an important concept when considering fractional parts.

"One," the children chorused.

I acknowledged, "OK, that was easy. You know about sharing." I continued with the directions. "You're going to do this activity several times," I said, "each time starting with a different number of cookies. And each time, you'll show on a recording sheet the equal shares you make."

I showed the students a sample *Dividing Cookies* recording sheet (see Blackline Masters). "You'll use a new recording sheet each time you share a different number of cookies," I explained. "Each time you share the cookies equally among the four of you, first cut the cookies out of the green paper and paste each person's share in a box. Then, at the bottom of the recording sheet, describe what you did by answering the question How much did each person get? Your group will do five problems, sharing cookies five times," I explained as I wrote:

Cookies	People
6	4
5	4
3	4
2	4
1	4

"First your group will share six cookies, paste the shares on a sheet, and record how much each person got," I said. "After you share six cookies equally, show me your paper so I can check that you did it correctly. Then you'll get another recording sheet and do the same for five cookies.

You'll do five sharing problems, using a different number of cookies each time."

I then talked with the class about how the groups should work. "Decide in your group who will do the tasks that need to be done," I said. "One person will get the recording sheet; another person will get two sheets of cookies; one person will get four pairs of scissors; another person will have a pencil ready to write everyone's name on the recording sheet. For each different worksheet, someone else in your group should do the writing.

"Together, cut out the cookies you'll need. You might want to cut out just the six cookies for the first problem, or figure out how many you'll need for all five problems and cut them all out."

I reminded the children what to do when their group finished sharing six cookies and recording the results. "Raise your hands so I can come and check. Remember, every member of your group should be able to explain your thinking."

OBSERVING THE CHILDREN

The children started work eagerly. Some groups cut out just the six circles they needed for the first problem; others cut out all of the circles.

I noticed that Afton, quick with numbers, added the numbers I had written in the Cookies column on the board. "We need seventeen," he said. Then he quickly counted to find there were nine circles on a sheet. "Hey, we don't need to cut two whole sheets," he announced to his group.

When a group had difficulty, I typically gave the students time to work out their problems. For example, Marco, Irina, Addie, and Beth got off to a rough start. Addie insisted on cutting out all of the cookies herself; Beth fiddled with the ones she had already cut out; Marco and Irina argued over who would write names on the recording sheet. The group finally settled

down and quickly solved the first problem, had me check it, and continued.

Other groups began work immediately, but not always as a team. Gib protested as Cami, without consulting anyone else in the group, immediately started cutting all the cookies in half. Carol and Kirk didn't say anything, but Gib insisted that Cami talk things over before cutting. Finally, Cami got up and went to another group, asking Troy, "Are you supposed to cut the cookies in half?"

Troy answered, "If you want to."

Cami returned to her group. By then, Carol had given everybody in the group one-half of a cookie. "It works," she said.

"See?" Cami said to Gib, who remained silent.

This group understood the idea of equal sharing: When they shared three cookies, they labeled each person's share as *a half and a $\frac{1}{4}$*. For five cookies, they wrote: *a whole cookies & $\frac{1}{4}$*.

When Marco, Irina, Addie, and Beth got to the fourth problem, sharing two cookies among four people, they were unsure about how to write each person's share. They had written $1\frac{1}{2}$ and called to me for help.

"Read your answer to me," I said to them.

"One-half," Addie and Marco said in unison.

Having them read gave me valuable information that they were able to construct equal shares and knew how much each person would get, but they weren't sure about standard fractional notation. I explained to them that what they had written indicated that each person got a whole cookie and a half.

"Oh, I see," Irina said. "I can fix it."

"Make sure that everyone agrees," I reminded her and left the group to continue.

Troy, Taylor, Kirk, and Breanna quickly solved the six-cookie problem. When they began to share five cookies, they discovered that they could create a new whole cookie if they grouped each person's fractional share in the center of the page. (See Figure 4–1.)

Breanna set herself the task of cutting all the cookies into quarters. She cut, and her partners figured out what kind of interesting arrangements they could make. These children concentrated on the design of the entire field of four rectangles. They wanted their answers to be right, but they also wanted them to look nice. (See Figure 4–2.)

Nicki, Jianna, Santana, and Rod showed that when they divided five cookies among the four of them, they each got one and one-fourth cookies. Jianna observed, "If five divided by four equals one and one-fourth, then four times one and one-fourth must equal five." Then Jianna counted aloud the four whole cookies and added the four-fourths to verify her thinking. (See Figure 4–3.)

Elijah and Joaquin worked as a pair. Their imaginary partners were Wort and Buck. As I checked their work, Elijah said, "We wrote the division part in three ways."

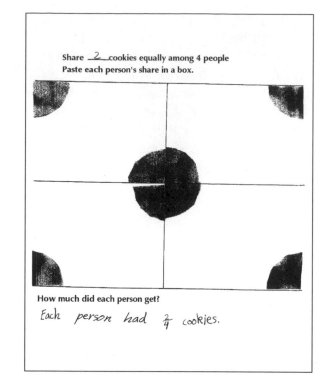

Share __2__ cookies equally among 4 people
Paste each person's share in a box.

How much did each person get?

Each person had 2/4 cookies.

▲▲▲▲▲▲Figure 4–2 *Troy, Taylor, Kirk, and Breanna arranged the cookie shares in a pattern that pleased them.*

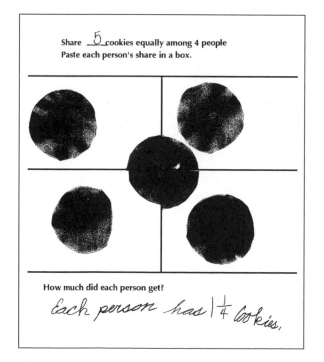

Share __5__ cookies equally among 4 people
Paste each person's share in a box.

How much did each person get?

Each person has 1¼ cookies.

▲▲▲▲▲▲Figure 4–1 *Troy, Taylor, Kirk, and Breanna shared five cookies and showed how each person got one and one-quarter cookies.*

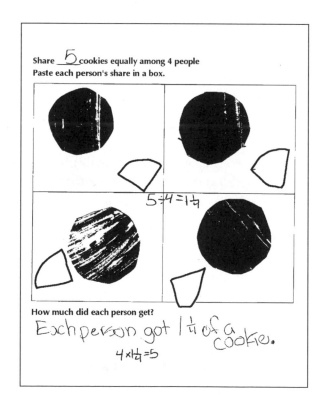

Share __5__ cookies equally among 4 people
Paste each person's share in a box.

$5 \div 4 = 1\frac{1}{4}$

How much did each person get?

Each person got 1¼ of a cookie.

$4 \times 1\frac{1}{4} = 5$

▲▲▲▲▲▲Figure 4–3 *Jianna, Nicki, Santana, and Rod used multiplication to confirm their division.*

42   Lessons for Introducing Division

Joaquin had a thoughtful yet hesitant look on his face. "When we wrote two-fourths equals one-half, I think we wrote two fractions. I drew a line to divide a cookie into fourths and I think I discovered that two-fourths is the same amount of cookie as one-half."

I was surprised by Joaquin's insight. "Let's check your thinking. What was the total number of cookies?"

"Two," Joaquin and Elijah responded. Elijah was also intrigued with Joaquin's insight.

"That's right," I said. "When you wrote two-fourths as a fraction to show the division problem, which number represented the total number of cookies?"

Joaquin and Elijah simultaneously pointed to the 2 in $\frac{2}{4}$.

"How many groups did you have to have?" I asked.

"Four," Joaquin replied.

"Why four?" I pushed.

"Because there were four people sharing the cookies," Joaquin said. "And the four is here," Joaquin added as he pointed to the denominator.

"And each person got one-half," Elijah said with surprise. (See Figure 4–4.)

Afton, Seth, and their two imaginary partners, Bob and Herb, were working on dividing four cookies among four people. This was not one of the assigned problems, but the boys decided to do it anyway. I noticed that they had distributed the four cookies, showing that each person got one. When they answered the question at the bottom of the page, they indicated each person received four cookies.

I interrupted their work and said, "I notice that you wrote when four people share four cookies they get four cookies each." The boys nodded their head in agreement with what I said. "How many cookies did you start with?" I asked.

"Four," Afton and Seth said together.

"The total cookies you started with was

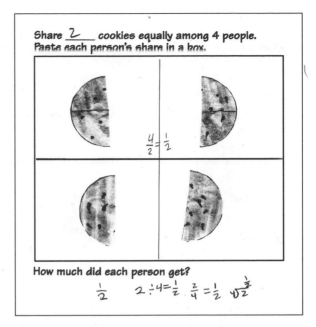

▲▲▲▲▲▲Figure 4–4 *Joaquin and Elijah used three number sentences to show the division.*

four," I repeated. "How many people have to share the cookies?"

"Four," the boys replied.

"You have four cookies and you have to share them among four people, or groups, so what question do you need to answer?" I asked.

"You want to figure out how many cookies in each group," Seth replied, and Afton nodded.

"If you only have four cookies to start with, how can four people each get four cookies?" I asked. Seth got a look of surprise on his face.

"For four people to get four cookies, you'd have to have sixteen cookies to start with," Seth said.

"Oh yeah," Afton agreed. "Four people getting four cookies when there are only four cookies to begin with doesn't make any sense! If we look at our paper, it shows that each person only got one cookie."

Afton wrote the correct division sentence on the paper, although he forgot to correct what was written at the bottom of the page. (See Figure 4–5.)

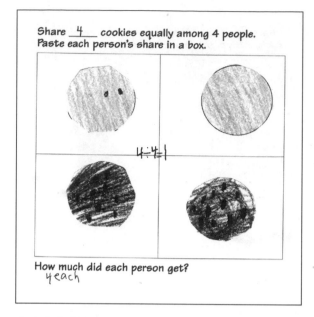

Share __4__ cookies equally among 4 people. Paste each person's share in a box.

4÷4=1

How much did each person get?
4 each

▲▲▲▲▲▲**Figure 4–5** *Afton and Seth indicated at the bottom of the page a possible lack of understanding.*

After solving the five required problems, Cindy, Jacob, Kareem, and Jody decided to do an extra one, sharing seven cookies among four people. (See Figure 4–6.)

Lindsey, Chandra, Kayla, and Andrea

Share __7__ cookies equally among 4 people Paste each person's share in a box.

How much did each person get? We each got 1 hole, one half, and one quarter.

▲▲▲▲▲▲**Figure 4–6** *Cindy, Jacob, Kareem, and Jody solved an extra problem: sharing seven cookies.*

completed the five required problems and then decided to share nine cookies among four people. (See Figure 4–7.)

Share __9__ cookies equally among 4 people. Paste each person's share in a box.

How much did each person get?
Each person gets 2 and ¼.

▲▲▲▲▲▲**Figure 4–7** *Lindsey, Chandra, Kayla, and Andrea shared nine cookies among four people.*

A CLASS DISCUSSION

When most students had finished and were working on extra problems, I asked for the students' attention. "It's interesting to see how people represented their thinking," I said. "When you had one cookie and you had to share it with four people, how much did each person get?"

"One-fourth," Cami answered, holding up half of a cookie.

Several hands went up, most likely in disagreement with Cami. Rather than telling Cami she was wrong, I asked her to explain her thinking. Cami explained, "When you cut up a cookie into four parts, each part is one-fourth." She looked at her piece. "Oh, wait! This is a half!" she corrected herself.

"Why do you think it's a half?" I asked.

"Because two of these make one whole cookie," Cami answered.

I wrote $\frac{1}{2}$ on the board, explaining, "This means 'one out of two,' and for four people, Cami needs 'one out of four.'" I wrote $\frac{1}{4}$ on the board.

"Suppose I take another cookie," I said. "If I talk about this cookie and one-fourth of a cookie, how much do I have altogether?"

"One and one-fourth," the class chorused.

"On your papers, when you shared five cookies," I continued, "some of you wrote one and a fourth in words for each person's share. How would you write it in numbers?" I called on Derryl, who walked up to the board and wrote:

$1\frac{1}{4}$

"What happened when you had to share three cookies?" I asked and called on Marco.

"We divided them in half and gave them out," he said. "But then we had two pieces left, so we divided them into quarters."

"How much did each person get?" I asked.

"A half and a quarter," Jenny volunteered. She showed the group's paper. (See Figure 4–8.)

"Can I show how to write it in numbers?" Kelsey asked. I nodded. Kelsey came up and wrote on the board:

$\frac{1}{2}+\frac{1}{4}$

"Did anyone divide three cookies a different way?" I asked.

Kendall was eager to show how his group had divided the cookies. "Each person got three-quarters," he said, showing their paper. (See Figure 4–9.)

"Do you know how to write 'three-quarters' in numbers?" I asked Kendall. He shook his head. Troy volunteered, however, came to the board, and wrote:

$\frac{3}{4}$

I commented about the solutions Kelsey and Kendall showed. "Their answers are different," I commented. "Did each group divide the cookies equally among four people?"

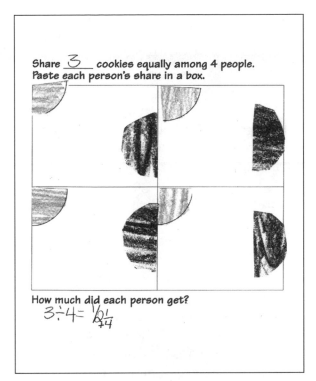

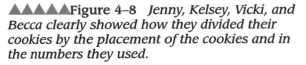

▲▲▲▲▲▲**Figure 4–8** *Jenny, Kelsey, Vicki, and Becca clearly showed how they divided their cookies by the placement of the cookies and in the numbers they used.*

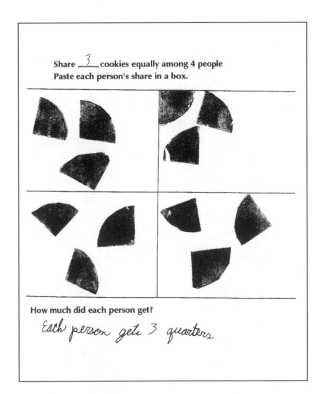

▲▲▲▲▲▲**Figure 4–9** *Kendall's group divided three cookies into quarters to share them.*

Children disagreed. "No," Robbie insisted. "Kendall's group got more cookies."

"Three-fourths means one-half plus one-fourth, so they're the same," said Afton.

Other children joined in the discussion. Some agreed with Robbie that more pieces meant more cookies. Others could see that the half was made up of two quarters.

"Look," Derryl said, going to the board and tracing a half-cookie portion. Then he taped two one-fourth pieces on it.

"Wow!" Robbie was impressed.

I explained, "Kelsey's group passed out halves, and then, when they needed to, they cut two halves in half, making quarters. Kendall's group cut the cookies into quarters first and then passed out quarters. These are two different ways to solve the same problem. Both groups came up with three-fourths of a cookie for each person. Three-fourths can mean one-half and one-fourth or one-fourth, one-fourth, and one-fourth." I wrote on the board:

$$\frac{1}{2} + \frac{1}{4} = \frac{3}{4}$$
$$\frac{1}{4} + \frac{1}{4} + \frac{1}{4} = \frac{3}{4}$$

I continued and gave the class an explanation of fractional symbols. "Let me explain why three-fourths is written as a three over a four," I said, writing the fraction on the board. I cut a circle into four parts. "The four tells us that we cut the cookie into four pieces. The three on top tells how many pieces I have. If I have three-fourths of a cookie, I have three parts of the four parts of the whole cookie."

I didn't introduce the words *numerator* and *denominator*. Instead, I used the cookies as a reference for the children. I drew on the board a diagram of what I had just done. I then asked a question that I frequently ask: "Did someone share three cookies a different way?"

Derryl explained, "We kind of did it two ways. We gave each person a half and a quarter, but we said that also means seventy-five percent." He showed his group's paper. (See Figure 4–10.)

I interpreted this explanation for the class. "Derryl's group said the whole cookie is one hundred percent. If you eat a whole cookie, you get one hundred percent of the cookie. If you eat half of a cookie, you get fifty percent. If you eat one-fourth of a cookie, you eat twenty-five percent. So three-fourths of a cookie is seventy-five percent."

Although this was the class's first formal work with fractions, it was clear that some students were familiar with the concept. Children seemed to have different pieces of information about fractions. By having the students share cookies and write and illustrate how much each person got, I learned what they knew about conventional notation and how well they grasped the abstract concept of fractional parts.

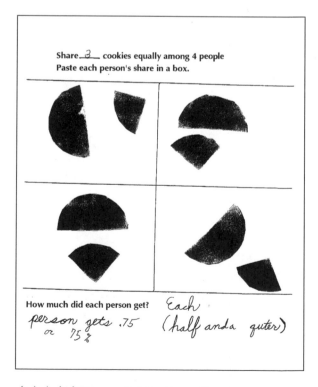

Share __3__ cookies equally among 4 people
Paste each person's share in a box.

How much did each person get? Each person gets .75 or 75% (half and a quter)

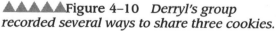Figure 4–10 *Derryl's group recorded several ways to share three cookies.*

EXTENSIONS

1. Ask students to explore the following: *Four people want to share cookies. They want only numbers of cookies that will result in no leftovers. For example, four people could share four cookies with no leftovers. What other numbers of cookies will work?*

Explain how you know. Repeat the activity for other numbers of people.

2. Pose the following problem: *There are twelve cookies. What numbers of people could share the cookies equally so there are no leftovers? Explain how you know.* Repeat the activity for other numbers of cookies.

Questions and Discussion

▲▲

▲ *In this lesson, remainders are expressed as fractions. Won't this confuse students? Why not just have whole cookies left over?*

Some students indicated remaining cookies as a whole number; for example, each person got two cookies and there was one left. This is by no means incorrect. The context of the problem, sharing cookies, is a natural way for children to discover that sometimes it makes sense to have a fractional part as a remainder. Splitting a cookie in half so each person gets one-half instead of having one left over makes sense. In other contexts, such as sharing pennies in the *Sharing Money* lesson, having one-half of the shared item (for example, one-half penny) doesn't make sense. Having a context gives meaning and helps children see when solutions make sense and don't make sense.

▲ *Why didn't you spend more time teaching the students how to write fractions and what the parts of fractions mean prior to teaching the lesson?*

The context of the lesson provided motivation and interest for the students, making their learning relevant and purposeful. Although some weren't sure how to write fractions, they asked for help when needed, making their questions and learning relevant, or they used ways other than standard fractional notation to express their ideas. The context gave a purpose for learning standard fractional notation.

CHAPTER FIVE
THE GAME OF LEFTOVERS

Overview

This game of chance gives children experience using the sharing model of division to divide quantities of color tiles into equal groups and think about remainders. Starting with fifteen tiles, the children play in pairs and take turns rolling a die, sharing the tiles among that many groups and keeping the tiles that are left over. They record a division equation for each roll. Children extend the game by creating their own dice and choosing how many tiles they wish to start with.

Materials

- ▲ dice, 1 per pair of students
- ▲ 1-inch color tiles, 15 per pair of students
- ▲ paper cups or other containers to hold 15 color tiles
- ▲ 3-inch squares of construction paper, 6 per pair of students
- ▲ chart paper, 1 sheet
- ▲ blank cubes, plus sticky labels for dice, 1 per pair of students (for extensions)
- ▲ optional: rules for playing the game of *Leftovers* to distribute to students (see Blackline Masters)

Time

- ▲ two class periods, plus additional time for repeated play and extensions

Teaching Directions

1. Tell the students that you're going to teach them how to play *Leftovers*, a game for partners. Show them the materials: a die, fifteen color tiles in a cup, and 3-inch squares of construction paper (called "plates").

2. Write the directions on the board or an overhead transparency or distribute a copy to each pair of students.

Leftovers

You need:
   a partner
   1 die
   15 color tiles
   1 cup to hold the tiles
   6 3-inch paper squares ("plates")

1. Take turns. On your turn, roll the die, take that number of paper plates or squares, and divide the tiles among them. Keep any leftover tiles.

2. Both players record the math sentence that describes what happened.

      For example: $15 \div 4 = 3 \text{ R}3$

   In front of each sentence, write the initial of the person who rolled the die.

3. Return the tiles on the plates to the cup before the next player takes a turn.

4. Play until all the tiles are gone. Then figure your scores by counting how many tiles each of you has. The winner is the player with the most leftovers. Add your scores to make sure that they total the 15 tiles you started with.

5. When you finish a game, look at each of your sentences with a remainder of zero (R0). Write on the class chart each sentence with R0 that isn't already posted.

---

3. Choose a student to model a game with you. Begin by asking your student partner to count out fifteen tiles. Decide who goes first.

4. The player who goes first rolls the die. This determines how many plates to lay out. So that the class can see what's happening in this model game, draw on the board the appropriate number of squares for each round.

5. The player who rolled the die then divides the total number of tiles in the cup into equal shares on the plates. He or she gets to keep all the leftover tiles for that round. Both players write a mathematical sentence to represent the division; for example, $15 \div 4 = 3 \text{ R}3$ or $15 \div 3 = 5 \text{ R}0$. During the demonstration, both you and your partner should record on the board so the others can see. (Having both players record gives all children practice writing the standard notation for division. Also, while including R0 if there is no remainder isn't conventional or essential, it is helpful to some children.) The first player hands the die to the second player at the end of the turn.

6. Return the tiles on the plates to the cup. The second person rolls the die, takes the correct number of plates, and divides up the tiles. Both players record again. The second player hands the die back to the first player at the end of the turn.

7. Continue playing until no tiles are left. If necessary, explain to students what to do if the number of plates exceeds the number of tiles. (See the "Teaching Notes" section for an explanation of this point.)

8. The winner is the player with the most leftovers. Check that all the leftovers total the original fifteen.

9. After you finish modeling the game, post the sheet of chart paper. Title it *Division with R0* and list the sentences from the board that have remainders of zero. (Do not write duplicates.) Tell the students that after they finish a game of *Leftovers*, they should record on the chart their sentences that have a remainder of zero. Remind them that they should check to make sure they write sentences that are not already on the chart.

10. Have students play the game in pairs. Circulate and check that they understand the rules and are playing correctly.

11. Begin class the next day with a class discussion about the game. Ask: "Which numbers were easy ones for getting remainders? Which were hard?" Students might have discovered that they got "stuck" on some numbers such as twelve, for which only one number (five) has any remainders. Also, with the class, examine the class chart of division sentences with remainders of zero and have the children look for patterns. For example, looking at the sentences that begin with ten ($10 \div 1 = 10$, $10 \div 2 = 5$, $10 \div 5 = 2$) may help children see that factors of a number can be used in two division statements. Also, children might notice that dividing by one produces the same answer as the number they started with.

Teaching Notes

The game of *Leftovers* provides students experience with the sharing model of division. The total number of tiles is known, the number of groups is known, and the unknown is the number of tiles in each group.

The game also focuses students' attention on remainders, or leftovers. Many students this age believe that something is "wrong" if there are leftovers. By playing the game, students see that leftovers in division are inevitable and make sense. Students also gain an understanding of what causes leftovers, or remainders, to occur.

As the students near the end of the game, it's likely that they will roll a number resulting in a greater number of plates than tiles. For example, there may be two tiles left and they roll a 4. Within the context of the tiles, it's impossible to place an equal number of tiles on each plate as there are only two tiles and four plates. So there are zero on each plate and the two tiles are leftovers. The mathematical sentence is $2 \div 4 = 0R2$.

At the end of a game, students should add up the leftovers recorded for that game. The total leftovers should equal fifteen, the number of tiles when the game started. When the game is played and recorded correctly, it isn't possible to have more or fewer leftovers than the original number of tiles. This happens because the leftovers come from the starting number and the game is played until all tiles have been distributed as leftovers.

One of the extensions provides students with the opportunity to number their dice in a way that's better for getting more leftovers. Students may think that 0 would be good to include on the die. They reason that dividing by zero would mean all the tiles are leftovers, so the person who rolls 0 first would be the winner. (See the Introduction for additional information about dividing by zero.) Limiting children to the numbers 1 through 6 for their dice, as suggested, avoids the situation of explaining why it's not possible to divide by zero.

The Lesson

▲▲

DAY 1

To introduce *Leftovers*, I asked the class, "If I had five candy bars and I wanted to share them among four people, how much would each person get?" The students had had previous experiences with sharing money and cookies. They were eager to respond to my question.

Elijah explained, "Each person would get one candy bar and there would also be one candy bar leftover."

"Put your thumb up if you agree with Elijah, your thumb down if you disagree, or your thumb sideways if you're not sure," I said. All thumbs were up in agreement with Elijah.

"What would you do with the leftover candy bar?" I asked.

Luke suggested, "Since there are four people and a candy bar is something you can break apart, then split it into four equal parts and give one part to each person. That would be one and one-fourth candy bars per person."

Brenna added, "You can show that one and one-fourth is right by using multiplication. Four times one candy bar is four candy bars. Four times one-fourth candy

bars is one candy bar. One candy bar plus four candy bars is five candy bars."

Seth had a question. "I've been thinking. We started with five candy bars and we knew we needed four shares. We had to figure the number in each share. Now that we know the number in each share, could we check it by thinking, 'There are five candy bars. Are there four groups of four and one-fourth in five?' I think it works because if I start with one and one-fourth and count by one and one-fourths, I end up with five. One and one-fourth plus one and one-fourth is two and one-half, and two and one-half and two and one-half is five." Some students nodded their agreement while others looked confused.

"Here's what I think Seth is thinking," I said as I wrote on the board:

$5 \div 1\frac{1}{4} = 4$

$1\frac{1}{4} + 1\frac{1}{4} = 2\frac{1}{2}$

$2\frac{1}{2} + 2\frac{1}{2} = 5$

Seth nodded his agreement. I continued, "So Seth thinks that's correct because he added one and one-fourth four times and it equaled five." I wrote:

$1\frac{1}{4} + 1\frac{1}{4} + 1\frac{1}{4} + 1\frac{1}{4} = 5$

"Hey, that's like my idea!" Brenna

responded. "That's repeated addition. My idea was multiplying by four to check that the division was right, and Seth's idea is repeated addition, but they're two ways of writing the same idea."

"Oh yeah!" "I get it!" were some of the students' responses.

I said, "I think both Brenna and Seth have ideas that are useful for checking division." This conversation indicated some students were increasing their understanding of division and were making sense of how division connects to other operations. Brenna, Seth, and others were applying this knowledge to check division. To redirect the conversation, I wrote on the board:

Dividing Candy Bars

$$\frac{5}{4} = 5 \div 4 = 4\overline{)5}$$

Then I said, "Everyone agrees that each person would get one and one-fourth candy bars. How would I record that to complete my division sentences?" I pointed to what I had written on the board.

Carlos answered, "You write a big one and then . . . can I come up and show?"

I nodded, and Carlos came to the board and recorded the answer in all three places:

$$5 \div 4 = 1\tfrac{1}{4} \qquad 4\overline{)5}^{1\tfrac{1}{4}} \qquad \frac{5}{4} = 1\tfrac{1}{4}$$

"So each person got one candy bar and one-fourth of a candy bar," I said. "Suppose you had a problem to solve that was almost the same, but this time you had to divide up five color tiles among four people." The children began to talk among themselves.

"You'd have to cut them up," Catalina said.

"Yeah, you need a knife," Robby added.

"It would be hard to cut them into pieces," Harrison said. "They're pretty small."

"You can't break them," Addie said, a voice of practicality. "You're not supposed to."

I interrupted their conversations. "Watch as I write the problem on the board." I wrote:

Dividing Color Tiles

$$5 \div 4 = \qquad 4\overline{)5}$$

"The problem looks the same, mathematically, as the *Dividing Candy Bars* problem," I said, "but you can't cut up the color tiles. How would you solve it? What should I write?" The children were quiet for a moment. Then several students raised a hand. I waited a bit more to see who else might have an idea. When a few more students raised a hand, I called on Cindy.

"Everyone would get just one color tile," she said.

"That makes sense," I said, "but that uses up four color tiles. What about the extras?"

"You'd just put it back in the box," Marco suggested.

"You could do that," I said, "but watch as I show you how to record mathematically when there is a leftover." I completed the recordings on the board:

$$5 \div 4 = 1\,R1 \qquad 4\overline{)5}^{1\,R1}$$

"The first one tells that each person gets one color tile, just like the one told that each person got one candy bar," I explained. "Then the 'R one' tells that there is one extra that's left over. The R stands for 'remainder,' and we say 'remainder one.' The answer is one remainder one."

I then posed another problem. "What if you were going to divide five color tiles among three people, instead of four people?" I asked. "Talk with your neighbor about what I could write to show the answer mathematically."

Some of the children used their fingers to figure out the answer. Robby, sitting near the color tiles, grabbed five of them to help him think. In a few moments, I called the children back to attention.

"Who can tell me what to write?" I asked. Almost half the students raised a hand. I called on Silas.

"It's one remainder two," he said, confidently.

"I'll record," I said, and wrote:

$$5 \div 3 = 1\ R2 \qquad 3\overline{)5}^{\,1\,R2}$$

To make sure the others understood, I drew on the board three stick figures and five squares to represent the three people and the five color tiles. "I can give each person one color tile," I explained, drawing a line from each stick figure to a square. "Then there are two leftovers, the remainder," I said, circling the two extra squares.

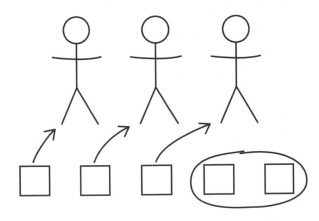

Introducing the Game of Leftovers

"Now I'm going to teach you how to play a game called *Leftovers*," I began. "It's a game of chance for partners and uses remainders. The winner is the person who gets more leftovers. I'm going to play the game with Irina so you can see the way it works." Irina came up and joined me at the board.

I cautioned the class, "The game isn't hard to play, but you have to count carefully and keep careful records."

I picked up a plastic cup containing tiles. "Your first job is to make sure you have fifteen tiles. Irina, will you make sure we have fifteen?" Irina counted the tiles and nodded her head.

"Also, you need a die and six squares of paper like this," I said, showing these items to the children. "We'll call these squares 'plates.' You go first," I said to Irina. "Roll the die."

Irina rolled a 4.

"The die tells you how many paper plates to lay out," I explained. "Irina, you lay out four plates and put the others aside for now. I'll draw four plates on the board so everyone can see."

"Next, the person who rolled the die takes the color tiles and divides them up so there's the same number on each plate," I explained.

Irina began to share the tiles. (Some of the children watched Irina place the tiles; others tried to figure out how many to put on each square.) Irina first put two tiles on each. She tried counting what was left in the cup, but abandoned that idea and put one more tile on each plate. Then she said, "There aren't enough to go around again. There are three left over."

To illustrate what Irina had done, I drew on the board three tiles in each of the four squares and drew the three leftovers separately.

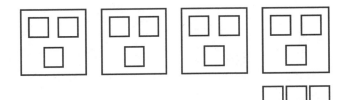

"Next, both people record the division sentence. You'll record on paper, but Irina and I will record on the board. I'll do it first. We'll record just one way for this game." I wrote the equation, then I wrote the letter *I* for Irina in front of the division sentence:

$I \quad 15 \div 4 = 3\ R3$

"This *I* will help me remember that Irina rolled the die," I explained. I designated a place on the board for Irina to record, and Irina copied what I had written.

"Irina rolled the die, so she gets to keep

the three leftovers and put the rest back in the cup," I said. "How many tiles do we have now?"

"Fifteen!" Robby exclaimed.

"We have fifteen altogether," I said, "but how many are in the cup now that Irina got to keep the three left over?" Irina counted and reported twelve tiles.

"Now it's my turn to roll the die," I said. "But before I roll I need to wait until Irina hands me the die. This way I know she's finished her turn." Irina handed me the die. I rolled a 6, put out six paper plates, and drew six squares on the board. "I have to divide the twelve tiles among the six squares," I said. I did this quickly and then drew on the board two tiles in each of the six squares.

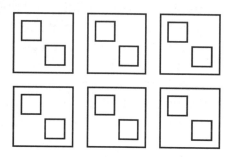

"There's nothing left over," Breanna said.

"That's right," I said. "Who can tell us what to write?" I called on Austin. Irina and I recorded as Austin dictated:

$12 \div 6 = 2\ R0$

Then I added a *W* in front to indicate that it had been my roll.

"There was no remainder, so do I get to keep any tiles?" I asked.

"No," the class chorused.

"That's right," I said. "So, how many tiles do we have now?"

"Twelve," they answered. I put the twelve tiles back into the cup and handed Irina the die.

Next, Irina rolled a 5. She put out five plates and divided the tiles as I drew on the

board. Afton dictated the equation, and Irina and I both recorded:

I $12 \div 5 = 2\ R2$

"Irina's winning," Shayna said, giggling. "She's lucky."

Irina and I continued to play the game, recording the plays on the board. The final list of equations was:

I	$15 \div 4 = 3\ R3$
W	$12 \div 6 = 2\ R0$
I	$12 \div 5 = 2\ R2$
W	$10 \div 3 = 3\ R1$
I	$9 \div 3 = 3\ R0$
W	$9 \div 6 = 1\ R3$
I	$6 \div 3 = 2\ R0$
W	$6 \div 3 = 2\ R0$
I	$6 \div 6 = 1\ R0$
W	$6 \div 4 = 1\ R2$
I	$4 \div 5 = 0\ R4$

"The last one is neat," Seth said. "Irina got to keep all four."

"She got stuck on six, though," Brenna said. "I bet you can get stuck forever."

"Not forever," Cami corrected. "Something has to happen."

"Maybe not," Brenna insisted.

"Who won?" Troy wanted to know.

"Let's count our tiles," I suggested. Irina reported she had nine and I had six.

"Do we have all fifteen together?" I asked. Irina counted the tiles; others figured in their heads or used their fingers.

Kelsey said, "Nine and six is fifteen so you have fifteen altogether."

"There's one more thing you and your partner have to do before you start another game," I said as I posted a large sheet of chart paper and titled it *Division with R0*.

"On this chart, write all the sentences from your papers that have a remainder of zero," I instructed. "But don't write the same one twice, like six divided by three equals two remainder zero."

As the children read the sentences on the board, I recorded the four different sentences that had remainders of zero.

Division with R0

$$12 \div 6 = 2 \ R0$$
$$9 \div 3 = 3 \ R0$$
$$6 \div 3 = 2 \ R0$$
$$6 \div 6 = 1 \ R0$$

"When you record your sentences on the chart," I said, "don't add any that Irina and I already wrote. Just new ones."

Observing the Children

When Joaquin and Skip began to play *Leftovers*, Joaquin rolled 3 and wrote: $15 \div 3 = 5 \ R0$. Skip copied it. Joaquin didn't bother to use the construction paper squares.

I said, as I pointed to the division sentence Joaquin wrote on his paper, "Show me with the materials what the fifteen means." While Joaquin's division sentence was correct, I wanted to be sure he could connect the meaning of the numbers to the activity.

Joaquin shrugged. "I know," Skip said. "It tells how many tiles we have."

"Oh yeah!" Joaquin said.

"What about the three?" I continued. "What does the three mean?"

"It tells how many plates to take," Skip said.

"Do you agree, Joaquin?" I asked. He nodded.

"The five tells how many tiles go on each plate," Joaquin said as he caught on.

"Which number tells how many groups?" I asked.

"The three," the boys chorused.

"The five says how many in each group," Skip added.

"Be sure to use the plates and tiles and think about what the numbers in your equations mean," I said. I left the boys to continue their game.

Jael and Luke ran into difficulties imme-diately. Jael rolled a 1, and Luke wrote the equation $15 \div 1 = 0$ before Jael had the chance to lay out the paper squares. Noticing the equation, I said to Luke, "What does the roll of the die tell you?"

"It means to put out one square," Luke said.

"Now you divide the tiles equally on however many squares you have," I explained. "How many tiles will be on the square?"

"Fifteen?" Luke asked, his tone indicating disbelief.

"If there is one boy and fifteen cookies and he gets all of them, how many cookies will he get?" I asked.

"Fifteen," replied Luke, astounded and pleased. He corrected the equation, writing $15 \div 1 = 15 \ R0$.

Shayna was playing with Vicki. Vicki had gone first, rolled a 2, and had one tile left over from the fifteen. Vicki handed the die to Shayna, and with fourteen tiles left, Shayna rolled a 5, put out five squares, and both girls recorded: $14 \div 5 =$. As Shayna began to divide up the tiles, Vicki punched the numbers into the calculator and said, "The answer is twenty-eight." She started to write it down.

"It can't be," Shayna protested. "We don't have twenty-eight tiles." She punched numbers into the calculator. "It's two point eight."

They didn't know what that meant and came to get help. "You have to count out the tiles on the squares to find out how many leftovers you have," I explained.

Shayna did this. "Four," she said, holding up the cup containing the extra four tiles. She took the extras and picked up the tiles on the plates and returned them to the cup. I watched the girls record: $14 \div 5 = 2 \ R4$.

I said, "For this game, the calculator won't help. It figures the problem as if you were dividing cookies or candy bars, not tiles. How many tiles will you be working with now?"

Shayna tried counting by eyeballing the tiles in the cup. After a few tries, she gave up, dumped the tiles on the table, and counted. "Ten," she concluded.

Shayna handed the die to Vicki, who rolled a 4.

Shayna wrote: *10 ÷ 4 =.* She put out four paper squares. Vicki dealt out two tiles for each square. She was excited because she had two left over.

I interjected, "Can you give every plate another tile?"

Vicki looked confused. "You can't," Shayna said, "you don't have enough. Let's write." Vicki followed Shayna's lead and both girls recorded: *10 ÷ 4 = 2 R2.* Vicki handed Shayna the die.

"How many tiles do you have for the next round?" I asked.

Shayna transferred the tiles from the paper squares to the plastic cup, counting as she did so. "Eight," she said. She rolled a 3, put out three squares, divided the tiles, and wrote: *8 ÷ 3 = 2 R2.* She did this by herself, with no help from Vicki or me. Then she told Vicki, "Copy this. Then you'll start with six." This time she didn't count the tiles. "I just know," she explained.

Vicki thought for a moment and said to clarify what Shayna told her, "OK, three groups of two is six and the two leftovers is eight. You keep the leftovers, so subtract two from eight and that's six."

I continued circulating among the groups, sitting with one group for a few minutes and then moving on to another. When children wanted to rush through the game, I tried to slow them down, encouraging them to be methodical. I showed them the importance of laying out the paper squares they were using as plates and counting the tiles they had at the start of each round. When children skipped steps, they got into trouble and the game didn't work out.

Marco and Irina were typical of children who didn't quite understand the activity

when they started. Both confident of their mathematical ability, both valuing speed, they didn't share their tiles on the paper squares and didn't count the tiles at the beginning of each round. They relied on thinking they knew the right answers to division problems. I scanned their paper. (See Figure 5–1.)

"You've made two errors," I told them.

"Where?" Marco demanded to know.

"You can find them if you replay the game," I said. I sat with them as they got started.

When Marco found the error he had made when dividing fourteen into four groups, he said, "Oh no! It all changes from here." I agreed and reminded them to slow down, lay out squares according to the roll of the die, count leftovers, and then count the tiles for the next round. I left them to redo the rest of their game.

I noticed that Addie and Jody had written *9 ÷ 4 = 2 with R2.* When I questioned that answer, the girls said they got the answer by counting tiles on the paper squares. I asked them to do it again so I could see. It turned out they had ten tiles, not nine. I explained that mistaking the

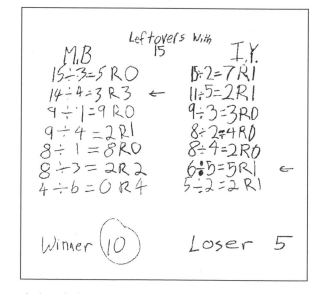

▲▲▲▲▲▲Figure 5–1 *I noticed two errors and asked Marco and Irina to replay the game.*

number of tiles at the beginning throws off the whole game. "Also," I told them, "you don't need to write *with*." The girls fixed their papers.

I noted that Jael and Luke were now off to a good start in their game, but I spotted a glitch on the seventh move. "Replay ten divided by five," I requested.

"It's two and no remainder," Jael reported.

"Right. But look at what you wrote here," I pointed out. (See Figure 5–2.) I asked the children to replay their game from that point on.

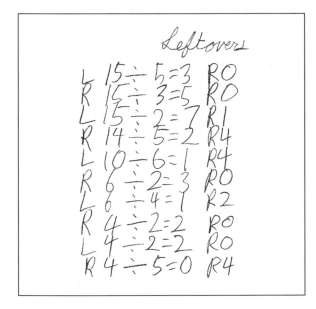

▲▲▲▲▲▲**Figure 5–2** *Another pair of students completed this game in ten rounds.*

DAY 2

I gathered the class at the front of the room for a class discussion. "*Leftovers* is a division game that can show us some interesting things about numbers," I began. "When you played *Leftovers*, what was a very hard number to get out of?"

Derryl and William exclaimed together, "Twelve! It's impossible."

I copied onto the board division sentences from the class chart that began with 12:

$12 \div 1 = 12\ R0$

$12 \div 3 = 4\ R0$

$12 \div 6 = 2\ R0$

$12 \div 2 = 6\ R0$

$12 \div 4 = 3\ R0$

"Now there's only one more number to roll," I commented.

"Five!" the class offered.

I added $12 \div 5 =$ to the list on the board.

"What happens with this number?" I asked.

"It's two remainder two," Marco said.

"Wow!" Derryl said. "Every number on the die except five comes out even, with no remainders. That's what makes it so hard. You need remainders for the game to work." (See Figure 5–3.)

"Who had another number besides

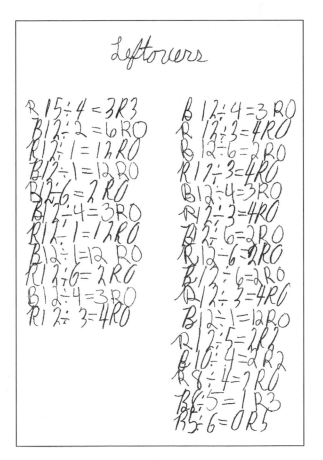

▲▲▲▲▲▲**Figure 5–3** *Robby and Brenna found that twelve was a hard number to move beyond.*

twelve that was hard to get out of?" I asked.

"Six," Troy replied.

"Can you explain why?" I encouraged.

"Every number on the die comes out even except for four and five," Troy explained.

I suggested that the children check the class chart for sentences that began with six.

"What other discoveries did you make about Leftovers?" I continued.

"You don't get remainders a lot when you roll a two," Austin said.

"Let's look at the chart," I said.

"It works for six, ten, eight, fourteen . . . ," Afton read from the chart.

"Hey, those are all even," Irina noticed.

"Of course," Marco said, "an even number always splits into two."

"Fourteen is a good number," Robby offered.

"Why is that?" I asked.

"You usually get something," Robby said, grinning.

EXTENSIONS

1. Based on what students have learned about division and how it relates to the game of Leftovers, encourage them to make their own dice. Provide students with blank cubes and sticky labels to use to number the faces of the dice. If you don't have blank cubes, have students cut six small squares of paper, putting one number on each. Then have them place the numbered squares in an envelope. Instead of rolling a die, students draw a number, replacing it in the envelope at the end of their turn. Students play the game of Leftovers with their new dice, recording as before. As a written assignment, students list the numbers on their dice and explain why they chose those numbers.

Note: Children should use numbers from 1 to 6, and they can use the same number more than once. Students should not use 0, as division by zero is undefined. See the Introduction for additional information on division by zero. Figures 5–4 through 5–6

New Die For Leftovers

On my die I put 3 fives I put them on because 5 is the only way to get out of 12. I put a 2 because it gets out of any odd number. I had 2 spaces left so I put on a 3 and a 2 and a 4.

▲▲▲▲▲▲Figure 5–4 *Ely explained why he included three 5s on his die.*

I picked 5, 4, 2, 6, 5, 3, because those numbers are more possible then the others like 1, 1 well have 1 pile, and you well never have remainders. I recommend it you make your one dice you good numbers.

▲▲▲▲▲▲Figure 5–5 *Shayna recommended making a die with "good" numbers.*

Left over, with 30

I picked 3, 2, 4, 5 and another 2 and 4 because you wouldn't get stuck with these numbers. as much I didn't pick one and six because you would get stuck on these number, I always get stuck on one.

▲▲▲▲▲▲Figure 5–6 *Kirk explained the discovery he made about rolling a 1.*

show three students' writing about the dice they made.

2. Allow students to choose the number of tiles to start the game. Students may use a regular die or one they create. Have them play the game as before. Remind students to write their starting number of tiles at the top of their recording sheets. Have students add their division sentences with R0 to the class chart. Lead a class discussion based on the following questions:

1. How many color tiles did you use? Why?

2. What numbers did you put on the die you created? Why?

3. What discoveries did you make about dividing different numbers?

Figures 5–7 through 5–9 show three pairs' games.

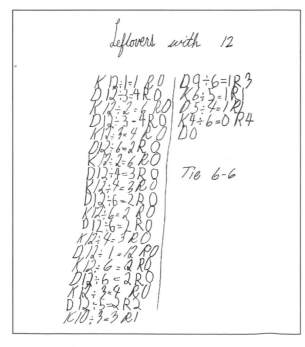

Leftovers with 12

K 12÷1=1 R0   D9÷6=1R3
D 12÷3=4 R0   K6÷5=1R1
K 12÷2=6 R0   D5÷4=1R1
D 12÷3=4 R0   K4÷6=0 R4
K 12÷3=4 R0   D0
D 12÷6=2 R0
K 12÷2=6 R0   Tie 6-6
D 12÷4=3 R0
D 12÷4=3 R0
D 12÷6=2 R0
K 12÷6=2 R0
D 12÷6=2 R0
K 12÷4=3 R0
D 12÷1=12 R0
K 12÷6=2 R0
D 12÷6=2 R0
K 12÷3=4 R0
D 12÷5=2 R2
K 10÷3=3 R1

▲▲▲▲▲▲Figure 5–7 *Kareem and Derryl's game ended in a tie.*

Leftovers

W 10÷5=2 R 0
K 10÷1=10 R0
W 10÷2=5 R0
K 10÷2=5 R0
W 10÷4=2 R2
K 8÷1=8 R0
W 8÷6=1 R2
K 6÷2=3 R0
W 6÷3=2 R0
K 6÷5=1 R1
W 5÷6=0 R 5

▲▲▲▲▲▲Figure 5–8 *Carlos and William started their game with ten tiles.*

The Game of Leftovers 59

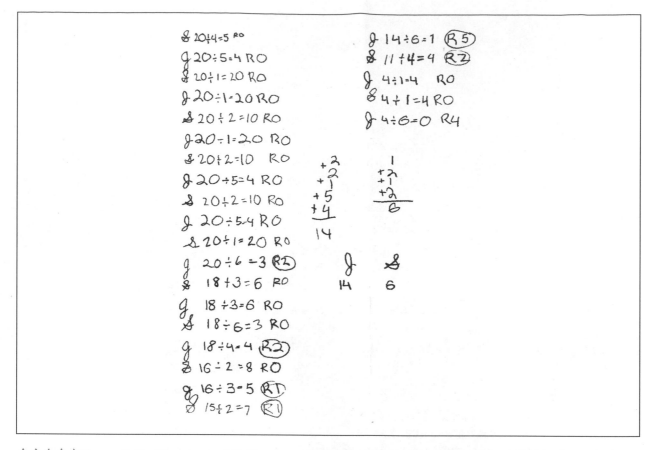

▲▲▲▲▲▲Figure 5–9 *Shayna and Beth were surprised at how many times they rolled before getting a remainder for twenty.*

Questions and Discussion

▲▲▲

▲ **What alternatives to dice can be used?**

Using alternatives to dice is appropriate for any number of reasons. For example, you may not have enough dice, you may want to have the children explain how to play the game to their parents and then play as homework, or in some cases, parents object to their children using dice. Alternatives include using spinners numbered 1 through 6 or having students cut out six small paper squares and write a number on each. They then place the numbered squares in an envelope or paper bag and draw a square. The number drawn represents a roll of the die. Remind students to put the square back in the envelope or bag before the next turn.

▲ **Why do you have children hand the die to the next player?**

First, waiting for the die to be handed to the next player is respectful. It prevents children from grabbing the die before a player is finished with his or her turn, thus preventing many arguments that often occur over who has the die and whose turn it is. This slows the game down so that both players can be fully involved and aware of what's going on. Slowing down the game in this way also encourages children to talk and exchange ideas.

▲ *Children get a lot of practice writing division equations during this activity. How do you make sure that they practice this correctly?*

Because students are involved in what they're doing, I'm free to circulate and look over their shoulders as they play the game. I'm able to quickly check what they're recording and intervene early when errors are made. This way students are less likely to practice writing division equations incorrectly. Because students are involved, I'm able to focus my attention on those needing help or an added challenge.

CHAPTER SIX
17 KINGS AND 42 ELEPHANTS

Overview

Margaret Mahy's book *17 Kings and 42 Elephants* employs playful, rhythmic language in the context of a royal procession through an exotic jungle. In this activity, students enjoy the book for its vibrant batik illustrations and semantic delights. The story then becomes a springboard for a division problem with remainders: The students figure out how seventeen kings can share taking care of forty-two elephants.

Materials

▲ *17 Kings and 42 Elephants*, by Margaret Mahy (New York: Dial Books for Young Readers, 1987)

Time

▲ one class period

Teaching Directions

1. Read the story aloud to the class.

2. Introduce the problem. Ask students to work individually or in pairs to determine how many elephants each king would get if the kings shared them equally. Tell students to write about how they solved the problem.

3. In a class discussion, have students share their solutions with the class.

Teaching Notes

Children especially enjoy *17 Kings and 42 Elephants* for its vibrant batik illustrations and semantic delights. The book describes a royal procession of seventeen kings and forty-two elephants through an exotic jungle. The language is infectiously rhythmic and the illustrations are a visual delight.

The students must figure out how seventeen kings can care for forty-two elephants. This is an example of a sharing problem. The students know the total number and the number of groups and they must determine how many elephants will be in each group. What to do with the remainder, or leftover elephants, poses an interesting challenge for the students.

The Lesson

▲▲▲

I gathered the students on the floor in the front of the room so they would be able to see easily the illustrations as I read aloud *17 Kings and 42 Elephants*, by Margaret Mahy. I held the book up and the colorful cover caught the children's attention immediately. Holding the book so the students could see the illustrations, I began reading aloud. I encouraged the children to savor the language and the art as I read aloud.

Cindy noted that "baggy ears like big umbrellaphants" sounded like the words in "Eletelephony," a poem she had read. I agreed that poets like to play with words and even invent them.

The class giggled with delight when I read, "Big baboonsters, black gorillicans / Swinging from the branches by their hairy knees."

When I finished reading the book, and the children shared their reactions to the language and art, I focused the class on the mathematical potential in the story. I asked, "How many kings were there?"

"Seventeen!" the children chorused.

"How many elephants?" I asked.

"Forty-two!"

"Subtraction!" exclaimed a half dozen children, confident they were anticipating my next question.

"We could do that," I agreed. "We could ask: How many more elephants are there than kings?" I paused for a moment, as I noticed some children starting to solve that problem. Several figured quickly that the answer was twenty-five.

"There's another problem we can consider," I commented as I started writing on the board:

If the kings divide up the elephants equally, how many elephants would each king get?

"Uh oh." This classroom murmur was followed by individual speculations: "Seventeen plus seventeen." "Five each." "No, six."

To focus the children on making sense of the problem, I asked, "How many elephants are there altogether?" The class responded with "forty-two." "How many kings?" They responded with "seventeen."

I asked, "Will each king get an elephant?"

"Yes, five," Addie responded.

"No, seven each," Robby quickly corrected her.

I didn't comment about whether either student was right or wrong. Instead I said, "You'll need to decide and then show on paper how you figured it out. The problem is to figure out how many elephants each king would get if they shared them equally. Your solution should explain how you reasoned."

I paused to give students time to ask questions, then continued, "If you think you want to discuss this with someone else, then you can work with a partner. Or you may work alone if you'd prefer."

OBSERVING THE CHILDREN

Afton and Derryl decided to work together. Afton got a calculator and punched in 42 ÷ 17. When he saw 2.4705882 for an answer, he was startled.

"What does it mean?" he asked Derryl. Derryl shrugged his shoulders.

Afton and Derryl then came to me. "We have no idea what the answer means," Afton said, showing me the calculator.

"If your answer doesn't make sense," I replied, "then try doing it another way."

Afton sighed. I decided to take this opportunity to talk with the boys about the frustrations sometimes provided by calculator answers.

"Show me what you did," I said. Derryl punched in 42 ÷ 17 and again got 2.4705882. Both boys groaned.

"Does any part of this number make sense?" I prodded.

"Nooo," the boys chorused.

"Hey wait, the two makes sense!" Derryl exclaimed.

"What do you think the two tells you about the problem?" I asked.

"I know," Afton said. "It means that forty-two divided by seventeen is two."

"What else does the two mean?" I asked, wanting to encourage both boys to make sense of what they were figuring.

Afton paused a moment and thought, then said hesitantly, "I think it means each king will get two elephants."

"Is there a way you can check to see if that makes sense?" I probed.

Both boys looked pensive as they thought about what I asked. "Well," Afton began, "if the two means each king gets two elephants and there are seventeen kings, then I could count by twos seventeen times and see how many elephants."

"But that's not right," Derryl said, "or else the calculator would just say two."

Meanwhile, Afton was counting by twos. "It's thirty-four elephants and there's forty-two in the story."

"Hey," Derryl said, "if each king gets three elephants then that would be . . . thirty-four and ten is forty-four, that means seven more, . . . , um, . . . fifty-one elephants."

"That's too many," the boys said together. They both paused and then Derryl said, "All those numbers after the two must be the leftover elephants!"

"That's weird, because really there are eight leftover elephants, not that funny number," Afton said.

I explained, "The decimal on the calculator represents a number that's bigger than two but less than three. You must learn how to interpret these numbers in order to use them. In the meantime, you'll need to think about another way to solve the problem." Afton looked glum.

"I know!" Derryl said. "Let's get tiles." The boys returned to their seats. (See Figure 6–1.)

Janie and Cami, also frustrated by the calculator, asked for help. I offered no immediate answer but suggested, "Think about another way to solve the problem." I left the girls.

When I returned a few minutes later, Janie reported, "We think each king gets three elephants."

I responded, "OK, let's check it out. What should we do first to check to see if your answer makes sense?" The girls talked this over a moment.

Cami suggested, "Write down a three." I did as Cami suggested.

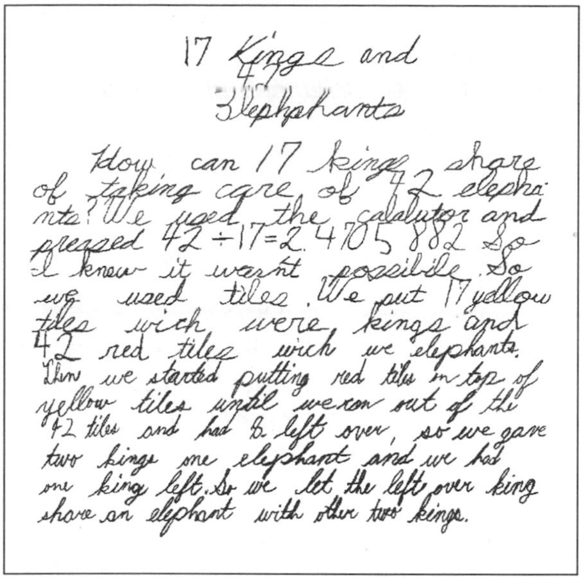

17 Kings and Elephants

How can 17 kings share of taking care of 42 elephants? We used the calculator and pressed 42 ÷ 17 = 2.4705882 So I knew it wasn't possible. So we used tiles. We put 17 yellow tiles which were kings and 42 red tiles which we elephants. Then we started putting red tiles on top of yellow tiles until we ran out of the 42 tiles and had 8 left over, so we gave two kings one elephant and we had one king left. So we let the left over king share an elephant with other two kings.

▲▲▲▲▲▲**Figure 6–1** *After they abandoned the calculator, Afton and Derryl used tiles to solve the problem.*

"What does the three mean?" I probed.

"That three means three elephants for one king," Janie explained. "Now write down another three."

"That takes care of elephants for how many kings?" I asked.

"Two," Janie said.

"How many threes do you need to write down to check your answer?" I asked.

"Seventeen," Cami answered.

"And what do seventeen groups of threes equal?" I asked.

Janie grabbed a calculator and punched in 17×3. "Fifty-one," she reported. "Too much."

Cami suggested, "How about two?" She wrote *2* on her paper seventeen times.

"There's another way," Janie insisted. She punched 2×17 into the calculator. When 34 appeared, Cami moaned, "Oh, that's not right, either." Cami, for whom numbers were only right or wrong, had no notion of how to look at a remainder. But she was conscientious and willing to keep working. Her method was to keep trying numbers until she got the one that she was looking for. If one number didn't work, then she'd try another—without taking any time to think about why the first number was incorrect. In this case, she did not look at whether thirty-four was too large or too small; all she noticed was that it wasn't forty-two.

Cami suggested, in more of a question than a hypothesis, "Maybe it's one?" She quickly started writing down a row of *1s*.

But Janie stopped her. "No, thirty-four is OK. That leaves eight elephants left over." She grinned. "We can have the kings cut up the remainder." The girls giggled at Janie's suggestion for the leftover elephants. In explaining her own thinking to Cami, Janie clarified what she herself knew.

Stopping to talk with Carol, I asked, "What are you going to do with the leftover elephants?"

Kareem overheard from a nearby table. "Make elephant stew," he quipped.

"Feed them to the tigers," said Ely, sitting next to Kareem.

I commented, "If you're going to use a mean solution, you need a nice one, too. Animal rights people will be upset if you are unkind to elephants."

Ely obliged and included two possible scenarios. He wrote:

$$17 \div 42 = 2 \, R8 \qquad \overset{2 \, R8}{17\overline{)42}}$$

I would say that each king should get two elephant and let the rest eight elephants free.

Mean Sulution: We will feed the eight remaining elephants to tigers and crocodiles.

Although part of his symbolism was reversed, his answer was right. (See Figure 6–2.)

Cindy had a more humane touch in her solution. She wrote: *Each king would get two elephants. The eight elephants that are left [go] to the tigers as slaves and tell the tigers not to eat them.*

I commented to her, "You need to show how you figured that out." Cindy added: *I*

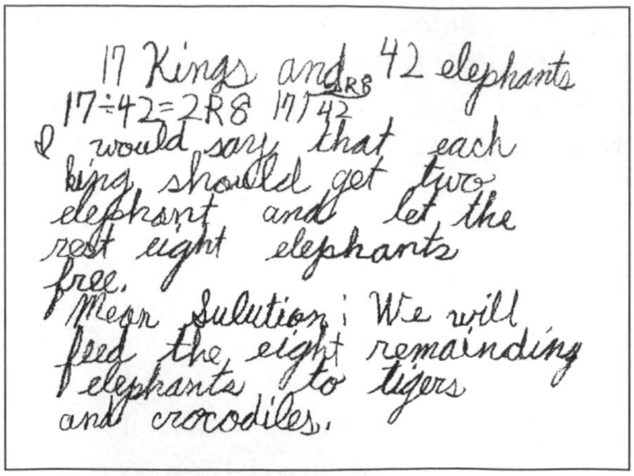

▲▲▲▲▲▲**Figure 6–2** *Ely provided two scenarios for what he might do with the extra elephants.*

got this answer by adding 17 + 17, and 8 were left over.

Gabby explained the problem of the leftover elephants: *We can not cut out the elephants. So I will gave the left over elephants to the zoo.* Her picture showed the seventeen kings walking away from the zoo, where they had left eight (sad) elephants. "They don't like being left behind," Gabby explained.

Taylor wrote: *If there [are] 8 Elephants I will get 8 [new] kings. then it is fair.*

Kareem corrected him, "If there were eight elephants I would get four more kings. Then it would be fair."

When I checked on Robby and Gib, Robby insisted, "Each king gets seven elephants."

"Let's see," I said. "Show me your thinking." Robby shrugged.

"Seven elephants equals how many kings?" I asked as I helped Robby and Gib construct the following chart:

7 elephants = 1 king

14 elephants = 2 kings

21 elephants = 3 kings

28 elephants = 4 kings

35 elephants = 5 kings

42 elephants = 6 kings

"Wow!" exclaimed Robby, admiring the chart. But his admiration was short-lived. "Uh oh, I'm in trouble. I didn't use up enough kings."

"If there were *six* kings, that would work," I said, emphasizing "six" and pointing to it on the chart.

"The solution is the others didn't want to be kings," Robby suggested.

Gib liked this solution. "They were probably scared of elephants," he added.

"OK, write it up," I agreed. I accepted Robby and Gib's solution.

At another table, I asked Harrison to explain his thinking. Harrison said, "Each king would get two elephants."

"Any leftovers?" I asked.

"No."

"How many elephants do you have?"

"I've got forty-two."

"But you only used thirty-four."

Harrison counted on his fingers. "Eight elephants left over."

"That's good that you did it all in your head," I said. "Now you need to write it down, so I can see your thinking."

A CLASS DISCUSSION

After all of the students had found solutions to the problem, I gathered them at the front of the room to share their thinking. I began by saying, "Even though there is only one answer, there are many ways to get it. I'm interested in having you hear all the different ways you used."

Jody went first. She showed her system of using tally marks and circles. (See Figure 6–3.)

Breanna demonstrated how she subtracted seventeen twice to get the answer. (See Figure 6–4.)

Troy commented to Breanna, "Ours are sort of the same, but backwards." He explained how he had added two seventeen times. (See Figure 6–5.)

Beth offered an unusual solution for the

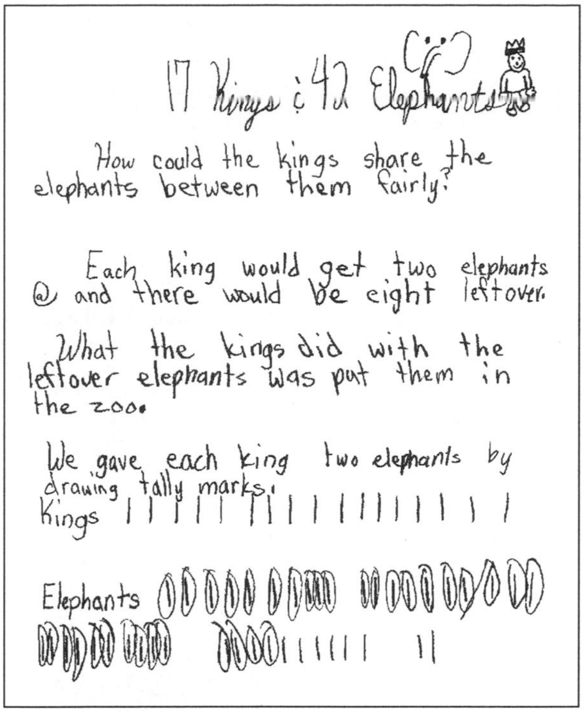

▲▲▲▲▲▲Figure 6–3 *Jody explained her system of using tally marks.*

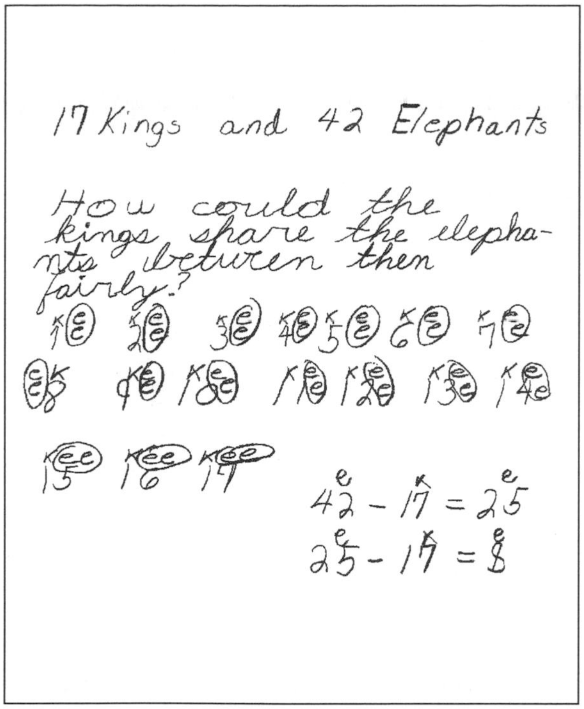

▲▲▲▲▲▲Figure 6–4 *Breanna subtracted to figure out the answer.*

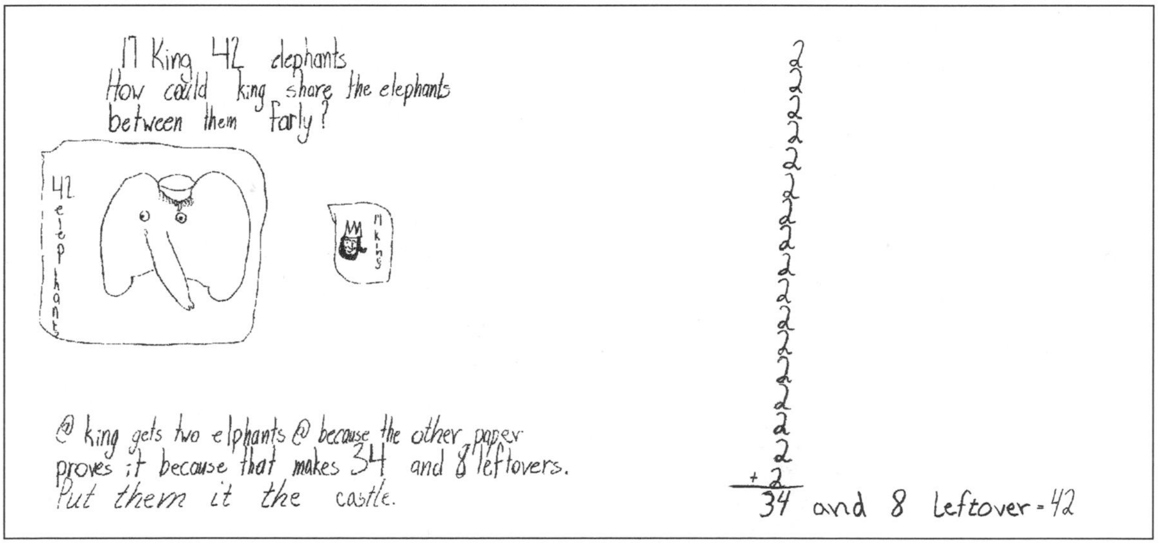

▲▲▲▲▲▲Figure 6–5 *Troy used addition to solve the problem.*

leftover elephants. "I added seventeen plus seventeen and got thirty-four," she explained. "That means there are eight leftovers. I think it would be fair to rotate the leftover elephants." She wrote: *The kings can share 8 elephants. Eight kings can each have one elephant from the leftovers. The* *next day another 8 kings can get one leftover then another.* (See Figure 6–6.)

Afton, who had followed Beth's argument carefully, objected, "Then one king would get one elephant by himself. That's not fair sharing."

Beth was frustrated, unsure of how to

> 17 King and 42 elephants
>
> How could the kings share the ele-
> phants between them fairly.
>
> There were 42 elephants & 17 kings.
>
> 17
> +17
> ‾‾‾‾
> 34 elephants
>
> Each king would get 2 elephants and
> there are 8 elephants leftover. The kings
> can share 8 elephants. Eight kings can
> have one elephant from the leftovers. The
> next day another 8 kings can get one
> leftover, then another.

▲▲▲▲▲**Figure 6–6** *Beth decided that the extra elephants should rotate among the kings*

answer Afton. I volunteered, "You're right, Afton. On the first day, eight kings each get an extra elephant; then on the second, eight different kings get the extras; but on the third day there is only one king left who hasn't had an extra elephant. But he can get his turn along with seven kings who already had an extra elephant on the first day and can have extras again."

"I get it," Afton said, smiling. "That's neat." Beth grinned.

"Robby and Gib have a different solution," I said, wanting to give status to the two boys for the thinking they did. Robby grinned as he announced, "Six kings got seven elephants each." He paused, "That's forty-two elephants because six times seven equals forty-two. We checked with a calculator."

"But that's only six kings!" protested several children.

"Because eleven kings were scared and didn't want any elephants," Gib announced, offering their punch line. He and Robby laughed, enjoying having surprised their classmates. Other children joined in the laughter, also enjoying this method of turning a mathematics problem into a shaggy-dog story.

The children were engrossed in this problem. They were intent on examining the thinking and problem-solving processes of their peers. They were anxious both to communicate what they knew and to learn from what their classmates knew.

It was nearly time to end math class and I asked, "Are there any more solutions?" Kareem volunteered.

"I had eight leftover elephants," he said, "and so I got four more kings. That means I have a new story. It's called *Twenty-One Kings and Forty-Two Elephants*."

I smiled. "That's great! Two new stories: Kareem's is *Twenty-One Kings and Forty-Two Elephants*. Robby and Gib's is *Six Kings and Forty-Two Elephants*."

Questions and Discussion

▲▲

▲ *What was your reason for allowing Robby and Gib to solve a problem different from the one you assigned?*

One of my goals is to recognize and nurture children's thinking. The boys were struggling to make sense of a difficult concept. Robby recognized his answer wasn't right, so when he came up with a clever solution for getting himself out of a numerical jam, I wanted to celebrate his humor and ingenuity, not stamp it as a 'wrong answer.'"

What's important is to listen to the children's thinking and help them verbalize their reasoning. The point is not merely for children to get answers but for them to communicate what they know and how they arrived at those answers.

CHAPTER SEVEN
SHARING CANDY BARS

Overview

In *Sharing Candy Bars*, children work in pairs to figure out how to share five rectangular "candy bars" equally among four people. Each candy bar is scored into six pieces. The problem presents an opportunity for children to think about fractions as they solve a sharing division problem.

Materials

▲ *Candy Bars* worksheet, 1 per pair of students (see Blackline Masters)

Time

▲ one to two class periods

Teaching Directions

1. Tell the children they're going to work in pairs to figure out how to share five "candy bars" equally among four people.

2. Hold up the *Candy Bars* worksheet and explain that each complete rectangle represents a candy bar. Tell the children that they should cut the candy bars as needed, decide how to divide them equally among four people, glue the portions to a sheet of paper, and finally write down how much each person's share is.

3. In a later class discussion, have students share their solutions, their methods for finding them, and the ways they represented each person's share.

Teaching Notes

This lesson presents students with the sharing model of division. The students must share the candy bars equally among four people. The total number of candy bars is known and the number of groups is known, so the students' task is to figure how much is in each group.

Like with *Dividing Cookies*, students can split the leftovers into fractional pieces of the whole. This gives students another opportunity to recognize that the context of the problem influences how the remainder is represented: as a fraction or as a whole number.

The class in the following vignette had done the *Dividing Cookies* lesson prior to doing this lesson. By repeating a similar lesson mathematically in a new context, I gave children the opportunity to apply and deepen what they had learned previously.

The Lesson

▲▲

I began, "*Sharing Candy Bars* presents a problem that is like the *Dividing Cookies* activity we did a few weeks ago."

"I bet they're just pretend candy bars," Harrison said.

"Yes, they are," I confirmed and showed the children the *Candy Bars* worksheet, on which there were five rectangular candy bars, each scored into six squares.

"Your task is to figure out how to divide the five candy bars among four people so that each gets a fair share," I continued. Because the children had experience sharing cookies, they needed no further explanation.

"Can we work together?" Beth wanted to know.

I nodded. Beth smiled.

OBSERVING THE CHILDREN

Wesley and Kendall decided to work together. They immediately set themselves the task of cutting apart all the squares. It took a long time. Kendall became tired of cutting, and while Wesley continued to cut, Kendall started dealing out squares, "Two for you and two for me." When the boys remembered that they were supposed to share the bars among four people, Wesley began numbering the squares *1 2 3 4, 1 2 3 4.*

"The answer is seven and one-half," Wesley announced.

Kendall asked, "Are you sure?"

Wesley nodded and so Kendall wrote: *Each person gets $7\frac{1}{2}$.* They brought their paper to me.

I asked, "Seven and one-half what?"

"Candy bars," the boys answered.

Rather than acknowledging right away whether the boys were right or wrong, I asked, "How many candy bars did you start with?" I felt this line of questioning would refocus the boys on making sense of the problem and their answer.

"Five," Wesley answered. Both boys said, "Uh oh." Wesley and Kendall returned to their table. They used scissors to cut off the first answer and, after a bit of figuring, wrote: *Each person gets 1 bar and $\frac{1}{6}$ and a half of a sixth.* They were pleased that they knew what one-sixth was and how to write it. (See Figure 7–1.)

Shayna and Cindy also used a numbering system, but they didn't use fractions to describe each person's share. They dealt out four of the candy bars whole, before

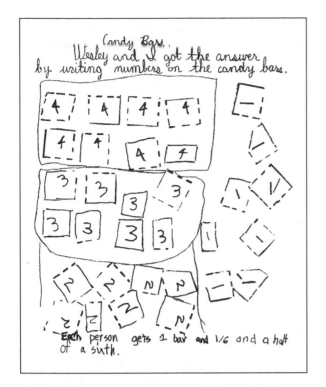

Candy Bars.
Wesley and I got the answer
by writing numbers on the candy bars.

Each person gets 1 bar and 1/6 and a half
of a sixth.

▲▲▲▲▲▲Figure 7–1 *Kendall described how he and Wesley solved the problem.*

pieces in half and finally pasted all the pieces down.

The girls then began to write about their solution. Shayna and Cindy were convinced they had solved the problem "in our head." They were becoming familiar with fractions but were not yet writing fractions symbolically. (See Figure 7–2.)

Cami and Gabby started by cutting each candy bar in half. But they then got stuck, distracted by the lines on the candy bars. I sat with them, helping them keep track of what a whole candy bar looked like. They glued their cut candy bars back together and decided that they needed four of them whole. Then they cut up the remaining candy bar—and discovered twelfths. (See Figure 7–3.)

Before noticing that each person would get a whole candy bar, Patricia and Breanna cut four squares off each and pasted them down. Then they pasted an additional two squares for each person.

"That was dumb," Breanna said. "They each get one whole." As others had done, they then gave each person another square and a half of a square. Unlike Cami and

they started cutting. Then they cut up the remaining bar, giving one square to each of four people. They cut the two remaining

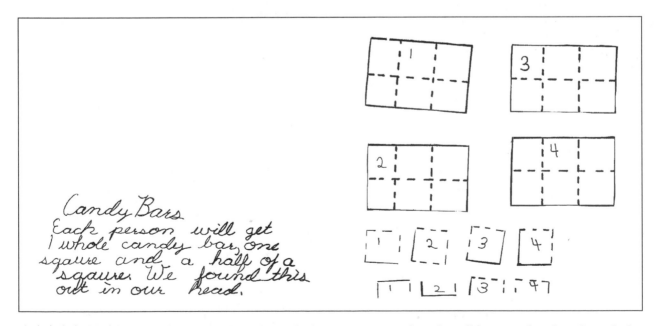

Candy Bars
Each person will get
1 whole candy bar, one
sgaure and a half of a
sgaure. We found this
out in our head.

▲▲▲▲▲▲Figure 7–2 *Shayna and Cindy's solution was correct, but they didn't use fractional symbols to describe each person's share.*

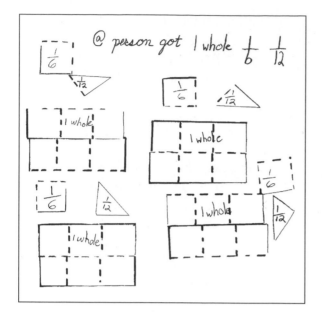

▲▲▲▲▲Figure 7–3 *Cami and Gabby described twelfths.*

Gabby, however, they did not use twelfths. They recorded each person's share as $1 + \frac{1}{6} + \frac{1}{2} of \frac{1}{6}$. (See Figure 7–4.)

Marco and Irina were working together. "Look," Irina said, "it's easy. They each get a whole bar, then a piece, and then half a piece."

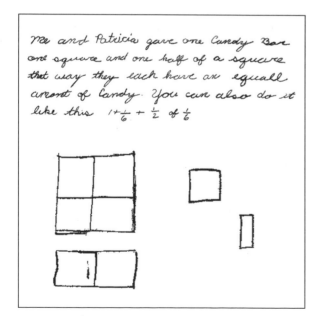

▲▲▲▲▲▲Figure 7–4 *Breanna recorded that she and Patricia gave each person $1 + \frac{1}{6} + \frac{1}{2} of \frac{1}{6}$.*

Marco agreed and began to record. "How about saying we did it in our heads?" he asked Irina.

Irina said, "OK. I'll cut them up."

While Irina cut the pieces, Marco wrote: *We just devided it in our head.* Then he drew four figures and pictured each with one candy bar, a piece, and half of a piece. Finally, Marco wrote: *Each person gets $7\frac{1}{2}$.* The two children showed me their solution.

As I did with Wesley and Kendall, I asked, "Seven and one-half what?"

"Little pieces," Irina said. "See?" She showed me what she meant.

"You need to be more specific in your sentence," I said. "Someone could think you meant seven and one-half candy bars."

They went back and added *pieces of candy* to their last sentence. Then they refined it further, ending up with: *Each person gets $7\frac{1}{2}$ individual pieces of candy.* (See Figure 7–5.)

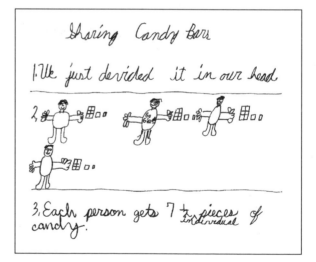

▲▲▲▲▲▲Figure 7–5 *Marco and Irina reported how many small squares each person got.*

A CLASS DISCUSSION

In a class discussion, the students reported their solutions and how they had represented them. I recorded on the board as they reported:

7 individual pieces

$1 + \frac{1}{6} + \frac{1}{2}$ *of* $\frac{1}{6}$

1 and $\frac{1}{6}$ *and a half of a sixth*

$1\frac{1}{4}$

1 whole $\frac{1}{6}$ $\frac{1}{12}$

1 candy bar and $\frac{3}{12}$

"What do you think of all these different solutions?" I asked.

"It's neat," Troy said. "There's lots of ways."

"Are they all right?" Valerie wanted to know.

"Do they make sense?" I asked.

"Ours is the same as Breanna and Patricia's," Wesley said, "but we used words."

"We had one like Marco and Irina," Kendall added, "but it wasn't finished."

"I think they're all the same," Afton said, "just different ways."

I responded, "That would mean that one-half of a sixth is the same as one-twelfth. Does that make sense?"

Troy was clear about this. "If you made twelve pieces and put them in twos, then you would have six of them. So they're the same."

I knew that not all of the children followed Troy's reasoning, but they suspected he was right since he was a strong math student. I didn't push for having each child understand all the fractional notations. However, I feel that a discussion like this is useful for all students. Those who get the chance to verbalize their understanding are confirmed; others have the chance to think about something that is new to them.

EXTENSION

Have students solve other problems. For example: *If there are five candy bars, and each person got one-half of a candy bar, how many people would get candy bars?* Or: *If you have five candy bars and you want to put them in bags of two, how many bags would you need?* Problems such as these use the same ideas as in the lesson, but rather than providing experience using the sharing model, they give students experience using the grouping model of division.

Questions and Discussion

▲▲

▲ *Do you think there is value in having students do both the* **Dividing Cookies** *and* **Sharing Candy Bars** *lessons? They are very similar activities.*

When children repeat activities or do similar activities that are of interest to them, they bring their prior experience to each new encounter. They are given the opportunity to cement their understanding and try other ideas to stretch their thinking. Ultimately students increase their confidence, deepen their understanding, and gain practice.

CHAPTER EIGHT
CLASSROOM GROUPS

Overview

In this lesson, children explore a real-world problem, one based on the kind of decisions that come up frequently in their own classroom. The problem gives children experience with the grouping model of division. The students have to figure out the number of groups there would be with 2, 3, 4, 5, 6, 7, 8, 9, and 10 students in each group.

Materials

▲ None

Time

▲ two class periods

Teaching Directions

1. Ask students to share reasons that you might want them in groups.

2. With your students, determine the number of children in the class. (You'll need to decide if you want to use the number of students enrolled or those present on that day.)

3. Ask the students how many groups there would be if they paired up into groups of two. Have several students explain their reasoning.

4. Tell the children they are to solve nine different problems and explain how they got their answers. They are to put the students in their class into groups of 2, 3, 4, 5, 6, 7, 8, 9, and 10 and tell the number of groups.

5. Lead a class discussion for children to share what they found out.

Teaching Notes

This lesson provides students with an experience using the grouping model of division. The children know the total, in this case the number of students in the class, and they know the size of the group, two students, three students, and so on. Their task is to determine how many groups of a particular size can be formed with the members of their class.

There are two different ways of thinking about a division problem. For example, $28 \div 2$ can be interpreted as putting twenty-eight into two groups or putting twenty-eight into groups of two. The answer to both situations is fourteen, but they have different interpretations: two groups with fourteen children in each or fourteen groups of children with two in each. Considered abstractly, both have the same numerical answer, but the meaning of the numerical answer is different when explained in the terms of each context. Providing students with experiences such as this one will help them better understand which interpretation makes sense.

As with most problems, children typically approach this problem in different ways. Some describe their solutions in writing; others prefer to draw diagrams. Some rely on addition; others use multiplication or subtraction. Some solve the problems using the grouping model by dividing the class into groups of two, three, four, and so on; others use the sharing model of division and divide the class into two groups, then three groups, four groups, and so on. The children's responses and insights can provide a rich foundation for a class discussion.

The students in the following vignette each did their own recording sheet showing their own thinking, although they talked with their table partners as they worked. I asked students to do this so I would have a written record of how each of them was thinking about this particular problem. I used the information to guide the class discussion and monitor the progress of the class. If you prefer, the activity is appropriate for students to work on in pairs.

The Lesson

▲▲

DAY 1

"We've been putting a lot of things into equal groups these last few weeks—tiles, cookies, raisins," I said to my students. "Sometimes teachers need to put children into groups. Can someone give a reason that I might want to put you into groups?"

"To work on problems together," Cody replied.

"Field trips," Cindy said.

Other children suggested, "To play a game." "To write stories."

"You get into groups for all sorts of reasons," I agreed. "Sometimes I put you in large groups, sometimes small. Today we're going to work on a problem about groups. To do it, we need to know how many students are in our class today."

"Thirty," Karina answered quickly.

"Two are absent," Carlos remembered. "That makes twenty-eight."

"Yes," I agreed, "and three are at student council, so how many are here right now?

"Twenty-five," the class chorused.

I wrote 25 on the board. "If I took the twenty-five of you and put you into pairs, how many groups of two would we have?"

Skip volunteered, "I know! It's twelve."

"Tell us how you figured out that answer," I encouraged Skip.

"Well, ten plus ten equals twenty. Five left over. Split them up, that makes two more groups and . . . ," he frowned and hesitated.

Kelsey offered, "It's twelve remainder one."

"What will I do with the leftover student?" I asked.

"One group gets three in it," Kelsey said.

Seth said, "I have another way!" He counted by twos to twenty-two, and I listed the numbers on the board:

2, 4, 6, 8, 10, 12, 14, 16, 18, 20, 22

"Now what?" I asked.

"Circle them to show they're groups," Seth directed.

After I did this, Seth noticed, "I didn't go far enough. I left out twenty-four." I added *24*. Seth counted the numbers and said, "Twelve groups of two . . . with one remainder."

I asked if anyone had a different way of thinking about the problem. No one did, so I introduced the rest of the task. "I'd like you to take a sheet of paper and show how we can put the twenty-five of you in these different groups." As I spoke, I wrote on the board:

Classroom Groups

How can we put our 25 students into groups of 2, 3, 4, 5, 6, 7, 8, 9, 10?

"There are nine problems to solve, one for each of the numbers. Be sure to show how you figured the number of groups for each problem," I explained. "Also, put your name and the date on your paper, write the title, and copy down the problem."

"What about the three people who will be back soon?" Afton wanted to know, referring to children who were at a student council meeting.

"You're right, Afton," I said. I erased the 25 and replaced it with *28*. To be sure all the students understood this change in the number, I asked for a volunteer to explain how he or she could solve putting twenty-eight students into groups of two.

Brenna volunteered, "You take the twenty and break it into ten and ten. Then take the eight and break it into fours. Add ten plus four."

When I asked the children to get to work, Lindsey asked, "Can we work with partners?" I often allow children to work with partners and felt it important to explain why I was asking them to work independently this time.

I shook my head "no" and explained, "Today I want each of you to have your own paper so I can see what you do to solve these problems. You can talk to people at your table, but I want you to do the problems your own way. It's important for me to see because you each have a special way to look at problems. I want to see Lindsey's way, Afton's way, Karina's way, Elijah's way—and everybody else's way. I like the way you cooperate in groups, but sometimes it's important for me to see how each one of you thinks."

Vicki wrote the problem on her paper. Then she jumped up from her desk and said, "I need help." I restated the problem.

"Oooh," Vicki said, smiling. "I get it."

Afton told me, "I'm going to kind of do it the way Silas did it."

"That's fine," I confirmed, "if that way makes sense to you."

Brenna found this problem particularly engrossing right from the start. For each number, she listed multiples until she reached or passed twenty-eight and then circled them. Her excitement grew as a chart emerged on her paper. "Wow!" she repeated over and over. (See Figure 8–1.)

A few minutes into the assignment, Karina exclaimed, "I know how you can split it one way. See, there are twenty-eight

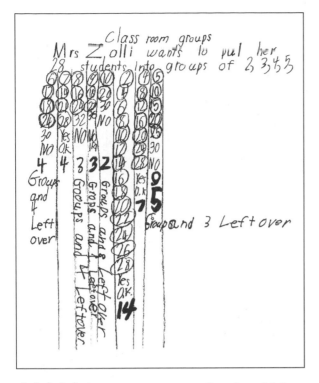

▲▲▲▲▲▲**Figure 8–1** *Brenna listed multiples to figure out how many groups there would be.*

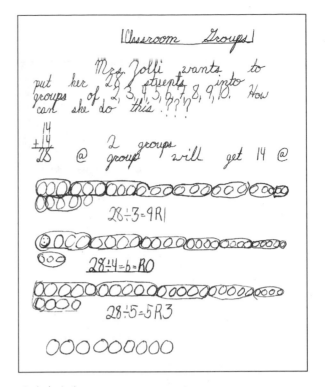

▲▲▲▲▲▲**Figure 8–2** *Karina's strategy was to draw twenty-eight circles and group them.*

kids, and that's fourteen plus fourteen." She was very pleased. I wasn't sure if Karina was thinking about students in groups of two, or about putting them into two groups. Rather than respond, I decided to watch for a few moments as Karina solved the next problem. Karina drew twenty-eight circles and began to circle groups of three. I moved on and checked back later. When she was finished, Karina's paper revealed that her strategy for each problem was to draw twenty-eight circles and then circle groups of two, three, four, and so on to put the students into groups. Karina was able to use the symbolism of division correctly, but she miscounted once and didn't have time to finish. (See Figure 8–2.)

Catalina also drew circles, but she organized them into groups of two, three, four, and so on. (See Figure 8–3.) I made a note to discuss the different interpretations later with the class.

Afton had a slightly different approach to the problem than most other students

did. He changed the total number of students for each problem by eliminating the number left over after grouping each time, his initial solution to dealing with leftovers. By the time Afton got to the last problem of making groups of ten, he had only nine students left. He wrote: *Get a kid to enroll and ÷ 10 by 10.* (See Figure 8–4.)

Elijah drew twenty-eight faces and used them over and over again to make groups to figure out the answers. He recorded his answers using standard symbolism, but in two instances he wrote incorrect answers: *28 ÷ 3 = 27 R1* and *28 ÷ 5 = 25 R1.* In each example, the incorrect answer had some mathematical connection to the problem; it was the multiple of the divisor that came just before twenty-eight. (See Figure 8–5.)

Luke used what he knew about multiplication to solve the problems, noting that *9 × 3* and *3 × 9* are *just switcharouds and they are the same. One means nine groups of three and three groups of nine.* When asked, "Are they really the same?" Luke replied,

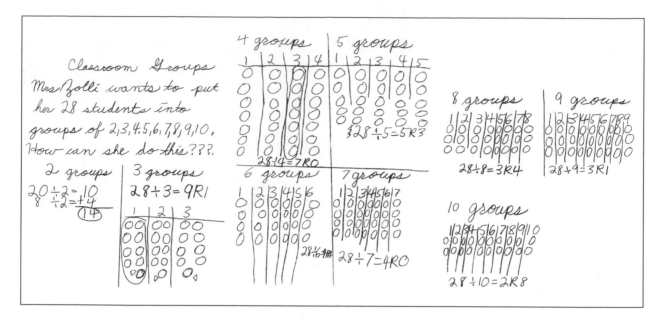

▲▲▲▲▲▲Figure 8–3   *After dividing twenty-eight by two, Catalina solved the rest of the problems by arranging circles into groups of three, four, five, and so on.*

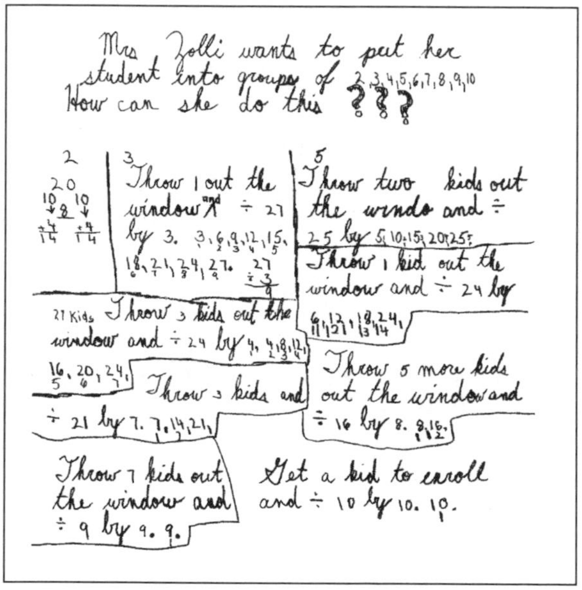

▲▲▲▲▲▲Figure 8–4   *Afton changed twenty-eight to numbers that would result in no remainders.*

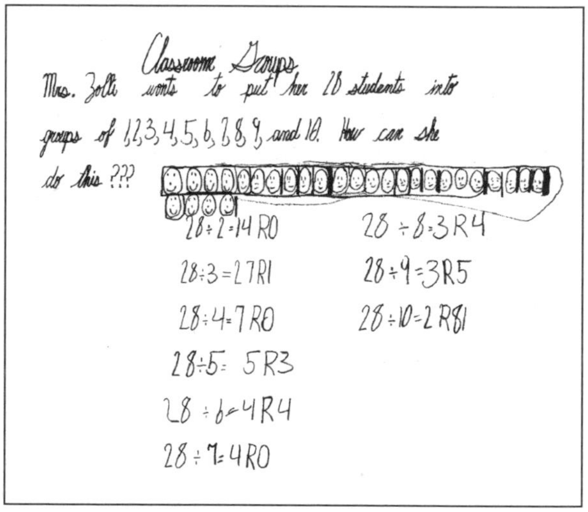

▲▲▲▲▲▲Figure 8–5   *Elijah used the same twenty-eight faces to figure out the answer to each problem, but he made two division errors.*

"One has more different groups but it's the same number total." (See Figure 8–6.)

DAY 2

I allowed time for all the students to complete their work, and then I asked for their attention. "I'm going to show you some things, and I'd like to see if you can explain what I'm doing. Actually, what I'm putting on the board is what you did yesterday."

I drew twenty-eight circles on the board in two rows of ten and one row of eight. I then turned to the class and asked, "What have I done so far?"

Classroom Groups

Mrs. Zolli wants to put her 28 students into groups of 2,3,4,5,6,7, 8,9,10. How can she do this???

$$\begin{array}{r}14\\ \times2\\ \hline28\end{array}\;\boxed{2's}$$
$$\begin{array}{r}9\\ \times3\\ \hline27\end{array}\;\boxed{3's}\;\text{and 1 Leftover}$$
$$\begin{array}{r}3\\ \times9\\ \hline27\end{array}\;\text{and 1 Leftover}\;\boxed{9's}$$
$$\begin{array}{r}10\\ \times2\\ \hline20\end{array}\;\text{10's}\;\text{and 8 Leftover}$$

$$\begin{array}{r}7\\ \times4\\ \hline28\end{array}\;\boxed{4's}$$
$$\begin{array}{r}5\\ \times5\\ \hline25\end{array}\;\text{and 3 Leftover}\;\boxed{5's}$$

$$\begin{array}{r}4\\ \times6\\ \hline24\end{array}\;\boxed{6's}\;\text{and 4 Leftover}$$
$$\begin{array}{r}4\\ \times7\\ \hline28\end{array}\;\boxed{7's}$$
$$\begin{array}{r}3\\ \times8\\ \hline24\end{array}\;\boxed{8's}\;\text{and 4 leftover}$$

$$\begin{array}{r}9\\ \times3\\ \hline27\end{array}\quad\begin{array}{r}3\\ \times9\\ \hline27\end{array}$$ because they just switcharouds and they are the same. One means 9 groups of 3 and 3 groups of 9.

▲▲▲▲▲▲**Figure 8–6** *Luke's solutions showed his understanding of the relationship between multiplication and division.*

"Made heads," the class answered.

"How many?" I asked

"Twenty-eight," the class responded.

I circled the twenty-eight heads in groups of threes.

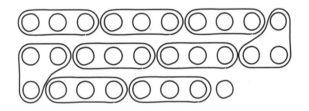

"I drew this the way it appeared on one of your papers," I said. "Who can explain what this girl did?"

"She circled every three," Keilani volunteered.

"She put them in groups of three," Skip added.

"What's the mathematical sentence?" I asked.

"I think it's 'Twenty-eight divided by three equals nine remainder one,' " Keilani said. I wrote:

28 ÷ 3 = 9 R1

"How did she figure the number of groups of three?" I asked.

"She counted circles. Nine circles," Jianna said.

"I'd like to give credit to Karina for the thinking in this problem," I said. "Now I'm going to draw a different way of thinking about the same thing." This time I organized twenty-seven circles into three groups and drew one circle to the side.

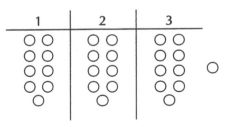

"Who can explain this thinking?" I asked.

Silas explained, "It's three groups of nine and one left over."

"What about the mathematical sentence?" I prompted. Silas repeated what Keilani had offered for Karina's solution.

"I'd like to give credit to Catalina for this

thinking," I said and turned to write on the board again.

"This next one is interesting, and I don't want the person who did it to give the method away," I cautioned. I drew a sample from Brenna's solution (refer back to Figure 8–1). In her paper, Brenna had inadvertently skipped solving the problem of putting students into groups of three. I, therefore, chose to record the way she solved the problem of putting students into groups of four. I listed the multiples of four, stopping at twenty-eight.

④
⑧
⑫
⑯
⑳
㉔
㉘

"Oooh!" children gasped in awe, amazement, and growing understanding.

"What are you thinking?" I asked.

"That's times and division," Jenny said with surprise.

I continued writing other lists of multiples as Brenna had done, adding *YES* or *NO* at the end of each column.

④	⑤	⑥	⑦	⑧
⑧	⑩	⑫	⑭	⑯
⑫	⑮	⑱	㉑	㉔
⑯	⑳	㉔	㉘	32
⑳	㉕	30	YES	NO
㉔	30	NO		
㉘	NO			
YES				

There were more "ooohs" as children saw more patterns. Some waved their hands

excitedly, wanting to talk about their revelations. "I know what she did!" "So do I!"

I paused, giving everyone a chance to study the board and think about the patterns. The room grew quiet as all the students studied the board intently. To give all students the opportunity to express their ideas, I asked the children to talk with their partners. I reminded them that first one person shares for thirty seconds while the other person listens carefully without interruption. At the end of thirty seconds the students switch roles, allowing the first listener the opportunity to speak and the first speaker the opportunity to listen. I timed the students, reminding them when to switch roles, and then asked for their attention.

I asked, "What do you notice?"

"The pattern gets shorter and shorter," Breanna said.

I pointed to the list of multiples of five and asked, "What does she mean by 'NO'?"

Nicki said, "There's extras, leftovers."

Addie asked, "Why did she say 'YES' on four?"

"It came out perfectly, no leftovers," Nicki explained.

"I'd like to thank Brenna for this thinking," I said. "Did you want to explain some more to us, Brenna?"

Brenna grinned. "I used my mind like a calculator. Like for groups of four, I thought, 'one times four is four, two times four is eight,' like that." Brenna used this metaphor often. She said that imagining her mind as a calculator helped her solve "hard math."

I added, "Brenna thought of solving the problem of dividing the class into equal groups by using what she knows about multiplication."

I reviewed the patterns in Brenna's scheme and invited the class to add the others I hadn't written. "Did anyone think about this problem in a different way?"

Afton said, "I did it like Brenna, but in

words. When I did groups of five, I started out by throwing three kids out the window, so then I could count by fives to twenty-five."

Cindy commented, "Wouldn't that be murder?"

"It wasn't a high window," Afton answered.

I said, "I always like to prove something before I believe it. We found out that twenty-eight divided by five equals five remainder three. Arrange yourselves into groups of five and sit down together. Then we'll check."

"But we're all here today," Kareem said.

"Then two of you will be helpers to help me prove the answer," I said and picked William and Janie.

After the intensity of "getting inside" one another's thinking, the physical activity of making these groups was a welcome relief. With a lot of laughter and friendly nudging, the students eventually grouped themselves and proved the equation: Three children stood as "remainders."

To end the class, I challenged the students to rearrange themselves into groups of seven and report the result in conventional mathematical symbolism.

Figure 8–7 shows another student's way of looking at this problem.

EXTENSION

Use some of the suggestions for reasons to group students made by the children early in the lesson as the contexts for additional problems to solve. For example, in this class a student suggested that students are grouped for field trips. Pose the following problem: *There are thirty-two students in our class going on a field trip. We'll be going by car and each car holds five students. How many cars will we need?* Then ask: *We have thirty-two students and five cars. How many will have to ride in each car?*

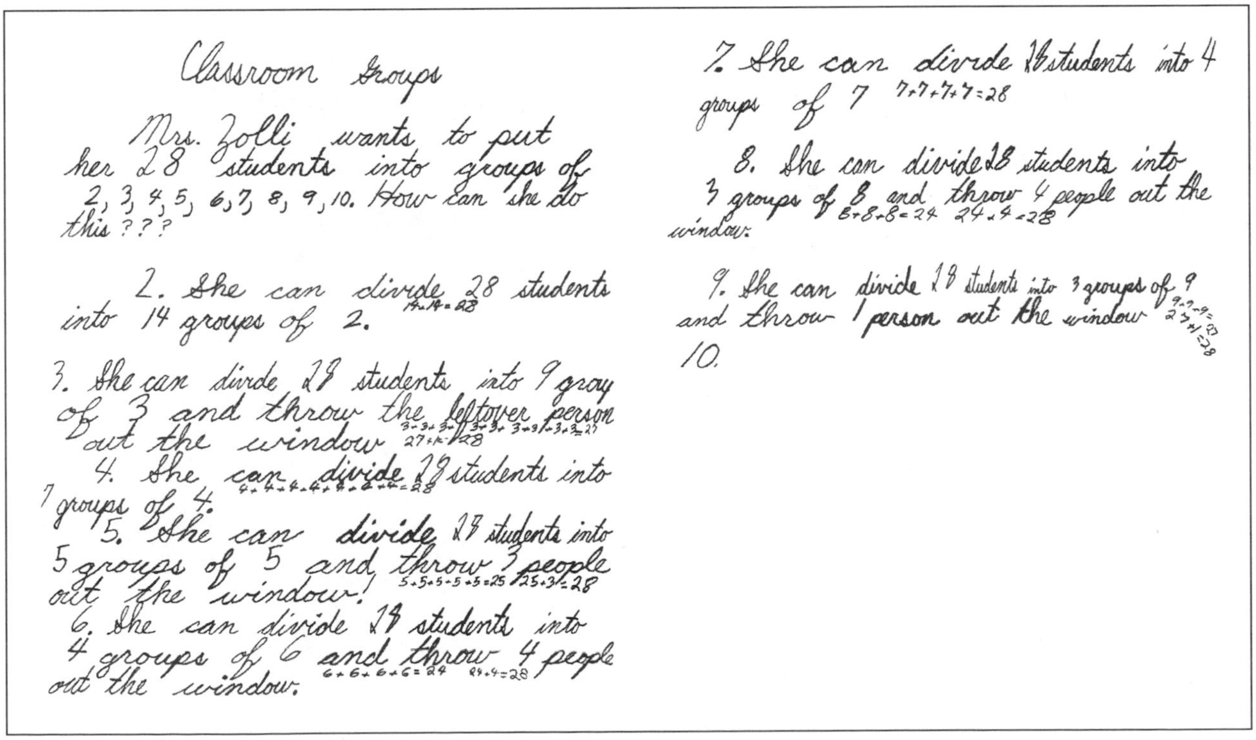
Classroom Groups

Mrs. Zolli wants to put her 28 students into groups of 2, 3, 4, 5, 6, 7, 8, 9, 10. How can she do this???

2. She can divide 28 students into 14 groups of 2. 14+14=28

3. She can divide 28 students into 9 groups of 3 and throw the leftover person out the window 3+3+3+3+3+3+3+3+3=27 27+1=28

4. She can divide 28 students into 7 groups of 4. 4+4+4+4+4+4+4=28

5. She can divide 28 students into 5 groups of 5 and throw 3 people out the window! 5+5+5+5+5=25 25+3=28

6. She can divide 28 students into 4 groups of 6 and throw 4 people out the window. 6+6+6+6=24 24+4=28

7. She can divide 28 students into 4 groups of 7 7+7+7+7=28

8. She can divide 28 students into 3 groups of 8 and throw 4 people out the window. 8+8+8=24 24+4=28

9. She can divide 28 students into 3 groups of 9 and throw 1 person out the window 9+9+9=27 27+1=28

10.

Figure 8–7 *Seth's paper showed how he connected addition and division.*

Questions and Discussion

▲▲▲

▲ *What is the benefit of having students talk with a partner?*

Having students talk with a partner provides the opportunity for every child to respond to a question or idea rather than just a few, as in a whole-group discussion. By listening carefully to a partner, children gain different ways of thinking about ideas. When a child shares, thinking is deepened and clarified. Having children share with a partner keeps more children focused and involved in the lesson, increasing learning for all.

Having children share with a partner before sharing with the class or on a writing assignment gives the child a chance to explore his or her own thinking before "going public." Listening to his or her partner may spark a whole new idea or insight that might not have occurred to the student otherwise. This improves the quality of what the student shares in a discussion or in a writing assignment.

▲ *Your students produced ideas that were ideal for the class discussion on the second day of the lesson. What if my students don't?*

While it's doubtful that your students will produce exactly the same ideas as in the vignette, it's likely they will use interesting strategies that can be shared with your students. In the unlikely event they don't, use the ideas shared in the vignette. Begin by saying, "In another class, a student did this . . . ," or "Here is what one student wrote. . . ."

▲ *You told the students that you wanted them to work independently, yet you allowed them to talk with their table groups. Why were they allowed to talk?*

By talking and listening to others, students can clarify their thinking or perhaps get ideas for ways to solve the problem. My goal was to see what strategies students used and how effectively they applied them. Students didn't copy one another, but they did share ideas. Once they had an idea, each individual student had to apply the idea meaningfully. This requires understanding and thinking.

CHAPTER NINE
PENNIES AND DIMES

Overview

In this lesson, the context of converting pennies to dimes helps students relate division to their real-world experience with money and investigate patterns that emerge when dividing numbers by ten. The lesson provides students experience with the grouping model of division. Students each take a handful of pennies and figure out how many dimes they would have if they exchanged their pennies for dimes. They record their problem with division equations, solve additional problems by combining their handfuls with others, and investigate patterns in the quotients and remainders from the problems they solve.

Materials

▲ play pennies (about 30–35 per student)
▲ transparent container for pennies

Time

▲ two class periods

Teaching Directions

1. Show students the container with the pennies. Ask them to estimate the number of pennies in the container. List their estimates on the board.

2. Model the task. Begin by taking a handful of pennies from the container. Shake your handful so any loose pennies fall back into the container.

3. Count the pennies in your handful by grouping them into same-size groups. For example, group them by fives and model counting by five. Record your total and draw how you counted on the board.

4. Ask students: "If I wanted to exchange all of my pennies for dimes, how many dimes could I get?" Have students share their thinking while you record on the board.

5. Ask students how to write a division equation for the problem. Model different ways to do so, for example, $27 \div 10 = 2$ R7, $10 \overline{)27}^{\,2\,R7}$.

6. Tell students they each will take a handful of pennies, record how many pennies are in their handful and how they counted them, figure out how many dimes their pennies equal, and write a division equation to show what they did.

7. Circulate as students work, asking them to explain what they're doing and why. Once students write a division equation, ask them to explain the meaning of the numbers they used. Ask a pair of students who finishes early to count the remaining pennies in the container. Do this before students replace the pennies in their handfuls.

8. Lead a class discussion. Draw a T-chart on the board with the columns labeled *# of Pennies* and *# of Dimes*. Leave a small space and write *10* in the # of Pennies column and ask students what number should go across from the ten in the # of Dimes column. Leaving space between each number as you list it, continue in this way with twenty, thirty, forty, and fifty pennies. Ask students to share patterns they see in the numbers on the T-chart.

# of pennies	# of dimes
10	1
20	2
30	3
40	4
50	5

9. Write *27* in the # of Pennies column between 20 and 30. Ask students what should be written in the # of Dimes column. Continue in this way, using numbers of pennies in some of the students' handfuls.

10. Ask students how to write division sentences to represent the ordered pairs on the T-chart. For example, the ordered pair (20, 2) could be represented with the following division sentences: $20 \div 10 = 2$, $10 \overline{)20}^{\,2}$, $\frac{20}{10} = 2$.

11. On the board, record the number of pennies in each of the students' handfuls of pennies. Ask students what they notice about the information on the chart. Record their ideas.

12. Explore with students the observation that when dividing by ten, the ones column determines the remainder. For example, any number of pennies with a two in the ones column will have a remainder of two, numbers ending with zero will have no remainders, and so on.

13. Have students pair up and combine their pennies. Ask them to find the total pennies and the number of dimes their pennies equal. Then have two pairs work together to find the total number of pennies for all four people and how many dimes those pennies equal.

14. Lead a second class discussion to gather and record information about the total pennies for each group of four. Find the class total and then add the pennies in the container that were left after the students took their handfuls. Together figure the number of dimes in the class total of pennies.

Teaching Notes

Ten is one of the landmark numbers in our number system, and we want students to be able to perform all four operations with ten easily in their heads—adding ten to any number, subtracting ten from any number, and multiplying or dividing any number by ten. This lesson focuses children on dividing by ten and gives them the opportunity to see how the quotient and remainder when dividing by ten relate to the dividend. They learn that the remainder from dividing by ten is the same as the number in the ones place in the dividend, and that the dividend with the number in the ones place removed is the quotient. For example, $32 \div 10 = 3$ R2, $163 \div 10 = 16$ R3, and so on.

Figuring out how many dimes there are for any number of pennies uses the grouping model of division. Each student figures out how many groups of ten, or dimes, are in his or her handful of pennies. Using pennies and dimes also reinforces for children the place value structure of our number system.

In this lesson, students include R0 as part of the quotient when there is no remainder. While this isn't conventional or essential, its use in this lesson helps children see some patterns. Also, the use of fractional notation to represent division wasn't included. When using fractional notation, it makes sense to write remainders as fractions. This is natural for children when considering cookies but becomes complicated when considering the number of pennies that remain after pennies are exchanged for dimes.

The Lesson

▲▲

DAY 1

Making Estimates
As I began the lesson, I handed each student a sheet of paper and asked them to have a pencil available. Then I held up a plastic transparent container with play pennies. The students were immediately interested and responded with "oohs" and "ahhs." "How many pennies do you think

are in this container?" I asked. Hands shot into the air as students were eager to share their estimates. I walked slowly through the room, holding the container so the students could see the pennies. As I walked I explained, "Please write your name and today's date on your paper. Then write the word *estimate* and a number that tells how many pennies you think are in the container. Remember, an estimate is your best guess about something." I walked to the board and wrote *estimate* on the board so the students could check how to spell it. After a few moments, when all the students had written an estimate on their paper, I asked them to sit on the floor where they could easily see the board, leaving their papers at their desks but remembering their estimates. The students talked excitedly about their estimates as they sat down.

After settling the class, I asked, "Who thinks your estimate of the number of pennies in the container is smaller than most other people's estimates?" Hands went up. I called on Jordan.

Jordan said, "I guessed ninety-three." I wrote Jordan's guess on the board and marked a check after it. I explained, "I made a check after Jordan's guess to show one person thought there were ninety-three pennies in the container."

"Did anyone make a guess that's less than ninety-three?" I asked. Krystin's hand went up.

"Eighty-seven," Krystin said. I wrote Krystin's estimate on the board above Jordan's, followed by a check mark. I did this to keep the estimates in numerical order. No one had a smaller estimate.

"It looks like eighty-seven was the smallest estimate," I continued. "Who thinks your estimate is a large estimate?"

Seth and Jason had their hands up immediately. "We both have five hundred," they said in unison. Some of their classmates looked surprised at the size of their estimate.

"Does anyone have an estimate larger than five hundred?" I asked. No one did. I wrote their estimate on the board, followed by two checks, leaving a large space between 93 and 500 to record the other students' estimates in numerical order.

"Does anyone have an estimate between ninety-three and one hundred?" I asked. No one did. "How about an estimate between one hundred and one hundred ten." Two hands went up. Kris reported his estimate of 100 and Belinda reported hers of 102. I added their estimates followed by checks to the list and continued until all students reported their estimates. Our final list looked as follows:

87	✔
93	✔
100	✔
102	✔
119	✔✔
120	✔✔
120	✔✔
123	✔
131	✔
135	✔✔
140	✔
145	✔✔✔✔
200	✔
212	✔
337	✔
350	✔
450	✔
500	✔✔

Introducing the Activity

"Today, we're going to think about pennies and dimes. First, you'll take a handful of pennies like I'm doing," I explained as I reached into the container and took a handful of pennies. "Take a handful, not a scoopful. Gently shake your hand so all the loose pennies fall back into the container. Then count your pennies in a way that will be easy for me to see how you're counting. For example, I'm going to count my pennies by fives." I laid out the pennies in five groups of five. There were two pennies left over. "Record how you counted on your paper." I drew the five groups of five with the two left over on the board so the students could see what I did and to model how to record. "Then record the number of pennies in your handful." I wrote *27* on the board near my drawing of how I counted the pennies in my handful.

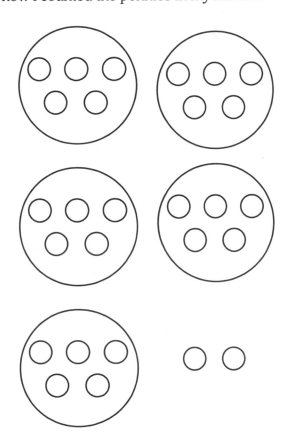

Next I said, "Now you figure out how many dimes you would get if you took your pennies to the bank and exchanged them

for dimes. How many dimes would I get for my twenty-seven pennies?" I paused and hands started to go up.

Casey explained, "You'd get two dimes. Ten pennies is one dime, ten more pennies is two dimes, and that's twenty pennies. Then you'd have seven pennies left over."

I wrote Casey's idea on the board:

2 dimes

10 pennies = 1 dime

10 + 10 = 20

1 dime + 1 dime = 2 dimes

7 pennies left

Casey added, "I think you could write a two for the dimes, then an R for remainder, and then a seven for the seven leftovers."

"Like this?" I asked and wrote on the board:

2 R7

Casey nodded her agreement, as did other students. There were no other comments.

To change the direction of the conversation, I asked, "How could I write this using a division equation?"

Eliza came to the board and wrote: $27 \div 10 = 2 \, R7$. The students indicated their agreement with Eliza with thumbs up. Ashlyn then wrote $10\overline{)27}^{\,2\,R7}$ and the students agreed with her.

"Let's review what you're to do," I said. "First take a handful of pennies. Then count them and show on your paper how you counted them, just as I did on the board. Then write the number of pennies in your handful on your paper. Next, figure out how many dimes you would get if you exchanged as many of your pennies as possible for dimes. Last, write a division equation for your problem."

"Do we use the paper with our estimates?" Jordan asked. I nodded.

"Do we have to count by fives like you did?" Belinda asked.

"No," I replied. "You need to group your pennies in a way that makes it easy for you to count them. How else might you group them other than by fives?"

"Twos," "Fours," "Tens," were some of the responses. Belinda nodded.

"Do we have to write all three ways for the division equation?" Dana asked.

"You may if you wish, but one way is enough," I replied.

"Do we work with partners?" Krystin asked.

"No, you'll each take your own handful," I explained. There were no further questions. I dismissed the students by table group, asking the students each to take one handful of pennies from the container as they returned to their seats.

Observing the Children

I circulated through the class, observing as children grouped their pennies. Anthony grouped his by twos, as did Eliza on the other side of the room. Anthony had twenty-two pennies in his handful. To figure the number of dimes, he circled five groups of two, showing that that was equivalent to one dime. He wrote: *2 dimes 2 leftovers 22 ÷ 2 = 2 R2*. I paused and thought for a moment about how to talk with Anthony about the equation he had written.

"How many pennies do you have?" I asked.

"Twenty-two," Anthony responded.

"How many pennies are needed in a group to make one dime?" I asked.

"Ten," Anthony replied.

I said as I pointed to the 2 Anthony had used as the divisor in his equation, "What was your reason for putting a two in that spot?" My thought was Anthony's picture showed two groups with ten in each, an interpretation with which he was more familiar. Anthony looked perplexed. I then said, "In this problem, you're trying to figure out how many dimes, or tens, there are in twenty-two. You know how many pennies,

and you know there are ten in each group; the question is how many groups of ten."

"Oh," Anthony said. "I see now. In my picture here's one group of ten and here's the other." He corrected his work. (See Figure 9–1.)

Eliza, who also counted by twos, thought there were forty dimes in forty-eight pennies. I asked her, "If you have forty dimes, how many pennies could you get if you traded them?"

Eliza paused then said, "Well, that's forty times ten . . . that's four hundred! I don't think there are forty dimes in forty-eight pennies."

"I agree with you," I said. "How could you figure out the number of dimes? Remember, one dime is worth ten pennies."

"I know," Eliza began, "if I count by tens I can figure out how many tens, or dimes, are in forty-eight. Ten, twenty, thirty, forty." Eliza kept track of the number of tens on her fingers as she counted. "There are four dimes and then eight pennies left over." She erased the 0, changing her answer from forty to four. (See Figure 9–2.) Like Anthony's error, Eliza's mistake was one several other students in the class made.

Amanda had little trouble with the task. She counted her twenty-seven pennies by tens and showed the seven left over. She wrote a division equation for her problem: *27 ÷ 10 = 2 R7*. She checked her answer using multiplication. She wrote: *10 × 2 = 20 20 + 7 = 27*. (See Figure 9–3.)

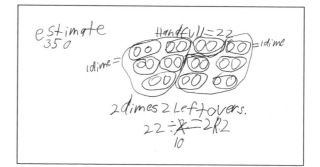

▲▲▲▲▲▲**Figure 9–1** *Anthony's corrected work.*

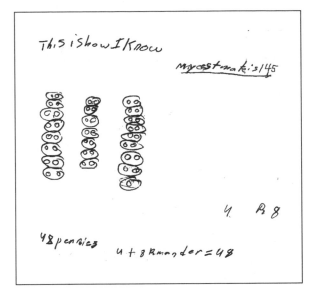

▲▲▲▲▲▲**Figure 9–2** *Eliza counted by twos, incorrectly figuring there were forty dimes and eight pennies in forty-eight pennies. She corrected her work to show there are four dimes with eight pennies remaining.*

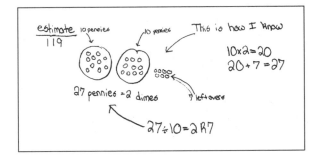

▲▲▲▲▲▲**Figure 9–3** *Amanda showed a clear understanding of the solution to the problem.*

Ashlyn was anxious to show me her work. She explained, "I counted by twos and there were fifteen groups of two and one leftover. To figure out how many pennies that was, I multiplied two times fifteen and that's thirty. Then I added the one that was left over, which made it thirty-one. Then I drew a picture of groups of ten because there are ten pennies in one dime. There are three tens in thirty, so that means there are three dimes. Then there is one penny left. I wrote three division sentences." I was impressed with the clarity of Ashlyn's explanation and the organization of her work. (See Figure 9–4.)

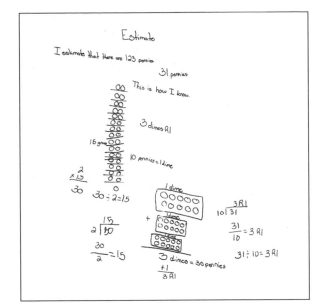

▲▲▲▲▲▲**Figure 9–4** *Ashlyn's organization and clarity indicated a strong understanding of the grouping model of division. Her recording of $\frac{31}{10} = 3\,R1$ isn't incorrect, although it isn't conventional.*

Briana and Amanda finished a few minutes early. I asked them to count the pennies remaining in the container while the others completed their work. I explained we would need the information later when we figured the total pennies in the container. They counted 112 pennies.

I asked for the students' attention. "You have one minute to put the final touches on your work. As soon as you're finished, please bring you paper and come sit on the floor." The students who were finished came and sat down while a few put finishing touches on their work.

A Second Discussion

I reminded the students to place their papers on the floor in front of them so they could see them. I find that doing this helps keep the papers from being rattled and creating a distraction, yet allows student visual access to their work. I began the discussion.

I drew a T-chart on the board and labeled the columns *# of Pennies* and *# of Dimes*. I put a *10* in the # of Pennies column and asked the class what should go in the # of Dimes column. The students correctly responded that a 1 should go in the # of Dimes column. I wrote this on the T-chart.

# of pennies	# of dimes
10	1

"What about twenty pennies?" I asked. "How many dimes?"

"Two," the class replied. I added the information to the T-chart, this time leaving space between numbers as I moved down the chart, stopping at 50. I left spaces so we could add numbers that came between those listed on the chart, for example, 42.

# of pennies	# of dimes
10	1
20	2
30	3
40	4
50	5

"What do you notice about the numbers in the Number of Pennies column?" I asked.

"They're all even," Krystin said.

"They all end in zero," Grant added.

"They're counting by tens," Dana said.

"What if I added my handful of twenty-seven to the Number of Pennies column?" I asked. "What would I write in the Number of Dimes column?" As the students thought, I wrote 27 on the T-chart between 20 and 30.

"I think I'm starting to get this," Dana said. "Twenty-seven pennies is between twenty and thirty, so there must be between two and three dimes. It's two dimes with

seven pennies left over." I added the information from Dana to the appropriate spot on the T-chart.

Thumbs up by most students showed agreement with Dana.

"Let's see where some of your handfuls would go on the T-chart," I suggested. Students were eager to share. I called on Maria. She reported that she had forty-two pennies in her handful.

I said, "First, think about the most possible dimes Maria could exchange for her pennies, then think about where to put this information on the T-chart." Most students raised a hand quickly. I called on Seth.

Seth was quick to answer. "That's easy. It's four dimes remainder two pennies. The forty-two goes between forty and fifty in the Number of Pennies column, and the four remainder two goes across from it in the Number of Dimes column."

I commented, "Things are easy once you figure them out." I added 42 and 4 R2 to the T-chart where Seth suggested.

Tony shared that he had fifty-four pennies in his handful. I wrote 54 on the T-chart under the # of Pennies column. Students were eager as they anticipated my question. "How many dimes in fifty-four pennies?" So many hands were up that I asked the students to reply together using a whisper voice.

"Five dimes with four pennies left over," the class whispered.

"Give us a hard one," Jason said.

"How about if a giant took a handful of seventy-seven pennies?" I said and wrote 77 on the T-chart. Again hands shot into the air.

"It's seven dimes and seven pennies! I get it!" Dana said.

"One last one," I said. I wrote 115 on the T-chart. The students got wide-eyed and then hands started to go up.

Briana explained, "In one hundred pennies, it takes ten dimes. You still have fifteen more pennies left. In fifteen pennies, there's one more dime. So that's ten dimes and one dime, which is eleven dimes. That leaves five pennies and that's not enough for another dime, so that means five are left over. It's eleven dimes with a remainder of five pennies."

I wrote Briana's thinking on the board:

100 pennies = 10 dimes

115 – 100 = 15

15 pennies = 1 dime and 5 pennies

10 + 1 = 11

115 pennies = 11 dimes remainder 5 pennies

Anthony had another way of thinking about the number of dimes in 115 pennies. He explained, "Five dimes equals fifty pennies. Five times ten is fifty. Eleven dimes equals one hundred ten pennies. Eleven times ten equals one hundred ten. One hundred fifteen minus one hundred ten leaves five pennies left over."

I recorded on the board:

5 dimes = 50 pennies

5 × 10 = 50

11 dimes = 110 pennies

11 × 10 = 110

115 – 110 = 5

11 dimes with 5 pennies left over

No one had any other ideas to offer. The T-chart looked as follows:

# of pennies	# of dimes
10	1
20	2
27	2 R7
30	3
40	4
42	4 R2
50	5
54	5 R4
77	7 R7
115	11 R5

To refocus the discussion, I pointed to the T-chart where it said 20 pennies. I asked, "How could I write a division sentence to show this?" I waited until several students had a hand raised.

Mason explained, "It's 'Twenty divided by ten equals two remainder zero.' " Next to the T-chart I wrote Mason's division equation.

# of pennies	# of dimes	
10	1	
20	2	20 ÷ 10 = 2 R0
27	2 R7	
30	3	
40	4	
42	4 R2	
50	5	
54	5 R4	
77	7 R7	
115	11 R5	

I continued asking the students how to write division equations for the pairs of numbers on the T-chart. Children suggested I use the various ways of writing division equations as we went along. The completed chart looked as follows:

# of pennies	# of dimes	
10	1	$10 \div 10 = 1\ R0$
20	2	$20 \div 10 = 2\ R0$
27	2 R7	$10\overline{)27}\ \ ^{2\ R7}$
30	3	$10\overline{)30}\ \ ^{3\ R0}$
40	4	$40 \div 10 = 4\ R0$
42	4 R2	$42 \div 10 = 4\ R2$
50	5	$10\overline{)50}\ \ ^{5}$
54	5 R4	$54 \div 10 = 5\ R4$
77	7 R7	$10\overline{)77}\ \ ^{7\ R7}$
115	11 R5	$115 \div 10 = 11\ R5$

"I think I learned a lot," Dana said. Others nodded their heads.

"I think I agree," I responded. "You just solved a hard problem in your heads." I wrote on the board: $10\overline{)115}$ and continued, "That's a big problem and you did it by using what you know and your number sense to help you." I ended the lesson there and collected the students' papers for safekeeping until the following day. I asked the students to return their pennies to the container on their way to recess. (If I hadn't had Briana and Amanda count the pennies that remained in the container after students took their handfuls, I would have emptied them into another container so they could be counted before the next day's lesson.) I left the T-charts and other sharing on the board for the following day.

DAY 2

I gathered the students on the floor and passed back their papers from the previous day. I planned to collect the information on their handfuls of pennies and then explore patterns presented by the information. Then I planned to have the students work in pairs to combine their pennies and figure out how many dimes their combined total equaled. Next, pairs would join and the students would repeat the activity, finding the total pennies among the four of them and the number of dimes the pennies were worth. I planned to lead a discussion to determine the number of pennies in the class total and the equivalent dimes, and last, to determine the number of pennies in the container.

To begin I said, "I'm going to go around and ask each of you to share with the class the number of pennies in your handful and how many dimes and leftovers that equals. I'll record your information on a chart. As each of you shares and I add new information to the to the chart, look for patterns." I drew a large T-chart on the board. Anthony was first to share. He reported twelve pennies in his handful, which equaled one dime remainder two pennies. I recorded as follows:

	# of pennies	# of dimes
Anthony	12	1 R2

Adam was next. He reported twenty-two pennies and two dimes remainder two pennies. Jason followed. He said he had forty-three pennies, which was nine and one-half dimes. I paused to consider if I wanted to sidetrack and discuss Jason's answer or come back to it. I decided to go on and return later during the class discussion of the information presented on the T-chart. We continued in this way until all students reported. The completed chart looked as follows:

	# of pennies	# of dimes
Anthony	12	1 R2
Adam	22	2 R2
Jason	43	$9\frac{1}{2}$
Seth	47	4 R7
Dana	54	5 R4
Eliza	48	4 R8
Annie	28	2 R8
Martin	32	3 R2
Natalie	31	3 R1
John	27	2 R7
Briana	19	1 R9
Ashlyn	31	3 R1
Amanda	27	2 R7
Mason	36	3 R6
Morgan	18	1 R8
Jordan	22	2 R2
Kris	8	0 R8
Randy	31	3 R1
Belinda	19	1 R9
Krystin	11	1 R1
Maria	42	4 R2
Tony	54	5 R4
Amelia	23	2 R3
Casey	20	2 R0
Grant	38	3 R8

"What do you notice about the chart?" I asked.

Natalie shared, "The number in the tens place of the pennies is the same as the number of dimes."

"Yeah," Briana added, "the dime is the tens place and the pennies is the ones place."

I wrote on the board:

Briana and Natalie: Dimes are the tens place, pennies are the ones place.

"Hey, that's right," Randy said. "I checked on some of them and it works. Anthony's handful is twelve; the tens place is one, and so is the number of dimes. The ones place is two and so is the number of leftover pennies. It works for Adam's, too." Many heads were nodding.

Kris shared next. "The ones column always tells the remainder."

I wrote:

Kris: The ones column always tells the remainder when you divide by ten.

I added, "I agree with you, Kris, as long as you're dividing by ten." The students were quiet for a few moments, considering the information on the board and what Kris had shared. Then Grant raised his hand.

"I think Jason's answer for how many pennies and dimes should be four remainder three. Ten pennies equals one dime. Forty divided by ten is four, so that's four dimes. Then there would be three pennies left over." If Grant or another student hadn't noticed Jason's error, I would have returned to it.

Jason responded, "I think Grant's right. My answer of nine and a half would be the answer for ninety-five pennies. I get it now."

Looking for Patterns

"Let's look at the results with a remainder of one," I said. "What number of pennies gave a remainder of one?" I wrote *R1*.

"Eleven and thirty-one have remainders of one," Belinda said.

I listed these under R1. "There aren't any more on the list," Kris said.

"What other numbers could go on the list?" I asked.

"Sixty-one," Jordan suggested.

"Forty-one," Amanda said. The students continued to suggest numbers as I listed them on the board.

```
                R1
                11

                31

                61

                41

                51

                21

                71

                81
```

"What do you notice about these numbers?" I asked.

"They all end in one," Anthony said.

"How many dimes in eighty-one pennies?" I asked.

"Eight with a remainder of one," Belinda said.

"What about one hundred one?" I continued. "Does it belong on the list?"

The students indicated with their thumbs that it did. I added *101* to the list. "What about one hundred eleven?"

"It belongs there," Ashlyn said. "It's one hundred eleven divided by ten. That's eleven with one left over."

"I think nine hundred ninety-one should be on the list," Krystin suggested.

"How about one?" Kris said with a giggle. "The division equation would be 'One divided by ten is zero remainder one.' "

"A million one!" Eliza said as her classmates giggled.

Kris raised his hand. "I believe that for every number you divide by ten, the ones place will tell you the remainder and the rest of the number tells you the number of tens. For eight hundred eighty-one, there is a remainder of one and eighty-eight tens. Ten times eighty-eight is eight hundred eighty, plus the remainder of one is eight hundred eighty-one." No one had anything to add after Kris finished, but most students nodded their agreement.

I used Kris's idea about the ones place in the dividend determining the remainder when dividing by ten to explore other remainders. Together we listed the numbers with remainders of two and then did the same with remainders of eight, each time discovering that the number in the ones place determined the remainder when dividing by ten.

Combining Pennies

I said, "I'd like you to work with the person sitting beside you. If you need to get the same number of pennies you had yesterday from the container, you may do so in a few minutes. You don't have to take pennies unless you think they would help you solve the next problem. Combine the number of pennies in your handful from yesterday with your partner's. Figure the number of pennies you have together and how many dimes they equal. Show me how you figured this on the back of your paper." I paused to see if there were questions. There were none.

The students got to work, only a few getting pennies from the container. I circulated through the class, reminding students to add labels to clarify how they were solving the problem and to write a division equation if they could. Most students had little difficulty with the assignment. Randy's work was typical of the class. He and Dana worked together. Randy indicated how many coins he had and how many Dana had. He added to find the total, then explained how he figured the dimes and leftovers. He indicated he understood that the ones place indicates the number of pennies left and the tens place indicates the number of dimes. Randy also wrote a division equation. (See Figure 9–5.)

As students finished figuring with their partners, I asked them to join the other pair at their table to figure the total number of pennies for their table group and then figure the number of dimes and leftovers. Briana wrote how her table figured: *Anthony and Mason got 58 pennies and*

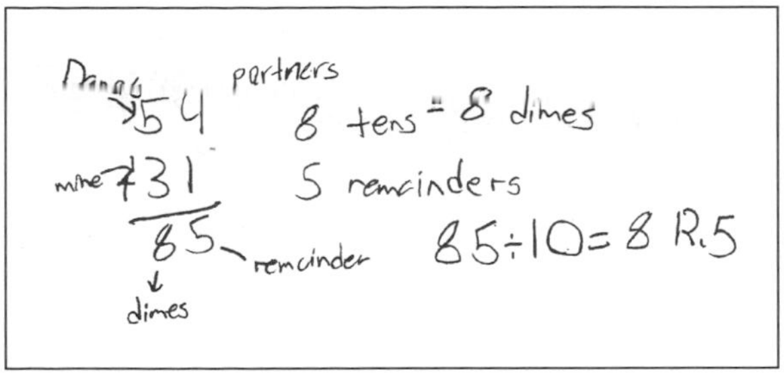

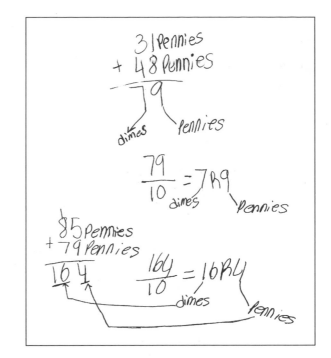

Figure 9–5 shows handwritten work in a box.

▲▲▲▲▲▲Figure 9–5 *Randy showed he understood that when dividing by ten, the ones place indicates the remainder.*

Briana and Amanda got 47 pennies. 58 + 47 = 105. There is 10 dimes and 5 pennies left-over. (See Figure 9–6.)

Natalie was pleased by her work. She explained as she showed me her paper, "I added up to find how many pennies my partner and I had. It's seventy-nine. I showed that the seven in the tens place tells the number of dimes because dimes are like tens, only money. The nine in the ones place is the pennies. Then I wrote a division sentence using a fraction. Then I did the same thing when our group figured out how many pennies altogether. It's one hundred sixty-four. The four in the ones place is the remainder of four pennies. The rest of the number means there are sixteen tens in one hundred sixty-four." (See Figure 9–7.)

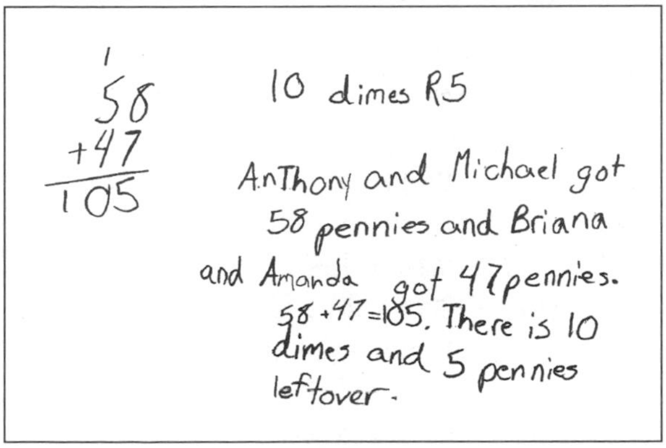

▲▲▲▲▲▲Figure 9–7 *Natalie clearly understood the number of dimes and pennies in her group's total. She represented the division using fractional notation. While the way she wrote the remainder is unconventional, it's not wrong.*

Most of the students finished with little difficulty as they cemented their insights about the relationship between pennies and dimes and ones and tens. I gave the students a one-minute warning, asking them to complete what they were doing. Then I asked them to bring their work with them to the floor for a discussion.

A Class Discussion

I began the discussion by pointing to the list of estimates the students made the day before about the number of pennies in the container. "The smallest estimate was eighty-seven and the largest was five hundred. Let's use the information you gathered about the number of pennies in your handfuls to help us figure the actual number of pennies in the container. When I call on your table group, please report the total number of pennies in the handfuls of your group." I called on the table groups

▲▲▲▲▲▲Figure 9–6 *Briana showed how her table figured the total number of pennies for their group.*

and they reported their totals as I recorded them on the board:

Table Totals

39

139

73

105

164

"Wow! I wonder how many that is," Ashlyn said.

"Let's figure it out," I responded. I paused and gave the students a few minutes to think quietly. Then I asked them each to work with their neighbor to find the total. The room was filled with the buzz of conversation as the students added the total. I asked for the students' attention.

"How many were able to find the total?" I asked. Most hands were up. "Who would like to explain?"

Kris explained, "We added the hundreds. There are three of them, so that's three hundred. Then we looked at the tens place. We noticed that three tens and seven tens made another hundred. That left another three tens and six tens and that's ninety. That's four hundred ninety. Then we added the ones. The ones are equal to thirty. Four hundred ninety plus thirty is five hundred twenty."

I wrote on the board:

300 + 100 + 90 = 490

490 + 30 = 520

No one had any other ideas to share. "Briana and Amanda counted the pennies left in the container yesterday. There were one hundred twelve left. How many were in the container when we started?" I wrote on the board:

520 + 112 = ?

Casey explained, "You can think of one hundred twelve in parts. There's one hundred, one ten, and two ones. You add one the hundred to five hundred and twenty and that's six hundred twenty. Then add the ten

to that and it's six hundred thirty, and add two more and it's six hundred thirty-two."

I recorded on the board:

112 = 100 + 10 + 2

520 + 100 = 620

620 + 10 = 630

630 + 2 = 632

"Oh brother, was my guess off!" said Krystin, who had guessed eighty-seven.

"Jason and I were closest," Seth said. "We guessed five hundred. But we were still one hundred thirty-two pennies off."

I said, "There were five hundred twenty pennies in your handfuls. How many dimes is that?"

"I really get this now," Dana said. He had struggled earlier and I was pleased to see his confidence. "There are no leftovers because there's a zero in the ones place. That leaves the fifty-two, so there are fifty-two dimes in five hundred twenty pennies. Can I write the division sentence?" I nodded and Dana came to the board and wrote:

$10\overline{)520}$ $^{52\ R0}$. Krystin asked if she could

write another division sentence. I nodded and she came to the board and wrote: $\frac{520}{10} = 52\ R0$.

"There's one more way. Can I write it?" Belinda asked with pleading eyes. I nodded and she wrote: *520 ÷ 10 = 52 R0.*

"These are three ways to correctly show the same division situation," I summarized. While it's not necessary to write R0 when the remainder is zero, it helps some children.

"How many dimes would all the pennies in the container equal?" I asked. "The total number of pennies is six hundred thirty-two." Eager hands shot into the air. "Tell me in a whisper voice."

"Sixty-three with two remainders," the class whispered. I nodded.

"What are the two remainders?" I asked.

"They're the two leftover pennies," Jordan answered.

"Give us a really hard one," Anthony requested. I smiled and wrote on the board: *1,657 ÷ 10 = ?* Again, hands popped up as the students wiggled in their spots with excitement.

Belinda said, "Easy! The seven means the remainder is seven. That means there are one hundred sixty-five dimes and seven pennies."

I asked her classmates to show their agreement with their thumbs. All thumbs were up.

"Would you like one more?" I asked, eager to continue their enthusiasm. Shouts of "Yeah!" and nods told me to go on. I wrote on the board: $10\overline{)52,674}$. Almost all hands were up. "Show me the remainder using your fingers," I said. Hands with four fingers were up instantly.

Randy explained, "The ones column is four. When you divide by ten, the ones column tells you the remainder."

"The number of dimes is big!" Natalie said. "I'm not sure I know how to say it."

"Would you like to try?" I encouraged.

Natalie paused, then said, "The number of dimes is five two six seven, and I think you say that five thousand two hundred sixty-seven."

"You figured it out just right," I said. I ended the lesson there.

Questions and Discussion

▲▲

▲ *When you were collecting the results from the students, Jason gave an incorrect answer. Why did you leave it on the chart rather than correct Jason immediately?*

I let Jason's answer stand for several reasons. It was clear that Jason was confused. By listening to other students' responses and considering why they made sense, he had the opportunity to make sense of his own answer and correct his own thinking. Also, I was interested to know if other students would consider the data as a whole and recognize that one answer was different. It's important for students to consider the big picture, not just their own response. Also, at that point in the conversation, I wanted to stay focused on collecting the data. Later, another student noticed Jason's error and presented a good explanation about why it didn't make sense. Jason made sense of the explanation and was able to see that his original answer didn't work.

▲ *What would you have done if another student hadn't noticed Jason's error?*

I would have pointed out to the class that one answer didn't look the same as the others. After asking the students which answer it was, I would have used a line of questioning to help them see why nine and one-half dimes wasn't equivalent to forty-three pennies.

CHAPTER TEN
HANDFULS OF CUBES

Overview

In this lesson, students take a handful of cubes, count how many there are, figure out the number of pairs there are if they put the cubes into groups of two, and then write a division equation to represent what they did. Next students add ten cubes to their handful and again figure out the number of pairs and record a division equation. After repeating this several more times, they look for patterns in the equations they recorded. The activity gives students experience with the grouping model of division.

Materials

▲ interlocking cubes (Multilink, Snap, or Unifix, approximately $\frac{3}{4}$ inch in size), about 60 per student

Time

▲ two class periods

Teaching Directions

1. Show students how to take a handful of cubes, not a scoopful, shaking the loose cubes into the basket.

2. Explain and model for the students that first they count the cubes, record the number of cubes on their paper, then figure the number of pairs of cubes in their handful and record. Next they write a division equation to show this.

3. Add ten cubes to your first handful. Figure and record the new dividend, or total. Find and record using a division equation the number of pairs in the new dividend.

4. Repeat Step 3 three or four times, each time recording with a division sentence.

5. Ask students to share what patterns they notice. Record on the board.

6. Have students each take a handful and conduct the activity independently as modeled in Steps 2 through 5.

7. Students who finish early can repeat the activity, this time finding groups of three in their handful.

8. Lead a class discussion to collect information about the students' investigations of pairs of cubes and to discuss patterns they notice in the information.

9. If time and student interest allow, discuss the results from investigations finding groups of three.

Teaching Notes

This lesson gives students experience with the grouping model of division. The number of cubes in a handful is the dividend. Because they group the cubes into pairs, or groups of two, the divisor is two. The quotient is the result of grouping the cubes into pairs.

After they add ten cubes several times to produce a new dividend and, therefore, a new problem, students search for patterns in the division sentences they've recorded. Patterns students notice may be variations of the following:

▲ The remainder is zero when you find the number of pairs in an even number.
▲ The remainder is one when you find the number of pairs in an odd number.
▲ Adding ten cubes to the handful results in adding five to the answer because there are five pairs in ten cubes.
▲ The remainder is always zero or one because a remainder of two or more would be enough to make more groups.

Keep in mind that the discussion in your class and the patterns your students notice will most likely vary from what is described in the vignette. Also, changing the activity to grouping into threes, fours, or other numbers extends the experience for students who are ready.

The Lesson

▲▲

DAY 1

Before class, I put interlocking cubes in baskets and placed the baskets on a counter in the back of the room. I prepared one basket per table group with about sixty cubes per student. Picking up one of the baskets and carrying it to the front of the room, I said, "Today we're going to do an investigation that begins with a handful of cubes." I showed the students how they should take a handful of cubes, rather than scoop them up, shaking their hand gently so loose cubes would fall into the basket. I continued, "Your job is first to figure out how many cubes are in your handful. Then figure out if you snap the cubes into pairs how many pairs of cubes are in your handful."

"What's a pair?" Dana asked. Several hands went up. I asked Dana to call on someone. He called on Krystin.

"A pair means two," Krystin explained matter-of-factly. Dana nodded.

I continued, modeling for the students what they were to do. "I need to count my cubes first and then record how many I have," I said and quickly counted nine cubes. I wrote on the board:

Handful of Cubes

9 cubes

"My next task is to figure the number of pairs, or twos, in my handful of cubes." I put the cubes in twos and set them along the chalkboard tray so students could see. "How many pairs, or groups of two, are there in nine?" I asked. "Show me with your fingers." Most students held up four fingers.

"There's a leftover," Amelia commented.

"In my handful of nine, I have four pairs, or groups of two, with one leftover," I summarized. I added to what I had written on the board:

Handful of Cubes

9 cubes

4 pairs, 1 leftover

"Who would like to write a division equation that shows this?" I asked.

Briana came to the board and wrote: $9 \div 2 = 4 R1$.

I pointed to each number in the equation as I explained, "I have nine cubes, and I put them into pairs, or groups of two. The four means I have four pairs, and the remainder of one is the leftover."

"I have nine cubes," I continued. "Now

I'm going to add ten more. How many cubes will I have?"

"Nineteen," the class chorused.

I took ten more cubes from the basket. "I have nineteen cubes. How many pairs is that?" Underneath the equation that Briana wrote, I wrote a division problem to represent what I was asking:

$9 \div 2 = 4 R1$

$19 \div 2 = ?$

Dana shared, "I think it's nine groups of two with one remainder."

"Put your thumb up to show agreement with Dana, put your thumb down to show disagreement, or put your thumb sideways if you're not sure," I said. Most thumbs were up. "Who would like to explain why Dana's answer makes sense?"

Belinda said, "You count by twos and it takes nine times to get to eighteen, and the nineteenth is the leftover."

I recorded on the board:

2, 4, 6, 8, 10, 12, 14, 16, 18

nine groups of two = 18

18 + 1 = 19

Randy said, "You can check by multiplying nine times two. That means nine groups of two. The answer is eighteen and then one more makes nineteen."

$9 \times 2 = 18$

$18 + 1 = 19$

I continued. "What if I add ten more cubes to the nineteen cubes?" The students were quiet as they thought about this. I gave them a moment to think then asked, "How many cubes will that make?"

"Twenty-nine," they chorused.

"How many groups of two, or pairs, do you think there are in twenty-nine cubes?" I asked.

Eliza said, "Nineteen remainder one." I wrote this on the board. Several hands were up.

"I disagree," Anthony said. "I think it's sixteen remainder one." I added Anthony's answer to the board. Amelia still had her hand up.

"It's fourteen remainder one," Amelia said. There were no more answers.

"We have three different answers," I said. "How could we find out which is correct?" Hands went up. I called on Jordan.

"Nineteen is too big. The problem before had nineteen cubes and nine pairs. The number of pairs is more than double what it was for the last answer, but the number of cubes didn't double," Jordan explained.

Briana added, "If you count by two nineteen times you get thirty-eight. There are only twenty-nine cubes. I think fourteen remainder one is right. Two times fourteen is like fourteen plus fourteen and that's twenty-eight. Add the remainder and it's twenty-nine."

Anthony raised his hand. "My answer of sixteen remainder one is wrong. I want to change it to fourteen remainder one." I nodded.

"Mine is wrong too," Eliza said. "I think it should be fourteen remainder one."

"If you think the answer is fourteen remainder one put your thumb up," I said. All thumbs went up.

"Let's use the cubes to check," I suggested. I paired twenty-nine cubes, setting each pair on the chalkboard tray and putting the remaining one at the end of the row of pairs. Together we counted the twos and confirmed there were fourteen pairs. I recorded on the board:

$9 \div 2 = 4 R1$

$19 \div 2 = 9 R1$

$29 \div 2 = 14 R1$

We continued in this manner, adding ten cubes two more times and finding the number of pairs. The list looked as follows:

$9 \div 2 = 4 R1$

$19 \div 2 = 9 R1$

$29 \div 2 = 14 R1$

$39 \div 2 = 19 R1$

$49 \div 2 = 24 R1$

"What do you notice?" I asked. The children studied the list and slowly began to put up a hand when they noticed something. I waited until about half the students had raised a hand. Then I called on Adam.

Adam shared, "I see a pattern in the ones place. It goes four, nine, four, nine, four, nine."

To encourage Adam and the others to be more specific, I asked, "When you say the ones place, to which number are you referring?"

"The answer," Adam responded. "The 'number of pairs' part of the answer." I pointed to the part of the answer I thought Adam meant and he nodded his agreement. I wrote on the board, paraphrasing Adam's idea:

There's a pattern in the ones column of the answer that tells the number of pairs. The pattern goes 4, 9, 4, 9.   Adam

"Is what I wrote correct?" I asked Adam to be sure I understood. He nodded.

Krystin shared next. "If you look at the number of blocks, it always ends in nine and the tens place goes up by one ten each time. I think that's because you keep adding a ten and that's how it comes out in the numbers."

I recorded Krystin's idea:

The ones place in the number of blocks is always nine. The tens place goes up by one each time because you add ten cubes. Krystin

Krystin nodded her agreement with what I recorded on the board.

Briana shared, "All the problems have a remainder of one."

I wrote on the board:

All the problems have a remainder of one. Briana

Adam shared, "The answer always increases by five."

I recorded:

The answer always increases by five. Adam

"I wonder why that happens?" I said. I paused. Several hands were up.

Jordan explained, "There are five twos in ten. Each time you add ten cubes, it's the same as adding five pairs." Several students nodded their agreement. There were no other comments.

I said, "In just a moment you'll need to send someone from your table to the back counter to get a basket of cubes. You'll share the basket of cubes with your table group, but you'll work by yourself and take your own handful of cubes. Count the cubes in your handful and record on your paper how many cubes there are. Then figure the number of twos, or pairs, in your handful. Record this on your paper, just as I did on the board." I pointed to the board where I had modeled how to record. "Add ten more cubes to your handful. Figure your new total and how many pairs are in your new total. Write this on your paper. Continue to do this four or five times. Then look at the information you have and write about the patterns you notice, just as we did on the board with my handful. To help you remember, I'll write the directions on the board." There were no questions. The students chose someone to get the cubes for their tables and I wrote the following directions on the board beside the work we did together:

1. *Take a handful of cubes.*
2. *Count them and record the total on your paper.*
3. *Figure the number of pairs in your handful. Record.*
4. *Add 10 more cubes. Figure the number of pairs. Record.*
5. *Do this 4 or 5 times. Record each time.*
6. *Write about the patterns you notice.*

Observing the Students

The students were eager and most got to work quickly. Jason and Seth were giving each other a difficult time by grabbing cubes away from one another. Krystin waited patiently as the boys fooled around. As I approached, Jason pulled his hand from the basket, allowing Seth to take his cubes. Jason took his, then Krystin. The three got to work figuring the number of cubes in their handfuls and the number of pairs in each handful. I watched a few moments.

Krystin commented, "I have an even number in my handful. I don't think I'll get any leftovers."

Jason responded, "I got an even number, too, and I'm not getting any leftovers, even when I add ten." I moved on.

"Mine's easy!" Amelia said. "I got ten in my handful. When I add ten cubes, it's like counting by tens." Amelia had figured the number of pairs in 10, 20, 30, 40, and 50 cubes. She was working on 60.

Kris explained, "I figured out some of my answers by doubling the number of pairs I thought would be in that number. Like for fifty-eight, I predicted it would be twenty-nine pairs, so I added twenty-nine and twenty-nine and it was fifty-eight."

I asked, "How did you know to try twenty-nine?"

"I saw a pattern in the answers," Kris explained. "The answers go up by five each time. If I add five to the answer that comes before, I should get the new answer."

"Why do you think that works?" I probed.

"I think it's because there are five pairs in ten," Kris said. "So when I add ten blocks, it's the same as adding five groups of two. Can I keep going?" I nodded. Kris had figured the number of pairs for 108 cubes. (See Figure 10–1.)

Grant was very involved with his exploration. He had paired cubes on his desk, and when he ran out of room on his desk, he started putting them on the floor. Unlike a few children who chose not to use the cubes, Grant took great delight in the visual representation of his work. He said, "There

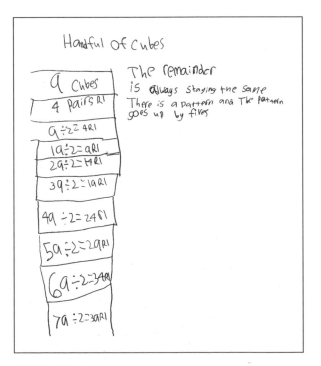

Figure 10–1 shows handwritten work:

Hand full of cubes

4 pairs

8 ÷ 2 = 4
18 ÷ 2 = 9
28 ÷ 2 = 14
38 ÷ 2 = 19
48 ÷ 2 = 24
58 ÷ 2 = 29
68 ÷ 2 = 34
78 ÷ 2 = 39
88 ÷ 2 = 44
98 ÷ 2 = 49
108 ÷ 2 = 54
118 ÷ 2 = 59
128 ÷ 2 = 64
138 ÷ 2 = 69
148 ÷ 2 = 74
158 ÷ 2 = 79
168 ÷ 2 = 84
178 ÷ 2 = 89
188 ÷ 2 = 94
198 ÷ 2 = 99
208 ÷ 2 = 104

▲▲▲▲▲▲**Figure 10–1** *Kris continued to figure the number of pairs of cubes up to 208.*

bigger by five and the number of cubes always ends in nine and the divided-by number is always the same, two."

"You see a lot of patterns," I replied. "You need to take what you told me and make it go from your brain, down your arm, and out your pencil onto your paper." Grant was a reluctant writer. "When you've done that, come get me and I'll give you a different problem to explore." Grant worked a few minutes, putting a couple of his ideas on his paper. He came to show me and I decided not to dampen his enthusiasm by pushing him to write more. (See Figure 10–2.)

I then gave him a different problem. To explain the new problem I said, "You started off with nine cubes in the first problem. You'll start with nine this time also. Instead of finding the number of pairs in your handful, see how many threes are in your handful."

"That's easy," Grant responded as he took nine cubes and divided them into groups of three. "There are three groups of

are seventy-nine cubes altogether. And that means there are thirty-nine twos. I can count them and show you." I watched as Grant proudly counted his cube pairs. "And there's one left over!"

"That's an accomplishment," I said. "What patterns do you notice?"

"Oh," Grant said, "I see a couple of patterns. One is that the remainder is always one. That's because I started with an odd number, nine. I keep adding an even number, ten. The number of cubes will always be odd because an even number plus an odd number is an odd number and an odd number has a remainder of one when you make pairs."

"Wow!" I said. "Can you write that down on your paper?"

Grant nodded and said, "There's another pattern: The answer always gets

Figure 10–2 shows handwritten work:

Handful of cubes

9 cubes
4 pairs R1
9 ÷ 2 = 4 R1
19 ÷ 2 = 9 R1
29 ÷ 2 = 14 R1
39 ÷ 2 = 19 R1
49 ÷ 2 = 24 R1
59 ÷ 2 = 29 R1
69 ÷ 2 = 34 R1
79 ÷ 2 = 39 R1

The remainder is always staying the same There is a pattern and The pattern goes up by fives

▲▲▲▲▲▲**Figure 10–2** *Grant wrote two of the patterns he explained aloud on his paper.*

three in nine." I reminded him to record on his paper. Then he added ten to the nine he had and figured the number of threes in nineteen. Soon he had trains of three cubes spread out on his desk.

It wasn't long before word was out in the class that Grant got to do a different problem. Soon other students were asking if they could do a different problem also. Many were excited about exploring with threes. Some went on to find out about fours. A few spent the time on their investigation of twos.

I checked back on Grant. He said with confusion in his voice, "I thought the number of threes was always going up by three. But that isn't what's happening and I've checked to be sure I didn't make a mistake. When the remainder goes from two to zero, the number of threes increases by four instead of three. I don't get it." I paused to think about how to help Grant see what was happening.

I began, "Put all your cubes back in the basket and let's start at the beginning. You took nine cubes in your handful, so take nine cubes." Grant did so. "Show me how many threes in nine." Grant carefully laid out three groups of three in a rectangular array.

"There are three groups," Grant commented.

"That agrees with what's on your paper," I confirmed. "Now take out ten more cubes and put them into threes and tell me how many cubes altogether and how many threes." Grant did this. He found there were nineteen cubes, or six groups of three with a remainder of one. I instructed Grant to take ten more cubes from the basket and make them into groups of three. This time he had twenty-nine cubes arranged in nine groups of three with two left over.

"Everything matches what's on my paper," Grant said as he checked what we were doing with what he'd written on his paper.

"Take ten more cubes and make groups of three," I said.

"Hey!" Grant said with surprise. "I'm going to add four groups instead of three this time. There are three groups of three each time I add ten, and one leftover, but this time I have enough leftovers for one more group of three. That makes four groups this time! Wow! I get it now. That's cool!" (See Figure 10–3.)

Jordan showed his addition as well as his division equations. He noticed several patterns and then began work on exploring groups of four. (See Figure 10–4.)

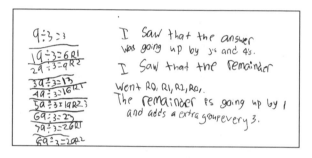

▲▲▲▲▲▲**Figure 10–3** *Grant wrote about the patterns he saw when dividing by three.*

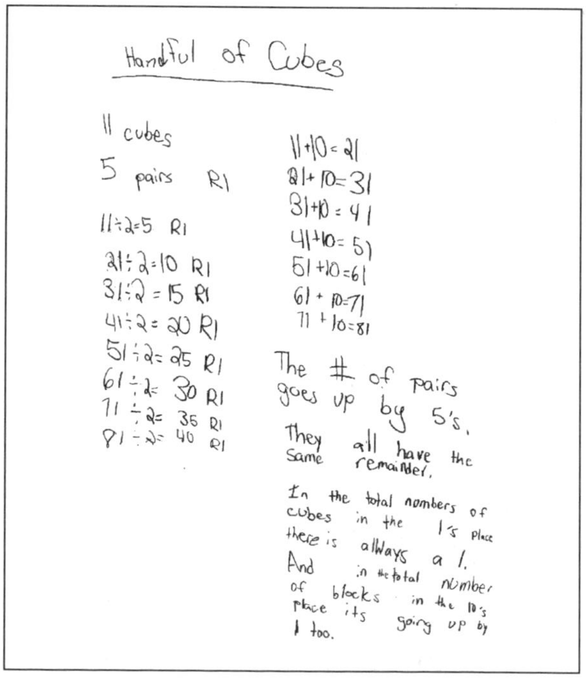

Handful of Cubes

Figure 10–4 *Jordan wrote addition equations to show how he figured the total number of cubes each time he added ten more.*

Casey spent her time exploring pairs. She was able to clearly explain her thinking about the patterns she noticed. (See Figure 10–5.)

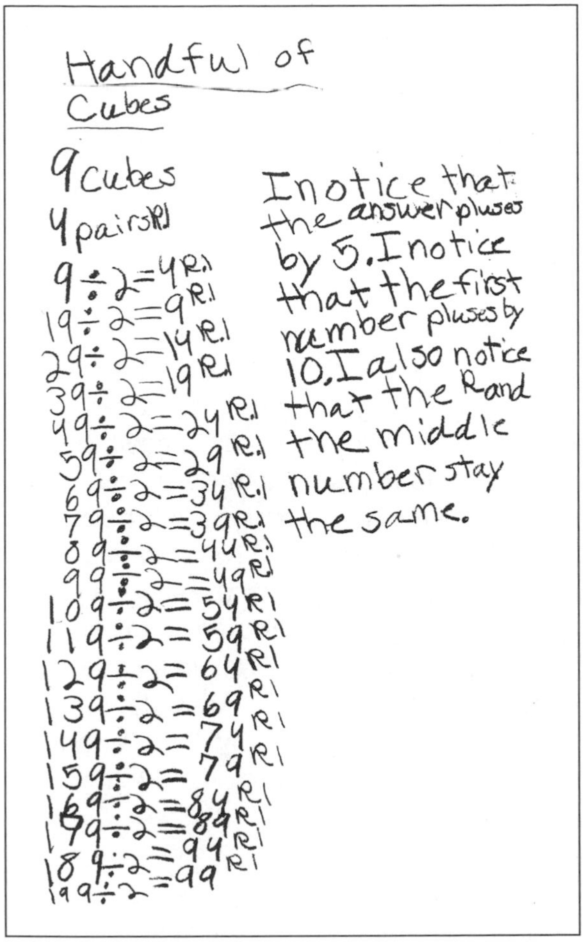

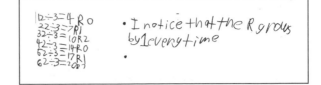

Handful of Cubes

9 cubes
4 pairs RI

$9 \div 2 = 4$ R1
$19 \div 2 = 9$ R1
$29 \div 2 = 14$ R1
$39 \div 2 = 19$ R1
$49 \div 2 = 24$ R1
$59 \div 2 = 29$ R1
$69 \div 2 = 34$ R1
$79 \div 2 = 39$ R1
$89 \div 2 = 44$ R1
$99 \div 2 = 49$ R1
$109 \div 2 = 54$ R1
$119 \div 2 = 59$ R1
$129 \div 2 = 64$ R1
$139 \div 2 = 69$ R1
$149 \div 2 = 74$ R1
$159 \div 2 = 79$ R1
$169 \div 2 = 84$ R1
$179 \div 2 = 89$ R1
$189 \div 2 = 94$ R1
$199 \div 2 = 99$ R1

I notice that the answer pluses by 5. I notice that the first number pluses by 10. I also notice that the R and the middle number stay the same.

▲▲▲▲▲▲Figure 10–5 *Casey enjoyed finding groups of two.*

Anthony brought his paper to me. He said, "I don't exactly know how to say this. I said the remainder is always going up by one when you do groups of three. The remainders go one, two, zero. It sounds like it goes down when it goes to zero, but it really went up, it's just there were enough remainders that there was a new group so then there weren't any remainders." I understood what Anthony was trying to explain and reassured him that his verbal explanation was

enough to communicate his idea. (See Figure 10–6.)

$12 \div 3 = 4$ R 0
$22 \div 3 = 7$ R1
$32 \div 3 = 10$ R2
$42 \div 3 = 14$ R0
$52 \div 3 = 17$ R1
$62 \div 3 = 20$ R2

• I notice that the R grows by 1 every time

•

▲▲▲▲▲▲Figure 10–6 *Anthony had difficulty writing about the pattern he saw when finding the number of groups of three.*

The students were interested and involved. I called for their attention and then said, "We need to stop for now. You'll have some time tomorrow to finish your work and then we'll have a class discussion to share what you've found out. You need to put your cubes in the basket and the basket on the back counter. Put your paper in your math folder so you'll be able to find it tomorrow."

DAY 2

I gave the students time to complete their work. Then I asked them to bring their papers with them and come sit on the floor. When the students were settled with their papers on the floor in front of them, I began. "What did you think of the investigation you just did?"

"It was cool!" Maria responded.

"You could go as long as you wanted finding pairs, and you could predict," Natalie added.

"I was a little confused at first and then I saw that I was adding five to the number of pairs every time I added ten cubes," Briana said.

When all who wanted had shared about their experience, I changed the direction of the conversation. "I'd like to gather some information from you. I'd like some of you to read the first five problems you investigated. I'll record them on the board while the rest of you look for patterns. Who would like to share?" I called on Krystin. She read her first five problems while I recorded on the board:

Pairs

Krystin
$$8 \div 2 = 4 \ R0$$
$$18 \div 2 = 9 \ R0$$
$$28 \div 2 = 14 \ R0$$
$$38 \div 2 = 19 \ R0$$
$$48 \div 2 = 24 \ R0$$

Anthony, Dana, Jordan, Natalie, Eliza, and Jason also shared.

Anthony
$$12 \div 2 = 6 \ R0$$
$$22 \div 2 = 11 \ R0$$
$$32 \div 2 = 16 \ R0$$
$$42 \div 2 = 21 \ R0$$
$$52 \div 2 = 26 \ R0$$

Dana
$$14 \div 2 = 7 \ R0$$
$$24 \div 2 = 12 \ R0$$
$$34 \div 2 = 17 \ R0$$
$$44 \div 2 = 22 \ R0$$
$$54 \div 2 = 27 \ R0$$

Jordan
$$11 \div 2 = 5 \ R1$$
$$21 \div 2 = 10 \ R1$$
$$31 \div 2 = 15 \ R1$$
$$41 \div 2 = 20 \ R1$$
$$51 \div 2 = 25 \ R1$$

Natalie
$$17 \div 2 = 8 \ R1$$
$$27 \div 2 = 13 \ R1$$
$$37 \div 2 = 18 \ R1$$
$$47 \div 2 = 23 \ R1$$
$$57 \div 2 = 28 \ R1$$

Eliza
$$9 \div 2 = 4 \ R1$$
$$19 \div 2 = 9 \ R1$$
$$29 \div 2 = 14 \ R1$$
$$39 \div 2 = 19 \ R1$$
$$49 \div 2 = 24 \ R1$$

Jason
$$4 \div 2 = 2 \ R0$$
$$14 \div 2 = 7 \ R0$$
$$24 \div 2 = 12 \ R0$$
$$34 \div 2 = 17 \ R0$$
$$44 \div 2 = 22 \ R0$$

Hands were in the air and students were eager to share the patterns they noticed as I wrote on the board. To give everyone the opportunity to share, I said, "Share with your partner about the patterns you see. First one of you will talk for thirty seconds while the other listens. At the end of thirty seconds I'll ask you to switch so the first talker gets to listen and the first listener gets to talk. At the end of the second thirty seconds, I'll ask for your attention. Remember not to interrupt your partner." I gave the signal to go and the room came alive as children shared their thinking. At the end of thirty seconds I reminded the students to switch roles. At the end of the second thirty seconds I asked for the students' attention. The students settled and raised their hands, eager to share. I called on Amanda.

"Every answer grows by five," Amanda shared. Several students nodded their agreement.

I wrote on the board:

Every answer grows by 5.   Amanda

Grant shared next. "I notice that the remainders are always zero or one."

"Why do you think this is happening?" I asked Grant and the rest of the class.

Grant continued, "Well it has to do with the size of groups. If you have groups of two, then if you have a remainder that's two or more, then you have enough for more groups. Zero and one are the only numbers small enough not to be another group. Besides, zero means there aren't any leftovers anyway."

"That makes sense!" Randy mused.

I wrote on the board:

The remainders are always one or zero. If the remainder is two or more then there is enough for more groups of two.   Grant

"Does what I wrote represent what you said?" I asked Grant. He nodded.

Annie shared, "Even numbers don't have remainders and odd numbers do."

"I know why," Jason interjected. "When you divide by two with an odd number, there's always an extra. That's why it's an odd number."

I wrote Annie's idea on the board:

Even numbers don't have remainders and the odd numbers do. Annie

Ashlyn had one last idea. "You always add ten to the number of cubes and five to the number of twos because there are five twos in ten."

I added Ashlyn's idea to the rest:

You always add ten to the number of cubes and five to the number of twos because there are five twos in ten. Ashlyn

There were no additional comments so I decided to have the students who explored finding groups of three share their information. I recorded in the same way as I did with twos. I recorded while Briana shared.

Threes

Briana
$$9 \div 3 = 3\ R0$$
$$19 \div 3 = 6\ R1$$
$$29 \div 3 = 9\ R2$$
$$39 \div 3 = 13\ R0$$
$$49 \div 3 = 16\ R1$$
$$59 \div 3 = 19\ R2$$
$$69 \div 3 = 23\ R0$$

"That's what I got, too," Grant said.

"Mine's different," Seth said. "I started with twelve." As Seth dictated his division sentences, I recorded them on the board.

Seth
$$12 \div 3 = 4\ R0$$
$$22 \div 3 = 7\ R1$$
$$32 \div 3 = 10\ R2$$
$$42 \div 3 = 14\ R0$$
$$52 \div 3 = 17\ R1$$
$$62 \div 3 = 20\ R2$$
$$72 \div 3 = 24\ R0$$

Kris raised his hand. "I think there's a mistake in Seth's. The number of groups of three goes up three until fourteen. That time it went up four."

Natalie was quick to respond. "I disagree with Kris. If you look at the other patterns in the answers, the ones place goes four, seven, zero, four, seven, zero like that."

Since Grant had bumped into this same problem during the work time, I was interested to see if he would volunteer to explain.

Briana shared, "I see why Kris thinks there's a mistake. But if you look at my division sentences, the same thing happens."

Amanda suddenly got a look of surprise on her face. She raised her hand with excitement. "I noticed something else. When four groups are added, the remainder always becomes zero." I saw Grant's hand go up.

Grant said, "When you add ten cubes, you're adding three groups of three and one leftover. After you add three groups of ten, you have three leftovers, which is an extra group of three. So for that time, it's like you added four groups of three instead of three groups."

Grant's classmates looked confused. To help more students understand, I asked Grant to get a basket of cubes and count out twelve cubes, the starting number that Seth used. I explained to the class, "Seth's handful had twelve cubes. If I make groups of three, then I have enough cubes for four groups of three with no leftovers." I put the groups of three on the chalkboard tray and pointed to the division sentences Seth shared. "Seth's first division sentence agrees," I commented. I asked Grant to count out several groups of ten. I took the first group as he continued to count and made it into groups of three. I said to the students, "I'm adding a group of ten to make twenty-two cubes altogether. Notice that from ten cubes, I can make three groups of three. How many are left?" I asked.

"One," the class chorused.

"Now we have seven groups of three with one remaining, or twenty-two cubes," I stated. "I'll add ten more cubes. How many groups?"

"Three groups of three with one left," Ashlyn replied. "Now you'll have ten groups of three with two left over." I added the groups of three cubes to the row already on the chalkboard tray.

"I can see what's going to happen," Dana exclaimed. "There are two leftovers, so next time there will be three. That's a new group!"

"Oh yeah!" "Cool!" "I get it!" were some of the responses.

"Let's try it and see," I said. Grant handed me another group of ten.

"You make three groups of three and add the leftover to the other two leftovers and that's actually going to be four groups of three," Belinda said. I did as Belinda instructed and verified she was correct.

"I see why that happens!" Krystin said. "And there are no leftovers."

I ended the discussion and the lesson on that note.

EXTENSIONS

Students can repeat this activity finding groups of four, five, six, and so on. Have the students write about the patterns they notice.

Questions and Discussion

▲▲

▲ *Why didn't you push Grant to write all the patterns he described to you?*

Making decisions about when to push and when to back off is part of the art of teaching. In this case, Grant, who was a reluctant writer, was very excited about the activity and could verbalize the mathematical patterns he saw. He was learning, thinking, and able to explain his understanding. By pushing him to write more, I felt I would be running the risk of dampening his enthusiasm for exploring the mathematics and possibly giving him a message that anything he said he'd have to write. Ultimately he could choose to remain silent for fear of having to write down everything spoken. On a different day with a different activity, I might choose differently. Because of the choice I made, Grant did some writing and then was able to explore more mathematics.

▲ *What if I don't have enough cubes?*

You can use objects other than cubes for this activity, or even a variety of objects. The purpose of the materials is to give students a way of solving the problem and verifying their results.

Also, consider that the smaller the objects used, the more there will be in a handful. Choose objects of a size that will keep the number in the handfuls of objects manageable for students.

▲ *Why don't you require all students to use the cubes throughout the activity?*

All students used the cubes initially. A few students were able to rely on abstract numbers only and no longer needed the cubes. To require them to use the cubes could act as a hindrance rather than a help to the growth of their mathematical understanding. The manipulative materials are tools to facilitate understanding, not the focus of the lesson.

▲ *What if my students don't notice any patterns?*

This is an unusual occurrence in my experience. Should this happen, ask questions that focus students' attention on a particular part of the information. For example, ask: "What do you notice about all the remainders?" "What do you notice about the divisors?" "What happens to the quotients each time ten cubes are added to the dividend?"

CHAPTER ELEVEN
HAND SPANS

Overview

In this lesson, each student measures his or her hand span and the length of his or her arm and then figures out how many of their hand spans are in their arm length. The lesson gives students experience with the grouping model of division as well as practice with measuring in inches.

Materials

▲ inch rulers, 1 per student
▲ inch measuring tapes, 1 per group of four students

Time

▲ one class period

Teaching Directions

1. Model for the students how to measure their hand span in inches. Using a ruler, with your fingers spread, measure from the tip of your little finger to the tip of your thumb. Round to the nearest inch. Record the length of your hand span on the board.

2. Model for students how to measure their arm length in inches. Using a student volunteer, measure from the student's shoulder joint to the tip of the student's longest finger. Then have the student measure your arm length. Record your arm length on the board.

3. Have students figure the number of your hand spans in your arm length. Record their strategies on the board.

4. Have students repeat Steps 1 through 3 independently, using their own measurements.

5. On a chart, gather the information from students about the length of their hand spans, arms, and how many hand spans are in their arm length.

name	arm length	hand span	# of hand spans in arm length

Lead a class discussion. Ask students: "What do you notice? What surprises you? Do some people have the same number of hand spans in their arm lengths?"

Teaching Notes

This lesson provides students with an experience with the grouping model of division. Students find out the number of groups—hand spans in this problem—in the length of their arms.

I used inches as the unit of measure because the numbers are more manageable than if they measured in centimeters. Children's hand spans typically fall between 5 and 8 inches. Their arm lengths usually fall between 20 and 26 inches. These numbers are appropriate and manageable for children. Using centimeters produces larger numbers with hand spans between 12 and 20 centimeters and arm lengths between 50 and 65 centimeters. The numbers that result from measuring in centimeters are more challenging and possibly appropriate as a later extension.

The Lesson

▲▲

I gathered the students on the floor. "How long do you think it is from the tip of my thumb to the tip of my little finger?" I asked as I held up my hand with my thumb and little finger spread as far apart as possible.

"Five inches," Randy said.

"A foot," Jason said.

"Twenty-seven centimeters," Krystin suggested.

I handed a ruler to Eliza, who was sitting on the floor in front of me. I asked her to hold the ruler still as I measured my hand span. It was between 7 and 8 inches. I said to the students as they watched, "I placed my thumb so the tip was even with the end of the ruler. The tip of my little finger is partway between seven and eight. Because my finger goes past seven, I'm going to round up and say it's eight. When you measure in a little bit, I'd like you to do the same. If your finger is partway between two numbers, use the closer number as the measurement of your hand span."

I wrote on the board to model for the children how to record:

hand span = 8 inches

"Who knows a shorter way to write *inches*?" I asked. Several hands went up.

Ashlyn suggested, "After you write the number you can make a sign that looks like a quotation mark and means inches."

I wrote:

hand span = 8 inches = 8"

Seth had his hand up. "You can write just I and N and a period after it and that stands for inches."

I added Seth's suggestion:

hand span = 8 inches = 8" = 8 in.

"These are three ways of recording the same measurement," I commented. "After you've measured and recorded your hand span, then you'll need to measure the length of your arm. I need a volunteer to help me show everyone how to do this." Hands shot up. I asked Belinda to help me.

I modeled what to do as I continued to explain, "First you'll need to find the joint where your arm connects with your body. You can find this by putting your fingers on top of your shoulder and moving your arm. When you do this, you can feel the joint." The students followed my directions and located the appropriate spot on top of their shoulders. Belinda showed me the correct joint, and using a measuring tape, I measured from that point to the tip of her middle finger. "The length of Belinda's arm is between nineteen inches and twenty inches, but closer to twenty inches. Just like with the hand span measurement, if your arm measure is between two numbers, use

the closer number. Now Belinda will help me measure." Because Belinda was short, I sat down so she could reach my shoulder and take the measurement. "My arm length is twenty-seven inches," I told the students and recorded this on the board:

hand span = 8"

arm length = 27"

I thanked Belinda for her help and asked her to return to her place. "If my hand span is about eight inches and my arm length is about twenty-seven inches, how many hand spans long is my arm length?" Hands began to go up. I waited until most were up.

Casey explained, "I think this is division because you have to figure out how many eights are in twenty-seven, but I used multiplication to figure it out. I know that three eights is twenty-four. So it's three hand spans with three inches left over."

"What division sentence could you use to represent the problem?" I asked.

Casey said, "Twenty-seven divided by eight equals three remainder three."

I wrote on the board:

Casey: 27 ÷ 8 = 3 R3

3 × 8 = 24

24 + 3 = 27

"Who has another way of figuring the number of hand spans in my arm length?" I asked.

"You could use a number line," Briana said. Briana came to the board, drew a number line, and used it to show how she could figure the number of eights in twenty-seven.

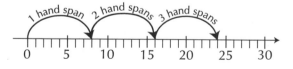

"You could draw twenty-seven circles and then circle groups of eight and then count how many groups that is," Kris said. I recorded on the board:

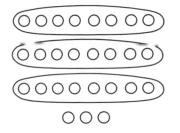

When all who wanted to had the chance to share their ideas, I said, "Let's review your task. First, use a ruler from your table basket to measure your hand span. Record the length of your hand span on your paper. Then ask someone at your table to help you use the measuring tape to measure the length of your arm. Record the length of your arm on your paper. Figure the number of hand spans in the length of your arm. Show how you figured and record the division equation. When you're finished, raise your hand. I'd like to check your work and then I have an additional problem for you to solve. I'll write the directions on the board so you can look up here if you forget what to do next."

"Do we work with partners?" Dana asked.

"Only to help you measure your arm," I said.

I asked the students to return to their seats. I passed out paper and tape measures, then wrote the following directions on the board:

1. *Measure the length of your hand span with a ruler. Record.*

2. *With a partner's help, use a measuring tape to measure the length of your arm. Record.*

3. *Figure the number of hand spans in the length of your arm. Show how you figured.*

4. *Write a division equation.*

5. *Raise your hand when you're ready for me to check your work.*

OBSERVING THE STUDENTS

The students were eager to explore this activity. Once at their seats, they reached for the rulers that are always kept in the supply baskets in the middle of their tables. They went to work measuring their hand spans and comparing the results with others at their table. A few students needed clarification about choosing a number if their hand span fell between two numbers. Students were surprised to discover that the sizes of their hand spans were similar.

The students helped each other measure their arm lengths, again comparing with great excitement. Anthony predicted, "Amanda is short and I'm taller, so I think my arms will be longer than hers."

They helped each other measure and Amanda replied, "Hey, your arms are two inches longer!" Anthony's arm length was about 24 inches while Amanda's was about 22 inches.

Belinda needed help on this activity. I asked her to explain the task using her own words. "I measured my hand span and I measured the length of my arm, but I don't know what to do."

Kris, who was listening, said, "Your hand span is six inches. How many sixes in twenty?"

Belinda lit up. "Oh, is that all? There are three sixes in twenty with two inches left over."

"What do the sixes represent?" I asked to make sure Belinda was making sense of the problem.

"Sixes . . . are . . . hand spans!" she said with a smile. "I figured it by thinking of cookies. In twenty cookies, I can make three groups of six."

"Write that on your paper," I encouraged. (See Figure 11–1.)

I moved on to check on another group. Amanda was proud of the number line she had made to show her solution. The hops on the number line represented her hand spans and she numbered them to show there were three hand spans in her arm length. (See Figure 11–2.)

Kris used repeated addition to solve the

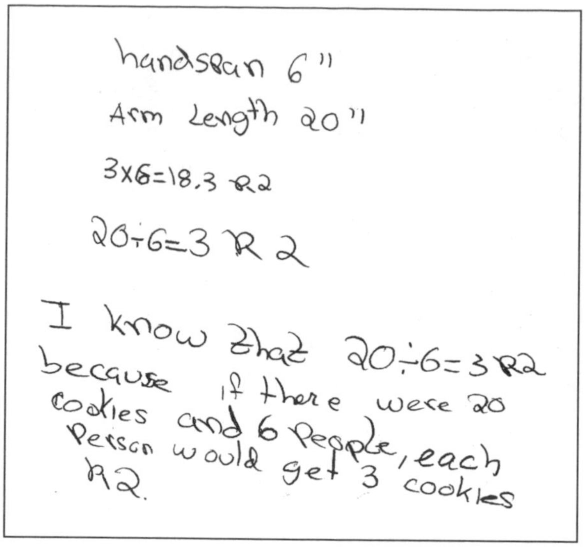

handspan 6"

Arm Length 20"

3×6=18, 3 R2

20÷6=3 R 2

I know that 20÷6=3 R2 because if there were 20 cookies and 6 people, each person would get 3 cookies R2.

▲▲▲▲▲▲**Figure 11–1** *Belinda used the context of cookies to help her think about the problem.*

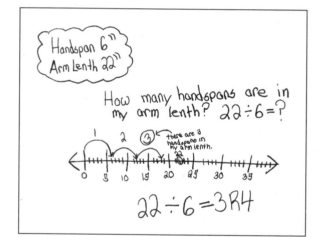

▲▲▲▲▲▲**Figure 11–2** *Amanda used a number line to show her solution.*

7" handspand

25

25÷7=3 R4

I know that 25÷7=3R3

25÷7=

3R4

I know that 25÷7=3R3

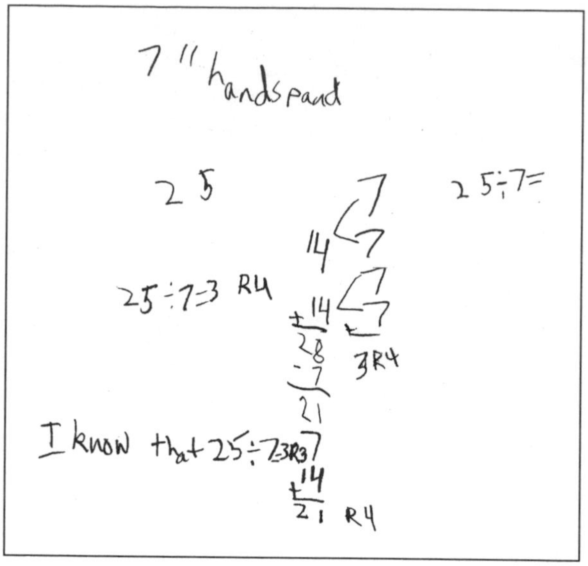

▲▲▲▲▲▲**Figure 11–3** *Kris used what he knew about repeated addition to help him figure the number of hand spans in his arm length.*

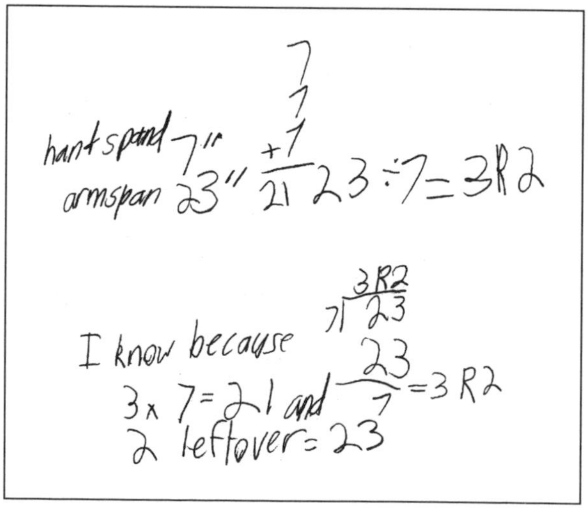

problem. His hand span was about 7 inches and the length of his arm was about 25 inches. He explained, "I added four sevens because I knew there were groups of seven and I thought there might be four in twenty-five. It was twenty-eight, which is too big. I subtracted out one seven and then it was twenty-one. Twenty-one to twenty-five is four, so there are four inches leftover and three groups of seven inches." (See Figure 11–3.)

Adam also used repeated addition to figure the number of 7-inch hand spans in his 23-inch arm length. He added seven three times to get twenty-one and found the remainder to be two inches. He showed multiplication as a second way to solve the problem. He multiplied three times seven and added the two leftovers to get twenty-three. He tried to use the division algorithm but was unable to do so correctly. (See Figure 11–4.)

handspand 7"
armspan 23"
7
7
+7
21
23÷7=3R2

I know because
3×7=21 and 2 leftover=23
3R2
7)23
23/7=3 R2

▲▲▲▲▲▲**Figure 11–4** *Adam used repeated addition and multiplication to help him solve the problem. He was unable to use the division algorithm correctly.*

A few students finished early. They were eager for an additional challenge. I suggested they measure their legs and find the number of hand spans in the length of their legs.

A CLASS DISCUSSION

I gathered the students on the rug where they could easily see the board. My goal was to collect the data and then ask what they noticed. As the students settled on the rug, I drew the following chart on the board:

name	arm length	hand span	# of hand spans in arm length

I began, "I'm going to take a few moments and go around the room and ask you to share your arm length, length of your hand span, and the number of hand spans in the length of your arm. As you give me the information, I'll fill in the chart." I began with Casey and called on each child until all had shared. The children were quiet. Gathering and recording the information only took a few minutes. I reminded them to look at the data as I gathered it.

As soon as Belinda finished sharing, Dana blurted, "Hey, look! Belinda and I both have the same number of hand spans and leftover inches, but the length of our arms and hand spans are different!" The students started talking among themselves and noticing other similar situations on the chart. I continued recording until all had shared and decided to return to Dana's observation (see top right).

"Dana noticed that he and Belinda had the same number of hand spans," I said. "What do you think about that?"

name	arm length	hand span	# of hand spans in arm length
Casey	22"	7"	3 R1
Maria	23"	7"	3 R2
Tony	25"	7"	3 R4
Morgan	24"	8"	3 R0
Adam	23"	7"	3 R2
Briana	22"	5"	4 R2
Anthony	24"	7"	3 R3
Amanda	22"	6"	3 R4
Mason	23"	8"	2 R7
John	24"	7"	3 R3
Jason	24"	7"	3 R3
Randy	22"	8"	2 R6
Dana	23"	7"	3 R2
Belinda	20"	6"	3 R2
Natalie	24"	8"	3 R0
Seth	23"	7"	3 R2
Grant	24"	8"	3 R0
Kris	25"	7"	3 R4
Annie	24"	8"	3 R0
Ashlyn	22"	6"	3 R4
Eliza	24"	8"	3 R0
Amelia	24"	7"	3 R3
Krystin	21"	7"	3 R0
Martin	24"	7"	3 R3

Natalie was eager to share. "I noticed that me, Eliza, and Grant all got the same number of hand spans. But we all have the same hand span and arm length."

Krystin noticed, "Kris and Ashlyn got the same answer with different numbers, too. They both got three hand spans with four inches left, but Kris's arm was twenty-five inches and Ashlyn's was twenty-two."

"Their hand spans were different, too," Jason noticed. "Kris's is seven inches and Ashlyn's is six inches."

"I checked Kris's and Ashlyn's by

multiplication," Briana said. "For Kris I multiplied three times seven equals twenty-one and added the remainder of four, which makes twenty-five. For Ashlyn I multiplied three times six is eighteen and added the leftovers of four and that's twenty-two. They both work."

Adam changed the direction of the conversation a bit and reported, "Most hand spans are seven inches. There are some that are five, six, and eight, but mostly they seem to be seven."

"The bigger kids have bigger hand spans and the littler kids have smaller ones," Amelia added.

Mason said, "All the arm lengths are in the twenties."

Amanda reported, "Briana's one of the littlest in our class and her hand span is the littlest, but she has the most hand spans in her arm length. She's the only person with four."

Dana commented, "Almost everyone has about three hand spans in their arm length. Even the teacher. I wonder if that's true of all people?"

"That's something we could explore another day," I suggested. The students were eager to investigate Dana's idea.

EXTENSIONS

1. Have students measure the arm lengths and hand spans of those at home and report back the following day. Lead a class discussion to explore Dana's idea. (If no one in your class makes this observation, tell your class about Dana's idea.)

2. Have students figure the number of hand spans in the length of their legs, the circumference of the heads, their heights, and so on. These kinds of investigations give them practice with measurement and division and also help them learn about the proportions of the human body.

3. Have students measure the distance they can jump, then find the number of their foot lengths in their jumps.

4. Repeat the initial experience but have the students measure in centimeters. Ask first: "How do you think the number of hand spans in you arm length will compare if you use centimeters instead of inches?" Most children will be surprised to learn that the answers will be the same both ways.

Questions and Discussion

▲▲▲

▲ *Can students work with partners rather than independently with this activity?*

Yes. This activity could easily be done with students working in pairs. To do this, have students do the activity in the same way, but record both their own measurements as well as their partner's on their individual recording sheets. Have students write about what they notice about the two sets of measurements.

▲ *Is there a way to gather the information about the students' measurements other than doing it as the beginning of a class discussion?*

Another way that works well is to post a chart and have the students record the appropriate information on the chart as they finish the activity. This saves time at the beginning of a discussion and allows students to be aware of the information as they're working. I chose to gather it at the beginning of the discussion to give the students a quiet time to focus on the information slowly as it was presented by their classmates. For some children, it's easier to take in large amounts of information in this manner. Also, auditory learners hear the information as well as see it as the students verbally share.

CHAPTER TWELVE
EXPLORATIONS WITH RAISINS

Overview

In this lesson, students first estimate the number of raisins in a $\frac{1}{2}$-ounce box, revise their estimates by counting only the raisins they can see from opening the box, and then count the raisins by arranging them in equal-size groups. Finally, students combine the raisins in their groups and figure out how many each will get if they share them equally. The lesson provides experience with both models of division. When they count raisins, students decide the size of the group to use and then see how many groups there are. When they share raisins in their groups, they know how many groups there are (the number of children in their group) and figure out how many are in each group.

Materials

▲ $\frac{1}{2}$-ounce boxes of raisins, 1 per student
▲ chart paper, 1 sheet
▲ $1\frac{1}{2}$-ounce boxes of raisins, 1 box for every three to four children (for extension)

Time

▲ one class period, plus one additional class period for the extension

Teaching Directions

1. Arrange students into groups of three or four. Ask students to clear their desks, and give each child a box of raisins and two sheets of paper, one lined and one unlined. Assure the children they will get to eat the raisins, but stress the importance of waiting until they complete their investigations.

2. Ask the children to guess how many raisins are in their boxes. Record their guesses, identify the smallest and largest, and, if you wish, talk about the range.

3. Demonstrate opening the top of the raisin box and looking at the visible raisins to estimate how many are in the box. Tell students to record their estimate of how many raisins are in the box. Write prompts on the board:

After opening the box my estimate is _____.

I think this because _____.

4. Invite children to empty their raisins out onto their sheets of plain paper. Ask them to group their raisins in some way so you can count them quickly as you walk by.

5. On a chart at the front of the room, record how many raisins each child reports and lead a general discussion about the results.

6. Explain to the students that for the next part they'll work together in groups. First, each group decides how many raisins it has altogether and explains how it knows. Then each group shares the raisins equally among the members, explaining how many raisins each person gets and how they were shared.

7. To end the activity, ask students how many raisins they think were eaten during the lesson.

Teaching Notes

This lesson makes use of both the grouping and the sharing models of division. To begin, students use the grouping model of division when they decide on the number of raisins that will be in each group, then find the number of groups of a particular size that make up the total. For example, a student might choose to group by fives. Using a small box of raisins, the students might discover there are eight groups of five raisins with two raisins left over for a total of forty-two raisins. Near the end of the lesson, students use the sharing model of division when they combine their raisins then divide them equally among each member of their group. The students also experience the close relationship between multiplication and division.

The data about the estimates and actual numbers of raisins in each box provide an opportunity to discuss the idea of range. To find the range, the least number in a set of data is subtracted from the greatest number. For example, if the least number of raisins in a box guessed is ten and the greatest number is fifty-two, the range is ten subtracted from fifty-two, or forty-two.

The Lesson

▲▲

"Today we're going to share raisins," I said to the class. "And these will be real raisins, not pretend ones like the cookies. So once you finish the mathematical exploration of sharing raisins, you can eat them."

I explained to the students that to get

ready for this activity, they needed to clear off their desks. "The only thing on your desk should be a box of raisins, two sheets of paper, and a pencil." Eager to find out what raisins had to do with mathematics, the children cleared their desks quickly. As they did so, I distributed a $\frac{1}{2}$-ounce box of raisins to each child. Also, I gave each child a sheet of lined paper and a sheet of unlined yellow copier paper.

"Here is how you should label your lined paper," I said, as I wrote on the board:

Name

Raisin Explorations

Robby announced, "I know what we have to do. We have to subtract."

I held up a small box of raisins. "Think about this box of raisins. Without opening your box, guess how many raisins you think are inside."

After a few moments, I asked the children to report their guesses. "Don't worry about what others think," I said. "These are only guesses, and you can always change your guess when you have more information."

Most of the students were eager to offer estimates. Numbers came as quickly as I could write them on the board:

33 13 30 10 16 31 20 12 33

I stood back and looked at what I wrote. I asked, "Does anyone think there are more than thirty-three raisins?"

Marco obliged, "Thirty-four."

Breanna quickly offered, "Forty-one."

I continued taking estimates until all who wanted to report had the chance to do so. I continued to write the estimates on the board. Then I asked the children, "What is the range of our estimates?"

To explain this new term, I said, "To find a range, look for the lowest number and the highest number. And when you report a range, you subtract the lowest number from the highest. Would someone like to report our range?" I used correct statistical terminology, knowing that my students enjoy trying out new vocabulary and that they become familiar with terms by hearing them used in the contexts of activities.

Afton was eager to demonstrate his understanding of this new concept and volunteered, "The range is ten and forty-one, that's thirty-one," he said.

"We say the range of our estimates is thirty-one," I said, again using the terminology correctly. "Does anyone think there are fewer than ten raisins?" No one responded.

"It can't be," Irina finally offered, "because raisins are small."

Cody said, "If there was forty-one, it would have to be a bigger box."

"Can I use a ruler to find out how long the box is?" Ely asked, holding up his ruler.

"Sure, and tell us," I responded.

"It's about two inches high," Ely said.

"And this way?" I asked, pointing to the width of the box.

Ely measured. "It's one and one-half inches," he reported.

"And this way?" I pointed to the depth of the top of the box.

"It's three-fourths of an inch," he said.

"Do you think the company puts the exact same number of raisins in every box?" I asked.

The class immediately chorused, "No!"

"But in packages of Lifesavers, there are always ten Lifesavers," I said.

"No, eleven," three students immediately corrected me, indicating social information for which students are more expert than teachers.

"They just stuff raisins in," Kendall said. "They don't count them."

I pointed out that sometimes products are packaged by weight, not number. I wrote on the board:

Net weight $\frac{1}{2}$ oz.

"'Net weight' means that's what the raisins weigh by themselves; you can find the net weight by weighing a box of raisins and then subtracting the weight of the box itself so you're left just with the weight of the raisins," I explained. "Find this information on your box."

Afton read aloud, "One and a half ounces."

"It says 'one-half ounce,'" I said gently to Afton. "If it were one and one-half ounces, it would have to have a one in front, like this." I wrote $1\frac{1}{2}$ on the board. Afton nodded.

"Did anyone find other weights on the box?" I asked.

"I see 'fourteen point one grams,'" Beth volunteered.

"The company weighs one-half ounce or fourteen point one grams of raisins, which are the same weight, and then puts them into the box," I explained. "Think about this: If you have big raisins in your box, will you have more or fewer raisins than if you have small raisins?"

A half dozen children responded quickly; "Less." A few responded "More" just as quickly. A conversation broke out among the students. In a few moments, all were in agreement that there would be fewer raisins in the box if they were bigger.

I continued, "All of you have made guesses about the number of raisins in this box. In just a moment, you'll open the top of your box and look inside. Listen carefully first. Don't touch the raisins, just look carefully at the ones on top. Then think to yourself about how many you estimate there are in all—and why. Don't talk with others yet; you'll have a chance to share your estimates in a bit. For now, think and record on your paper." I wrote on the board:

After opening the box my estimate is _____.

I think this because _____.

When the students opened their boxes, some stared for a bit at the top layer; some immediately started counting the visible raisins; others tried to count layers, using their fingers to measure. After I checked

that all of the students had recorded, they reported their estimates and reasons.

"I thought there were ten, but now I see there are more," Addie said. "They're more squished up than I thought." (See Figure 12–1.)

Cindy thought there were twenty raisins in her box. "Because they don't come all the way to the top," she reported.

Kareem guessed thirty-one. "I still think thirty-one," he said, "because I counted ten and I think there's space for two more tens and an extra. Ten times three is thirty and an extra is thirty-one." (See Figure 12–2.)

Derryl estimated twenty-two. "I looked at the top, and I found seven, and then I measured how high the box was . . . and counted seven, eight, nine, ten. . . ."

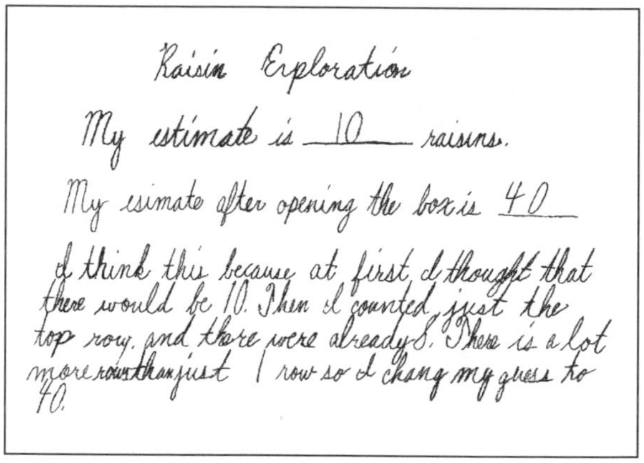

Raisin Exploration

My estimate is __10__ raisins.

My estimate after opening the box is __40__

I think this because at first, I thought that there would be 10. Then I counted just the top row, and there were already 8. There is a lot more rows than just 1 row so I change my guess to 40.

▲▲▲▲▲**Figure 12–1** *Addie revised her estimate from ten to forty.*

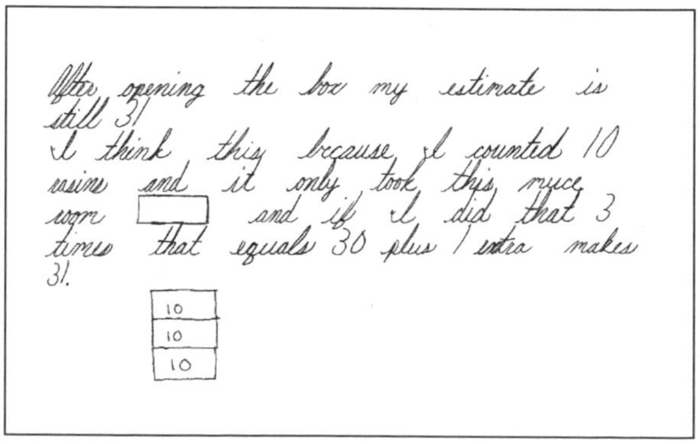

After opening the box my estimate is still 31.
I think this because I counted 10 raisins and it only took this much room [ ] and if I did that 3 times that equals 30 plus 1 extra makes 31.

| 10 |
| 10 |
| 10 |

▲▲▲▲▲**Figure 12–2** *Kareem didn't change his first estimate of thirty-one.*

Kendall guessed thirty and explained, "I tried fifteen and then I doubled it."

"I'll guess twenty five," Robby said. "That's more than I thought before." When I asked him to explain his reasoning, Robby insisted, "I just know there's more."

Some children reported how they used layers to come up with estimates. Shanna said, "I counted six, and I think there are six layers and some extra, so I changed to thirty-eight. I thought six times six is thirty-six, then I added a few extra."

Marco said, "I thought ten, but I can see seven on top, and it looks like there's seven down. But I don't think there's seven in each row. I guess forty-six." (See Figure 12–3.)

After the children had the opportunity to report their estimates, I asked, "Is there anybody who thinks there are fewer than twenty?"

"I say sixteen," Troy said, smiling.

"How many think there are more than twenty raisins?" I asked.

Most of the hands went up. "More than thirty?" I asked, upping the ante.

Janie wanted to backtrack. "I think there are more than twenty-two but less than thirty; I think there are twenty-nine."

"There are thirty-three!" Harrison exclaimed.

"What did you think before?" I asked.

"I thought thirteen," Harrison said. "But that was before I looked."

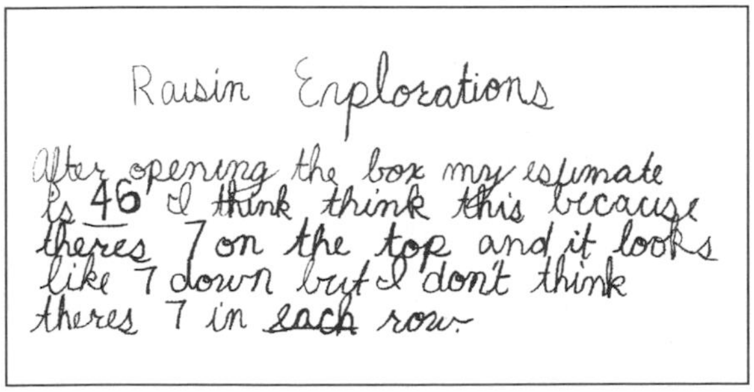

Raisin Explorations

After opening the box my estimate is 46 I think think this because theres 7 on the top and it looks like 7 down but I don't think theres 7 in each row.

▲▲▲▲▲▲Figure 12–3 *Marco thought his box had seven layers with seven or fewer raisins in each layer. He estimated forty-six.*

"You've increased your estimate because you have more information now," I commented, offering students the rationale for changing their guesses.

"I guess forty," Ely said, "because my raisins are really small."

"How many are on your top layer, Ely?" I asked, prompting him to think about his reason a different way.

"Six," he responded.

"How many layers do you think are in the box?" I pressed.

Ely looked closely at his box. "Ten? No, maybe six," he said. He thought a moment and said, "And six times six equals thirty-six, so I think there are thirty-six raisins in my box." He changed his estimate on his paper.

"I think there are twenty," offered Gib, grinning. "I opened both ends and guessed at the middle."

COUNTING THE RAISINS

"Please put your boxes down now and look at me," I instructed, to get the students' attention. "Next, you'll count your raisins. That's what the yellow paper is for, so you can dump out your raisins and count them. But don't eat any yet." I added, "We'll eat the raisins, but please wait so that we can do some more mathematics first." I paused until all students settled and were listening.

"Group your raisins in a way so that as I come around I can quickly see how many you have," I continued. "Once you've decided how to group your raisins, circle each group, drawing the raisins or writing the number in each circle. That way, when you take the raisins away there will still be a picture of how many raisins you had to start with." I paused to give students a chance to ask questions. There were none.

"OK, go ahead. Dump out your raisins and represent them on your paper."

The students began excitedly. Several of them had trouble getting all the raisins out of their boxes because they stuck together. I suggested that they open both ends of the box and try pushing them out.

Each child concentrated intently on his or her own box of raisins. "I have a lot of raisins!" Troy exclaimed. Meanwhile, Gib carefully counted his one by one.

Across the room, Marco also counted one by one. When Irina told him, "It's quicker if you group them," Marco grouped by fives, but he couldn't seem to figure out how to use the groupings to determine how many he had altogether.

Irina lined up her raisins in horizontal rows of tens. Once she had four rows, she commented, "My estimate was way off." (See Figure 12–4.)

Many children grouped their raisins by twos, but in different ways. Harrison counted out loud by twos as he put his raisins into groups of two. Janie and Kareem grouped their raisins the same way. (See Figure 12–5.)

Carol, however, put all of her raisins on one side of the paper and moved them, two by two, into a pile on the other side, counting by twos as she did so. Shayna and Addie did this as well. Shayna got mixed up in the middle and had to start again. When she

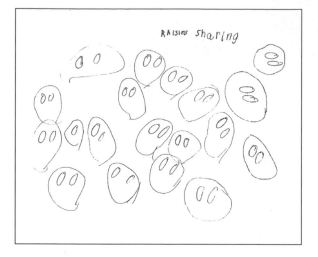

▲▲▲▲▲▲Figure 12–5 *Kareem put thirty-seven raisins into groups of two.*

noticed what Janie had done, she began arranging her raisins into groups of two.

Breanna arranged her raisins into groups of five. Shanna watched Breanna make one group of five and began to group her own raisins the same way.

Seven children grouped by twos, nine grouped by fives, and ten grouped by tens. Derryl grouped by threes and Cody by fours. Cindy grouped twenty-five of her raisins by fives and then switched to threes. She wrote: *I have thirty-three*, but she pictured forty-three. She saw her error and erased two groups of five. (See Figure 12–6.)

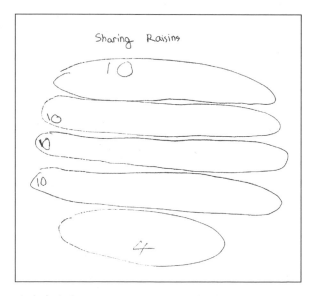

▲▲▲▲▲▲Figure 12–4 *Irina grouped by tens; she had four tens and four extra raisins.*

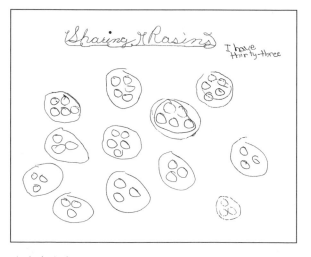

▲▲▲▲▲▲Figure 12–6 *Cindy started grouping by fives, then switched to threes.*

A CLASS DISCUSSION

Once the students had recorded their raisin groups, I asked them to put their raisins back into the boxes and then come to the front of the room. "Bring your yellow papers," I said as I posted a large sheet of chart paper.

When the children were seated, I said, "I'm going to record your counts. I wonder who has the smallest number of raisins. Does anybody have less than thirty-three?" A few hands went up. "Less than thirty-one?" No one raised a hand.

"I don't have less than thirty-one, but I have thirty-one," Carol reported. I wrote *31* to begin the chart.

"When I call your number," I said, "tell us how you grouped your raisins." I started with Carol, who had counted thirty-one.

"I did it by tens," Carol said.

"How many groups of ten and how many extras?" I asked.

"Three tens and one extra," Carol replied.

"That's three groups of ten and one left over," I said, recording on the chart. As other students reported, I recorded the data:

31:	3 groups of 10 and 1 left over
32:	6 groups of 5 and 2 left over
32:	3 groups of 10 and 2 left over
33:	3 groups of 10 and 3 left over
33:	6 groups of 5 and 3 left over
34:	3 groups of 10 and 4 left over
34:	17 groups of 2s
35:	8 groups of 4 and 3 left over
35:	7 groups of 5
36:	12 groups of 3
36:	12 groups of 3
36:	3 groups of 10 and 6 left over
36:	3 groups of 10 and 6 left over
37:	7 groups of 5 and 2 left over
37:	5 groups of 7 and 2 left over

When I wrote the two descriptions for thirty-seven, Robby excitedly exclaimed, "Hey! There's two different ways: seven groups of five or five groups of seven—both with two left over. It's the same thing." I smiled, and the students continued reporting. They were interested in the counts and how their classmates had grouped raisins to get them.

37:	18 groups of 2 and 1 left over
37:	3 groups of 10 and 7 left over
38:	18 groups of 2

After Harrison reported he had eighteen groups of two for a total of thirty-eight raisins, Addie protested, "You'd better count again. I had the same method, and I have nineteen groups of two."

"Oops, I skipped a number. It's nineteen groups of two," Harrison agreed.

38:	3 groups of 10 and 8 left over
38:	7 groups of 5 and 3 left over
39:	3 groups of 10 and 9 left over
39:	3 groups of 10 and 9 left over
39:	7 groups of 5 and 4 left over

When I reached forty, Gib reported, "By fives."

"Count how many groups," I suggested.

Gib counted what he had drawn. "Eight groups of five," he said.

40:	8 groups of 5
40:	20 groups of 2
40:	4 groups of 10
44:	4 groups of 10 and 4 left over

I invited the class to look at the information on the chart. I acknowledged the many different ways students found to group their raisins.

"What's the range of our actual counts?" I asked.

Cindy responded, "It's twelve, no thirteen. It's thirteen."

"How did you figure?" I wanted to know.

"I went thirty-one . . . forty-one, then

forty-two, forty-three, forty-four. That's ten and three more," Cindy explained.

"The range of our counts is much smaller than the range of our estimates," I pointed out. "Why do you think that might be?" Many hands went up.

Cody explained, "Maybe because we were guessing before."

Kelsey added, "The more information we had, the better guesses we could make."

"And when we counted, we had real information," Shayna said. Had the students not made these suggestions, I would have pointed out that our estimates improve when we have additional information.

Then I held up an unopened box and asked, "If I were going to guess how many raisins were in this box, what would be a good guess?"

"Forty!" Robby exclaimed.

"Explain your thinking," I prodded.

"That's how many I had," Robby replied.

"Thirty-five," Shayna offered. "Look at the chart. Most people got that number."

"But lots more people got more than thirty-five," Afton observed. "I think thirty-seven or thirty-eight would be a better guess."

I chose not to go into the formal idea of averaging but noted the children's intuitive explanations.

GROUP COMBINING AND SHARING

I then explained, "You need to work together in groups for the next two problems. First, you need to decide how many raisins your table has altogether and write about how you reached that decision. Then you need to share the raisins equally among the members of your group." I distributed one sheet of paper to each group, saying, "On your papers, you'll report how many raisins each person got and explain how you did the sharing." I wrote the following on the board to remind the children what to do:

1. Decide how many raisins your group has altogether. Explain how you know.

2. Share the raisins equally among the members of your group. Explain how many raisins each person got and how you shared them.

The children responded eagerly to this task. Their approaches varied widely. Shanna immediately started counting everybody's raisins one by one. Cindy and Jody wrote down each person's total and used a calculator to find the grand total. In another group, Ely and Afton recorded each person's total and added, using paper and pencil. Irina did the same for her group. Carol, Cami, Gib, and Kareem dumped their raisins in the center of the table and then, in turn, began taking raisins one by one. Valerie and Janie talked about what they should do, but Robby exclaimed, "I'm the champion! I have forty." He started eating.

Valerie protested, "He's eating them!"

William, another member of the group, silently started adding the totals.

"Did you eat raisins?" I asked. Robby denied doing so. I advised the group, "Tell him what to do. When you work in groups, you must keep group members advised of what they need to do."

"We need to take turns," Valerie said to Robby. "Everybody take a raisin." They each took a raisin from the center, and then another.

"Could you do it in a faster way?" I asked. No one answered. "How about ten? Could you each take ten raisins?"

Janie grinned and instructed her teammates, "Everybody take ten!"

In her group, Jody tried to convince William, who had the most (forty) to give two raisins to the person with the least (thirty-five). She tried to explain, but

William didn't see why he should give away two if nobody else at the table was giving away any. They decided to use the calculator and divide their total by four. When the calculator showed 35.5, they didn't know what to do. After some discussion, they decided to push all the raisins into the center and dole them out one by one.

I returned to Irina's group and asked, "So how many did your group end up getting?"

"We can't figure it out," Breanna said.

"What happened?" I asked.

Irina said, "I don't know," and laughed.

"Do you have a total?" I persisted.

"Yeah, it's one hundred forty-nine," Irina replied.

"What happens next?" I probed.

Marco offered, "First, we're going to try figuring it out. Maybe we should put them all together and then pass them out and see what we get."

"We tried the calculator," Beth explained for her group. "We added all our raisins and got the answer. Then we divided by four, but it didn't work. It's thirty-seven point twenty-five."

The group decided to try Marco's idea. They spent a lot of time arguing over who would draw raisins first from the center pile. The students explained that they wanted to take ten each but couldn't decide who should go first. I suggested that they take raisins simultaneously. Each child took three groups of ten and one group of five. Three raisins were left over. They gave the extras to me. "That will save more argument," Irina said.

Then they worked on writing their solution. The math was not quite right, but the children had persevered with a difficult division problem, in the process discovering something about division, something about the benefits and liabilities of the calculator, and something about group process.

Afton, Ely, Kendall, and Harrison used a calculator successfully to help them divide their raisins. They weren't stumped when the answer appeared as 37.25. They reported that each person would get thirty seven and a quarter, deciding one-fourth raisin is possible mathematically, if not in the real world. "You wouldn't really divide a raisin into quarters," explained Afton, "but you can write one-fourth anyway."

Kirk, Taylor, and Troy constituted a group of three. Once they had added their raisins, they noticed that they could simplify the division by first giving everybody thirty. Then they had twelve left over. At this point, they ran into trouble and said that each person would get two out of the twelve. By now, everyone was eating raisins, and no one noticed that the shares were not equal. (See Figure 12–7.)

When Gib was asked what he thought of this activity, he was enthusiastic. "I got to tell the class what our group did. I reported for our group. And I liked trying to help other people. My partner next to me said he had trouble counting out the raisins, so I helped." Gib grinned. "And in the end I ate my math."

As the math period ended, I decided to introduce the class to one more number sense activity. "How many raisins did we eat today? More than one hundred?"

"Yes!" the children responded.

"More than one thousand?" The children were doubtful. A hum of murmuring spread through the room, but no one volunteered.

"More than a million?" I asked.

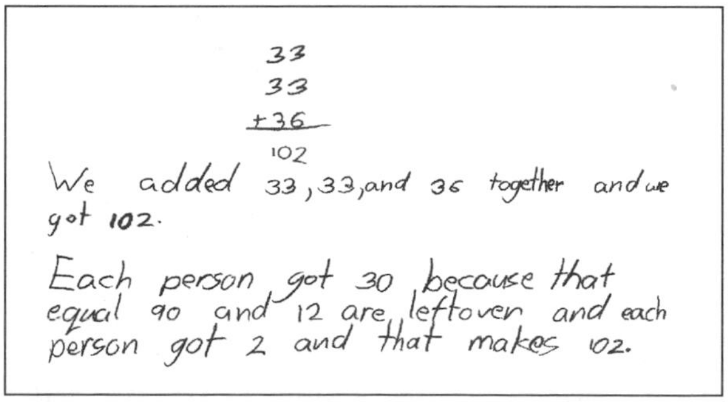

$$\begin{array}{r} 33 \\ 33 \\ +36 \\ \hline 102 \end{array}$$

We added 33, 33, and 36 together and we got 102.

Each person got 30 because that equal 90 and 12 are leftoven and each person got 2 and that makes 02.

▲▲▲▲▲Figure 12–7 *Kirk, Taylor, and Troy didn't notice their mathematical error.*

"Noooo." The children were sure of themselves, certain that a million was too many.

"How many do you suppose we did eat? Does anyone have a guess?"

Troy's guess sounded tentative. "Maybe six hundred ninety-five?"

"I say seven hundred." Cindy was more positive.

"I bet it's one hundred seventy-five," Robby said confidently.

"Let's see," I suggested. "What about for six people? How many would six people get altogether?" Janie used a calculator to multiply 6 by 36 and figured that six children might receive 216 raisins. I wrote this number on the board.

"Do you want to change your guess for thirty children?" No one responded. I suggested that students might use the chart to find out how many raisins the class ate. Robby rushed to the front of the room with a calculator, entered some numbers, and then turned to the group and reported, "It's going to be a very, very high number."

Figure 12–8 shows how one other group divided their raisins.

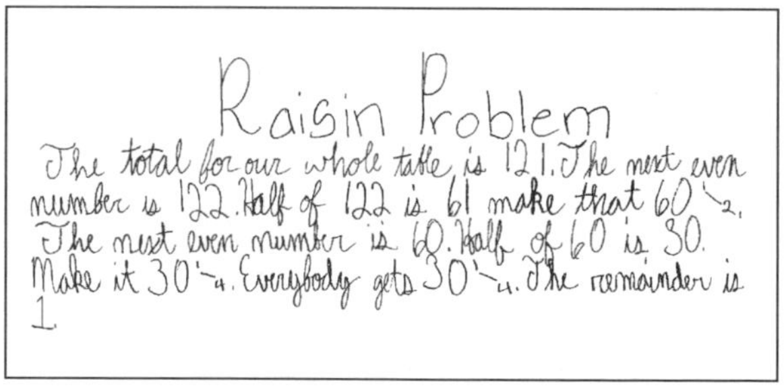
Raisin Problem

The total for our whole table is 121. The next even number is 122. Half of 122 is 61 make that 60 ÷ 2. The next even number is 60. Half of 60 is 30. Make it 30 ÷ 4. Everybody gets 30 ÷ 4. The remainder is 1

Figure 12–8 *Maria, Martin, Annie, and John worked to make sense of the numbers.*

EXTENSIONS

Have students repeat the investigation, only this time give each group of three or four one $1\frac{1}{2}$-ounce box of raisins. Have students begin by estimating the number of raisins in the box without opening it. Encourage them to use what they learned from the first experience to help them make their estimates. Students then individually write their estimates on a sheet of paper. Next, students pore out their raisins, count them, record their total, and explain how they grouped their raisins to be counted. Then, students divide the raisins among the members of group, record how many each received, and how they were divided. (See Figures 12–9 and 12–10.)

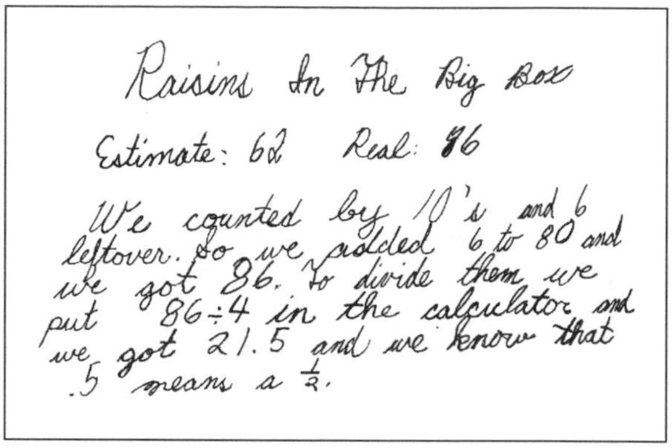
Raisins In The Big Box

Estimate: 62 Real: 86

We counted by 10's and 6 leftover. So we added 6 to 80 and we got 86. To divide them we put 86÷4 in the calculator and we got 21.5 and we know that .5 means a ½.

Figure 12–9 *Derryl, Kirk, Troy, and William explained their understanding that .5 is the same as $\frac{1}{2}$.*

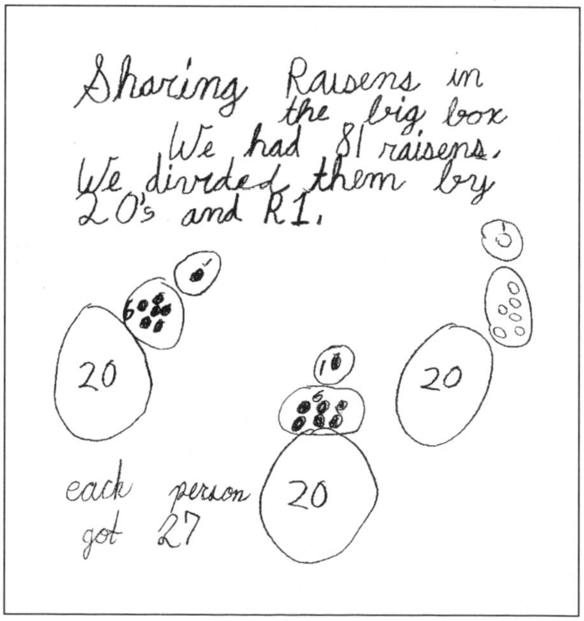

Figure 12–10 *Even though the R1 is incorrect, this paper showed that Robby, Marco, and Cami had divided the raisins correctly.*

Questions and Discussion

▲ *Why didn't you teach the meaning of the word range prior to teaching the lesson?*

While I did explore the range with the students, this wasn't the main focus of this lesson. However, even if it were the main focus, I still would have used the context of the lesson to teach the meaning of the word. Students understand, remember, and use vocabulary when it is taught within a context.

▲ *During the work times, students seemed to argue a lot. Isn't the arguing a waste of instructional time?*

The students did argue at times. For the most part, I allowed them to work through their difficulties, and only when necessary did I intervene with a question or suggestion aimed at moving them forward. Learning to resolve differences is an important life skill. Students can't learn this skill if they aren't given opportunities to work through difficulties. In the cases in this lesson, students worked through their problems, learned about working with others, and successfully interacted with the mathematics.

▲ *It seems students in your class use a calculator whenever they want. Why is this allowed?*

Students are allowed to use calculators to solve problems, just as they are allowed to use paper and pencil and manipulative materials. Calculators are tools that adults use commonly and with which children should have experience. Whenever a child uses a calculator, I require that the child make sense of the answer. There are times when the answer on the calculator makes no sense to the student. When this is the case, the student must find another way to solve the problem that does make sense. Sometimes finding the answer in a different way helps children understand the calculator's answer. Children also discover that they must understand the problem clearly enough to know what to do with the calculator. And, they discover that just because the calculator gives an answer doesn't mean it's the right answer. Children also find that sometimes they can do a calculation more quickly in their head or with paper and pencil.

CHAPTER THIRTEEN
DIVISION STORIES

Overview

This lesson gives children the experience of connecting real-world situations to division equations and also demonstrates the difference between the grouping and sharing model of division. After discussing two word problems, children create their own problems. For each, they write an equation, estimate the answer, and show at least one way to solve the problem. The lesson helps develop children's understanding of division, their number sense, and their ability to compute accurately. Also, the lesson introduces how to use a number line to solve division problems.

Materials

▲ *Division Stories* worksheet (see Blackline Masters)

Time

▲ two class periods; can be repeated

Teaching Directions

1. Begin the lesson by listing the multiples of five from 0 to 50 on the board. Encourage the children to say the numbers with you as you record them on the board. Explain that you are going to give them some problems and they are to think about which of the numbers on the list would be a good estimate for the answers.

2. Before class, write the following problem and the problem in Step 6 on an overhead transparency. Show the first problem, or write it on the board:

Jackie has 24 pails of water to carry to Jill, who is collecting frogs. Jackie can carry 2 pails at one time. How many trips will Jackie need to make?

(**Note:** This problem is an example of the grouping model of division.)

3. Ask children to choose an estimate from the list. Put a tally mark next to each of the choices the students make.

4. Have students talk in pairs about the solution and then have volunteers explain how they solved the problem. As students explain their thinking, record their solutions on the board. Ask students how their estimates relate to the answer.

5. Ask the children how you might write math equations to represent the problem. This may be difficult for children and this is a good time to help them with this skill.

6. Repeat Steps 2 through 5 with the following problem:

Jackie got tired after carrying 2 pails. She sat down to rest. Jill has 24 frogs. The frogs need to be put into pails of water. If Jill divides the frogs equally between the 2 pails, how many frogs will be in each pail?

(**Note:** This problem is an example of the sharing model of division.)

7. Explain the individual assignment. For the division equation $32 \div 4 = \square$, students are to estimate the answer, write a problem that fits the equation, and figure the answer. Remind students that division problems involve equal-size groups and their story problems should indicate this. Distribute the worksheet to students.

Division Stories

Estimate   Equation _____

Problem _____

_____

_____

_____

_____

_____

_____

_____

Figuring

---

8. The next day have students share the different problems they wrote for the equation, their solutions, and their methods of figuring the answer. Point out that many different situations can be represented by the same division equation.

Teaching Notes

Asking students to write stories that represent a division equation provides an opportunity for students to make connections between the symbolism of division and real-world situations. In addition, you can gain insight about what your students understand and can apply to the task, and what areas of their understanding and skill need additional work. Prior to this lesson, students have learned how to represent division situations with three types of equations: $12 \div 2 = 6$, $2\overline{)12}$ with 6 above, $\frac{12}{2} = 6$. This lesson reinforces these representations.

Using the number line as a strategy to solve a division problem was introduced in this lesson. Students found this strategy especially helpful when trying to determine the number of groups rather than the number in each group. For example, consider Jackie's twenty-four pails and the two pails she can carry each trip. A move from 0 to 2 on the number line represents the first trip and the two pails that Jackie carried on that trip. Each "hop" on the number line represents a trip with two pails carried to Jill.

$$24 \div 2 = 12$$
grouping

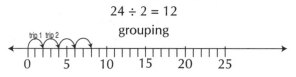

The second problem in which Jill must divide the twenty-four frogs between two pails seems more difficult for children to represent on a number line. Splitting the distance from 0 to 24 into two parts is a challenge for some.

$$24 \div 2 = 12$$
sharing

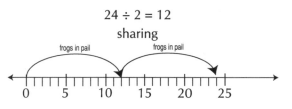

The Lesson

▲▲▲

DAY 1

I began the lesson by listing the multiples of five on the board from 0 to 50. I encouraged the students to count with me as I listed the numbers. I had listed 0, 5, and 10 when Jason interrupted and said, "There's a pattern!" I paused.

"Jason says he sees a pattern," I replied. "Does anyone else see a pattern to the numbers I'm listing?" Many hands went up. "What do you predict I'll write next? Tell me in a whisper voice."

"Fifteen," the students whispered. I added *15* to the list.

"What's next?" I prompted. The students responded with twenty and I added *20* to the list. We continued in this way until we reached fifty. I listed fifty as *> 50* and explained to the children that what I wrote meant "greater than fifty."

0

5

10

15

20

25

30

35

40

45

> 50

I summarized what we did by writing *multiples* on the board and saying, "The numbers we listed are some multiples of five. Listing multiples of five is like counting by fives. Just like we could keep counting by five, we could also continue to list multiples of five, but I think we have enough for now." I paused to give the students a moment to consider what I said.

I continued, "In just a moment, I'm going to share a problem with you. Think about which number on the list would be the best estimate for the answer to the problem." To remind the children what estimate meant, I said, "Remember that when you estimate, you are thinking about a reasonable guess for the answer to the problem. Another way of saying it is, 'The answer is *about*. . . .' " I emphasized "about."

"If I thought the answer was about nine, what's the best number on the list to show my thinking?" I asked.

"Ten," the students chorused.

"What about eighteen?" I asked.

"Twenty," responded most.

Anthony said confidently, "Fifteen!"

I replied, "Hmm, I heard fifteen and I heard twenty. Let's use a number line to check which is closer to eighteen." I drew a number line on the board.

"Where would I mark on the number line to show eighteen?" I called on Jordan, who came to the board and correctly marked 18.

"Oh, I see," Anthony responded. "I can see that eighteen is one closer to twenty than to fifteen." Others nodded their agreement.

Introducing the First Problem

Prior to class I had written two problems on overhead transparencies, and I projected the first one.

Jackie has 24 pails of water to carry to Jill, who is collecting frogs. Jackie can carry 2 pails at one time. How many trips will Jackie need to make?

I gave the students a few moments to quietly read and consider the problem, then asked for a volunteer to read the problem aloud.

I said, "Look at the list of numbers. Think about which number is the best estimate for how many trips Jackie will have to make to carry all the pails to Jill. When I say the number you think is the best estimate, put your hand up. When you raise your hand, I'll make a tally mark next to the number to show that's your estimate." I read the list, beginning with zero. As I did so, the students raised their hands to indicate their estimates. I recorded a tally mark beside the appropriate number for each hand raised. Most of the students indicated an estimate of ten, although a couple thought fifteen and one thought twenty.

I said, "Talk with your partner about what you think the answer is. Also, share with your partner how you solved the problem and why your solution makes sense. I would like for each of you to be sure to have the opportunity to talk. I'll time for thirty seconds while one person talks and the other listens. At the end of thirty seconds, switch roles so the first talker listens and first listener talks. Remember, no interrupting." I timed for thirty seconds, then asked the students to switch roles, timed for another thirty seconds, and then asked for the students' attention.

I said, "Using a whisper voice, tell me what you think the answer is. How many trips will Jackie have to make?"

"Twelve," the students whispered.

"Who would like to share how you solved the problem?" I asked. Hands shot into the air as students were eager to share. I called on Briana.

Briana explained her thinking, "One-half of twenty-four is twelve. It's like a multiplication problem. I thought in my brain, 'Two times something equals twenty-four.' I knew that twelve plus twelve equals twenty-four, so two times twelve must equal twenty-four. Twelve is half of twenty-four."

I recorded Briana's thinking on the board:

$\frac{1}{2}$ of 24 is 12

$2 \times \square = 24$

$12 + 12 = 24$

$2 \times 12 = 24$

$12 = \frac{1}{2}$ of 24

$\square = 12$

"Does this represent your thinking, Briana?" I asked. She nodded.

Mason shared next. "I counted by twos to twenty-four. Two, four, six, eight, ten, twelve, fourteen, sixteen, eighteen, twenty, twenty-two, twenty-four."

As Mason counted by twos, I recorded on the board:

2, 4, 6, 8, 10, 12, 14, 16, 18, 20, 22, 24

"How did you know to count by twos?" I asked. I didn't expect the answer Mason gave.

"It's an even number and it's easy to count by twos," Mason replied.

"How does counting by twos relate to the problem of how many times Jackie will have to carry pails?" I probed. Mason shrugged.

"Let's review the problem to see if we can make sense of what you did," I began. "What are we trying to figure out?"

"How many trips Jackie has to make," Mason responded confidently.

"What else do you know about the problem?" I pushed.

"There are twenty-four pails and she can take two each time. . . ." Mason paused and grinned. "I know where the two comes from! It's how many pails Jackie carries each time." Several students nodded and I agreed with Mason.

"How many trips will Jackie have to make, Mason?" I asked.

Mason began counting by twos in a quiet voice, keeping track of the number of times he counted by two on his fingers. When he reached twenty-four he said, "Twelve. I know because I used all the fingers on both hands then two more. Every time I use all my fingers on both hands, that's like a ten. So one ten and two ones, that's twelve." I was glad I took the time to help Mason make sense of the problem.

"Does Jackie always carry the same number of pails?" I asked. The class nodded. "How do you know?"

"The story says Jackie could carry two pails at a time," Randy said. I wanted to reinforce to the students that the story told them the pails were carried in equal-size groups of two.

To introduce the number line as a tool for solving the problem, I said, "How could we use the number line to show Mason's thinking?" I pointed to the number line I had drawn on the board. I paused to give the students a moment to consider. Several hands went up. When about half the students had a hand up, I called on Anthony.

"You could make hops on the number line by twos," Anthony suggested.

"Come show us," I said, inviting Anthony to come to the board. Beginning with 0, he marked hops of two, finishing at 24. Then he counted each of the hops and announced, "There are twelve hops in twenty-four. That's twelve groups of two."

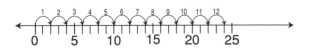

"Put your thumb up if you agree with Anthony, thumb down if you disagree, or sideways if you're not sure," I said. All thumbs were up.

"Does anyone else have a different way to use the number line or a different way to solve the problem?" I asked.

"I think you could circle groups of two on the number line instead of hopping," Ashlyn suggested. Several students nodded.

Dana said, "You could draw the pails and then do what Ashlyn said, circle twos." I drew on the board, starting with pails and changing to squares to save time. Dana came up and circled groups of two.

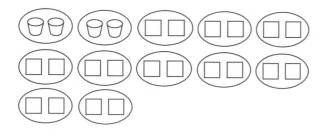

"I agree," I replied. There was one hand still up. I called on Seth.

Seth explained, "I took twenty-four apart. First I thought about the four. I figured half of four is two. Then I did half of two is one."

I wrote on the board:

$\frac{1}{2}$ of 4 = 2

$\frac{1}{2}$ of 2 = 1

"Where did you get the four?" I asked.

"It's in the ones place in twenty-four," Seth said.

"Hmm, if the four is in the ones place, then where did you get the two?" I probed.

"From the tens," Seth said.

"Do you mean 'two' or 'two tens'?" I asked.

"Oh yeah! It's two tens, which is twenty," Seth said. "I knew my idea should work, but it wasn't coming out. I see why now. It should be half of twenty is ten, not half of two is one." I made the correction on the board:

$\frac{1}{2}$ of 4 = 2

$\frac{1}{2}$ of 20 = 10

"Now what, Seth?" I asked.

"Add them up and that's the number of times Jackie has to carry pails," Seth concluded with a sigh. I added the last part to Seth's explanation:

$\frac{1}{2}$ of 4 = 2

$\frac{1}{2}$ of 20 = 10

10 + 2 = 12

There were no more comments.

Writing an Equation

"What division equations can we write for this problem?" I asked. Students were eager to share. I called on Casey, who came to the board and wrote:

12 ÷ 24 = 2

Several hands went up. "I disagree with that," Dana said. I asked Dana to explain. "I think the way Casey wrote it, the answer would be one-half, not two."

Casey's error is a common one. To give Casey a chance to correct herself, I said, "Casey, please read your number sentence aloud." Casey did so, but didn't correct herself. "What do each of the numbers in your number sentence mean?"

Casey looked confused and shrugged. I explained, "Twenty-four tells the number of pails. The two tells how many pails Jackie can carry at once. Your equation says Jackie has twelve pails to carry and she'll carry them twenty-four at a time. This doesn't make sense to me," I replied.

"Oh!" Casey said with surprise. "I see how to do it now. Can I fix how I wrote it?" Casey asked. I nodded and she rewrote the equation correctly.

Eliza came to the board next and wrote:

"I'm not sure about this," Eliza said. "Can I ask someone for help?" She called on Natalie. Natalie came to the board. She and Eliza talked a moment, then Eliza erased what she wrote originally and replaced it with:

$$2)\overline{24}^{\,12}$$

"Show your agreement with your thumb," I said. Most thumbs went up.

"I know another way," Amanda said. "Can I show?" I nodded. Amanda came to the board and wrote:

$\frac{24}{2} = 12$

The students agreed with what Amanda wrote.

Solving a Second Problem

I projected the second problem.

> Jackie got tired after carrying 2 pails. She sat down to rest. Jill has 24 frogs. The frogs need to be put into pails of water. If Jill divides the frogs equally between the 2 pails, how many frogs will be in each pail?

As before, I gave the students a few moments to read and consider the problem quietly, then asked a student to read it aloud. I asked, "What is it we're trying to figure?"

Amelia answered, "We want to know how many frogs will go into each of the two pails that Jackie carried." The students showed their agreement.

"Do the pails have to have the same number of frogs?" I asked. The students nodded. "How do you know?"

"It says, 'if Jill divided the frogs equally,'" Belinda answered. The others nodded.

As before, I asked the students to use the numbers on the list for their estimates and I recorded their estimates using tally marks. The students shared with their partners what they thought the answer was and how they solved the problem. I called the students to order to lead a discussion about how they solved the problem. Dana shared first.

"I divided the frogs into two parts because there were two pails," Dana said. "I know twelve plus twelve is twenty-four. That means twelve frogs per pail."

I wrote:

$12 + 12 = 24$

"I know how you could use a number line," Mason shared. I encouraged him to explain further. He said, "I think it's harder than the first problem, but you have to split the space between zero and twenty-four in two equal parts. Can I show?" I nodded. Mason came to the board and, using the number line from the first problem, he put one index finger on 24 and the other on 0. Then he moved each finger one line toward the middle of 0 and 24. He explained, "I have to find the middle, so if I move my fingers together one line each at a time, they'll meet in the middle." Mason continued to move his fingers as he explained, and they met at 12.

"Oohs" and "ahhs" could be heard from the others as they expressed their appreciation for Mason's thinking.

Eliza shared next. "You could draw two circles and then put a mark in one, then a mark in the other, like that, until you did twenty-four marks."

I drew Eliza's idea on the board.

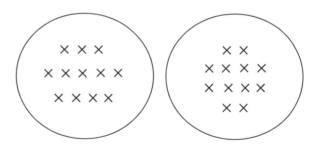

Grant had one last idea. "You could take ten frogs and put them in one pail and ten in the other. That's twenty. If you subtract twenty from twenty-four, that leaves four frogs. Then you put two frogs in each pail. Ten and two is twelve. Two times twelve is twenty-four. So twenty-four divided by two is twelve. It's related!"

I wrote:

$10 + 10 = 20$

$24 - 20 = 4$

$$10 + 2 = 12$$
$$12 \times 2 = 24$$
$$24 \div 2 = 12$$

There were no more comments.

Next I asked the students how to write a division equation for the problem. Grant came to the board and wrote: $24 \div 2 = 12$.

"Hey! That's weird. It's the same equation as the first problem," Dana said.

"That seems strange," Randy added. "In one we had to count how many groups of two and in the other problem we split the total in two."

"Oh yeah!" Briana and Amanda said together. While some students understood what Dana, Randy, Briana, and Amanda noticed, others looked confused. I was pleased about the students who showed understanding that division can have two interpretations and made note of those who looked confused, knowing we would have many other discussions like this during the year.

To finish the discussion, Belinda came to the board and wrote the division equation $\frac{24}{2} = 12$ and Jordan wrote the equation $2\overline{)24}^{\,12}$.

Writing Division Stories

To introduce the writing assignment, I said, "We've explored two story problems. For each, we estimated an answer, wrote a division equation that fit the problem, and showed different ways of figuring the answer." I pointed to the different parts on the board as I explained. Then I projected an overhead transparency of the worksheet the students would use to record their work.

I continued, "Now you're going to write a story problem for the equation 'Thirty-two divided by four equals box.' " I wrote the equation on the appropriate line on the transparency: $32 \div 4 = \square$. "First, when you get your paper, copy the equation. Next, under the word *Estimate*, list the multiples of five from zero to fifty." I stopped to demonstrate this on the transparency. I continued, "Then circle a number that is an estimate of what you think the answer will be. Next, write a story that fits the equation. Remember, division problems involve equal groups and your story problem should indicate equal groups are needed. Then show at least one way to solve your problem." I asked for questions as I handed each student a copy of the worksheet.

"Can we work with a partner?" Natalie asked.

"Not today," I replied. "I'm interested in seeing what each of you thinks and understands. That will help me know how to better help you." My answer seemed to satisfy Natalie and the others. There were no other questions and the students got to work.

Observing the Students

As the students worked, I circulated through the class, answering questions and asking some of my own. I noticed that almost all the students wrote problems involving the sharing strategy. Mason wrote: *There was 32 pumpkins and there where 4 pumpkin pickers how many pumpkins does each pumpkin picker get.* Mason's solution shows four pumpkin pickers with eight pumpkins for each. (See Figure 13–1.)

Anthony wrote about bugs and people who wanted to share them. As Mason did, Anthony drew a picture of his solution and also showed how he could solve the problem numerically. Anthony also revised his estimate after figuring the answer. (See Figure 13-2.)

Like Anthony and Mason, Casey wrote a sharing problem. She wrote: *There were 32 tigers and 4 zoos. How many tigers at each zoo? There 8 tigers at each zoo.* Casey explained her thinking about how to solve $32 \div 4$ and included a revised estimate. (See Figure 13–3.)

Briana called me over, frustrated that

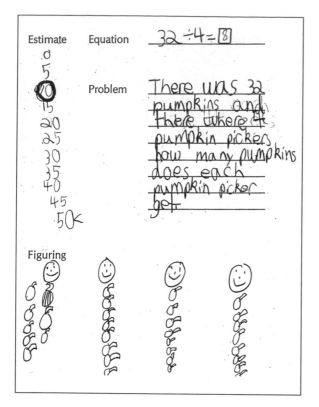

Estimate   Equation $32 \div 4 = \boxed{8}$

Problem   There was 32
pumpkins and
there where 4
pumpkin pickers
how many pumpkins
does each
pumpkin picker
get

Figuring

▲▲▲▲▲▲**Figure 13–1** *Mason later revised his story problem to show equal groups were needed.*

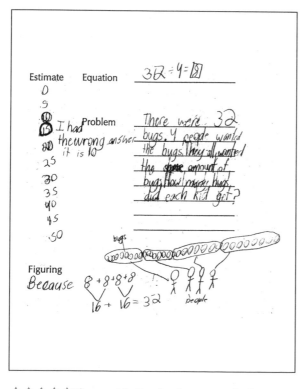

Estimate   Equation $32 \div 4 = \boxed{}$

I had   Problem   There were 32
the wrong answer   bugs. 4 people wanted
it is 10   the bugs. They all wanted
the same amount of
bugs. How many bugs
did each kid get?

Figuring
Because $8 + 8 + 8 + 8$ bugs
$16 + 16 = 32$ people

▲▲▲▲▲▲**Figure 13–2** *Anthony's solution included the use of repeated addition.*

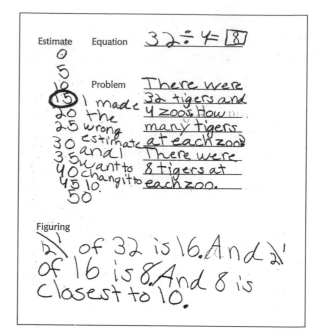

Estimate   Equation $32 \div 4 = \boxed{8}$

Problem   There were
32 tigers and
4 zoos. How
many tigers
at each zoo?
There were
8 tigers at
each zoo.

I made
the
wrong
estimate
and
I want to
changit to
10.

Figuring

$\frac{1}{2}$ of 32 is 16. And $\frac{1}{2}$
of 16 is 8. And 8 is
closest to 10.

▲▲▲▲▲▲**Figure 13–3** *Casey's initial story problem didn't indicate equal groups were necessary. Her problem solution indicated she understood division involves equal groups and her later revision also indicated this understanding.*

she couldn't make sense of her answer and how it related to the number line. She explained, "I made a number line. I hopped across it in fours because the problem says to divide by four. I got eight hops of four. My problem is about thirty-two puppies and four girls. I know each girl gets eight puppies because eight times four is thirty-two." Briana was tenacious in her attempt to make sense of the situation. I paused and thought a moment about how to best help her.

"Let's think about the number line and the puppies," I began. "How does the number line represent the puppies?"

Briana thought a moment then said, "Each mark on the line means one puppy."

"Show me how many puppies on the number line," I said. Briana pointed to the 32. "Your problem says the four girls want to divide the puppies equally. How can you show that on the number line?" Briana looked confused.

"How many groups do you have to divide the puppies into?" I asked.

"Oh, four," Briana said.

"If you have to divide the puppies into four groups, and the number line can represent the puppies, then how many parts do you have to divide the number line into?" I asked.

"Oh, four!" Briana said. To do this, she split the line from 0 to 32 in half first at 16. "That's two equal groups," she said as she worked. Then she split each half into half again at 8 and 24. "That's four equal groups and each of the new groups has two of the groups of four in it!" she observed with surprise, thought about it a moment and then said, "Of course that's right, two fours equals eight!" As a final thought, she drew four stick figures and showed two groups of four going to each. (See Figure 13–4.)

Amanda had a similar problem, but was able to reason through it herself. (See Figure 13–5.)

The students enjoyed the activity. As

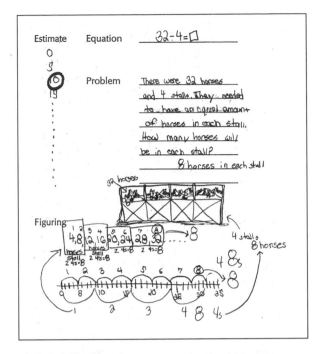

▲▲▲▲▲▲**Figure 13–5** *Amanda drew a picture of horses in their stalls. Her initial story problem indicated equal groups were needed.*

they finished, I checked their work and asked them to show another way to solve the problem. I noted that about half hadn't indicated in their story problems that equal groups were needed. I planned to bring this up as part of the class discussion the following day. I collected their papers for safekeeping and ended the class.

DAY 2

I handed the papers back to the children and asked them to gather at the front of the room. When the students were settled, I began a class discussion to share the problems they'd written the day before and their solutions. Grant had worked very hard on his paper and was proud of how he used both a picture and the number line as ways to solve the problem.

Grant began by reading his paper. "There are thirty-two leaves and four pools. How many leaves fell in each pool? Each pool has eight leaves." I bet the pool owners

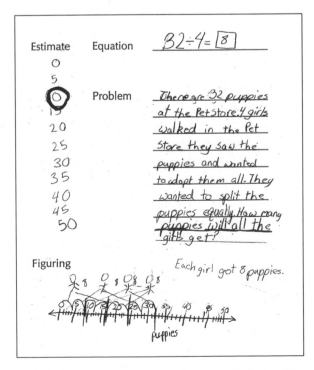

▲▲▲▲▲▲**Figure 13–4** *Briana struggled and eventually figured out how to use a number line to solve her problem.*

were mad because they had to get the leaves out! But to solve the problem, I drew four pools and then put one leaf in each until I had counted thirty-two leaves. Then I did the number line. I knew I had to have four groups on the number line, so I counted by eights. Eight, sixteen, twenty-four, thirty-two." (See Figure 13–6.)

Grant's problem was typical of the students' first division stories in that he didn't specify that the groups had to be equal. While Grant assumed that the same number of leaves were in each pool, he didn't state this in the problem. Because of this, the problem Grant wrote had many possible solutions.

To bring this to the students' attention, after Grant shared his paper, I said, "If I'm figuring out the answer to the division equation, then I know it has to be eight because thirty-two divided by four means that we have to have equal groups. But if

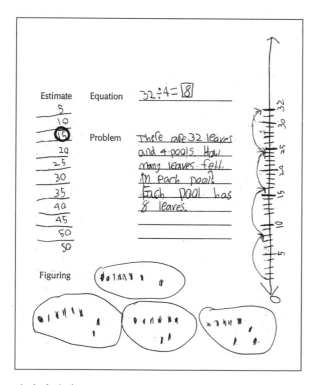

▲▲▲▲▲▲**Figure 13–6** *Grant was proud of the solutions he showed on his paper, but he forgot to indicate in his story problem that each pool should have an equal number of leaves.*

I'm figuring out the answer to the story problem you wrote, then I could answer in other ways as well. For example, I know there are four pools and the thirty-two leaves are in them, but maybe there were twenty leaves in one, ten in another, and one leaf in each of the other two. Your story doesn't say that each pool has the same number of leaves."

Grant reread his problem to himself. "Do I have to change it?"

"Let's do it together as a class," I said. I wrote Grant's problem on the board:

There are thirty-two leaves and four pools. How many leaves fell in each pool?

"Who has an idea about what we can add to Grant's problem so it's clear that he wants us to divide the leaves into four equal groups?" I asked the class.

Briana said, "Write at the end: *Each pool has the same amount of leaves.*"

Seth said, "Or put a sentence in the middle, something like: *The same number of leaves fell in each pool.*"

I recorded both of their suggestions on the board. Because I knew this was a common error in students' first problems, I then had the students share their problems with a partner to check to be sure that they had included the importance of equal groups. I said, "Look at each other's papers and be sure that it really is a division problem. If it's not, see if you can figure out what to add to be sure the problem is about equal groups." Several of the students made revisions. (See Figures 13–7 through 13–9.)

"Can I share next?" Kris asked. "I discovered two things by this assignment." I nodded, not wanting to squelch Kris's pleasure with his discoveries.

"I discovered that multiplication and division really are connected!" Kris exclaimed. "Look right here," he said as he pointed to $4 \times 8 = 32$ and $32 \div 4 = 8$. "Take four times eight equals thirty-two, presto-

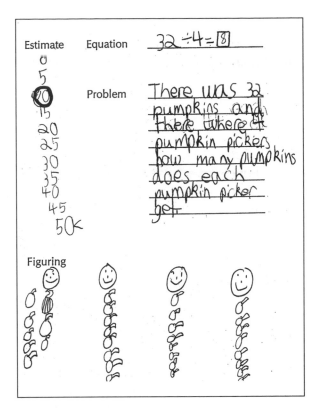

Estimate: 0, 5, (10), 15, 20, 25, 30, 35, 40, 45, 50X

Equation: 32 ÷ 4 = ⬜8

Problem: There was 32 pumpkins and there where 4 pumpkin pickers how many pumpkins does each pumpkin picker get

Figuring

▲▲▲▲▲▲**Figure 13–7** *With the help of his partner, Mason revised his story problem to indicate it was a division problem requiring equal groups.*

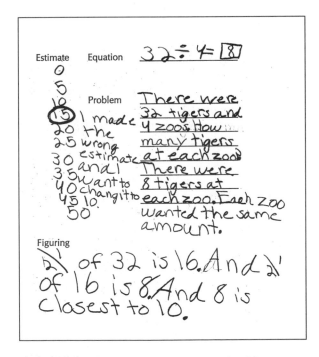

Estimate: 0, 5, 10, (15), 20, 25, 30, 35, 40, 45, 50

Equation: 32 ÷ 4 = ⬜8

Problem: I made the wrong estimate and I want to change it to 10. There were 32 tigers and 4 zoos. How many tigers at each zoo? There were 8 tigers at each zoo. Each zoo wanted the same amount.

Figuring: ½ of 32 is 16. And ½ of 16 is 8. And 8 is closest to 10.

▲▲▲▲▲▲**Figure 13–8** *Casey revised her story problem by adding a sentence indicating the zoos wanted the same amount.*

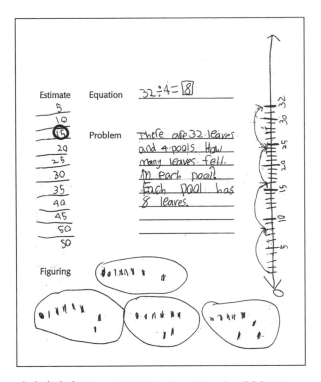

Estimate: 5, 10, (15), 20, 25, 30, 35, 40, 45, 50, 50

Equation: 32 ÷ 4 = ⬜8

Problem: There are 32 leaves and 4 pools. How many leaves fell in each pool? Each pool has 8 leaves.

Figuring

▲▲▲▲▲▲**Figure 13–9** *Grant revised his story problem to indicate equal groups were needed.*

chango, turn it around, and it's thirty-two divided by eight is four. Magic! Except it really isn't. I'm the magician because I know why it works. When I drew my picture I could see how both equations were in the picture! The cookies," he said, pointing to the dots that represented cookies in his picture, "are in eight rows of four, that's four times eight. Or I could think, hmm, there are thirty-two cookies in this picture and they are arranged in eight rows. I wonder how many in each row? I count the number in a row and it's four! Math is magnificent! Then I listened to what Grant said and now I know how to fix my number line. I divided it into eight parts of four when I should have divided it into four parts of eight!" (See Figure 13–10.)

Jamie shared next. "I counted by fours first, drew a line above where I showed my counting, then numbered each time I counted by four and found I had eight fours." Jamie's solution indicated she thought of the problem as a grouping problem rather than

Division Stories   139

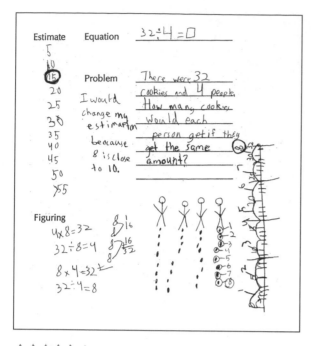

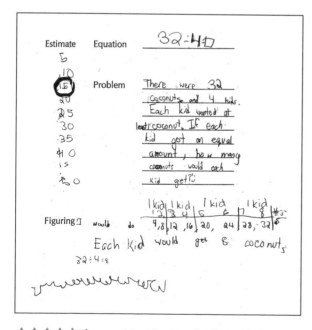

▲▲▲▲▲▲**Figure 13–10** *Kris used two ways to show how to solve 32 ÷ 4 = ☐.*

a sharing problem, as most of the other students did. (See Figure 13–11.)

Dana was the last student to share. "I wrote three equations for how to solve the problem. I also drew four circles and then

▲▲▲▲▲▲**Figure 13–11** *Jamie figured the number of fours in thirty-two, then figured how many coconuts each child received.*

divided up the thirty-two among the circles. Then I drew four people and put eight candy bars under each. It made a rectangle that is eight rows of four." (See Figure 13–12.)

When all who wanted to share had done so, I indicated I was impressed with the variety of division stories they wrote and all the ways they thought to solve them. I ended the lesson by saying, "As you've heard by listening to all the different division stories, there are many situations that can be represented by one equation."

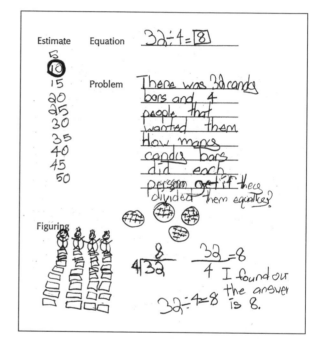

▲▲▲▲▲▲**Figure 13–12** *Dana solved the problem in two ways and showed three ways to symbolically represent the situation.*

EXTENSIONS

Have students choose their own equations and repeat the activity. As students gain experience, the complexity of their problems and solutions will increase. Ask students to write a division story on one side of a sheet of paper and, on the back, solve the problem. Collect the stories and make them into a class book. Also, you may want to choose a different division problem each day for the class to solve together.

Questions and Discussion

▲▲

▲ *What do you do if students present a solution that has an error in it?*

I record what the student reports. Then I turn to the class and ask if the students agree. This encourages all students to check the calculations for errors. If a student notices an error, it is discussed so that all understand. Often the student who made the error finds the error and corrects it without help from the class. Also, I make it a part of the classroom culture that errors are an important part of learning.

▲ *Why do you always probe and push students to explain their thinking?*

When I push students to explain their thinking, they must clarify their understanding. This deepens their learning. Also, just because a student gives a correct answer doesn't mean the student understands. Maybe the student does understand and maybe the student doesn't. Additional questioning can reveal brilliant ways of thinking or it can reveal misconceptions that can be corrected early. Asking students to explain their thinking is a part of the classroom culture. As such, students expect to be asked questions and they understand that questions are not red flags from me that they did something wrong.

CHAPTER FOURTEEN
HUNGRY ANTS

Overview

One Hundred Hungry Ants, written by Elinor J. Pinczes, tells the story of one hundred ants hurrying to sample the food at a nearby picnic. The book adds to children's understanding of division through having them examine rectangular arrays and having them represent them symbolically with division equations. Children work individually to explore how to group other numbers of ants.

Materials

▲ *One Hundred Hungry Ants*, by Elinor J. Pinczes (Boston: Houghton Mifflin, 1993)

Time

▲ one to two class periods

Teaching Directions

1. Read the story aloud to the class.

2. Reread the story or have a class discussion in which the children retell what happened. This time, have children figure out how many ants were in each line whenever the ants regrouped.

3. Show the children how rectangular arrays connect to division by using division symbolism to record how to represent each way the ants regrouped:

$$100 \div 2 = 50 \qquad 2\overline{)100}^{\,50} \qquad \tfrac{100}{2} = 50$$

$$100 \div 4 = 25 \qquad 4\overline{)100}^{\,25} \qquad \tfrac{100}{4} = 25$$

$$100 \div 5 = 20 \qquad 5\overline{)100}\,^{20} \qquad \frac{100}{5} = 20$$

$$100 \div 10 = 10 \qquad 10\overline{)100}\,^{10} \qquad \frac{100}{10} = 10$$

4. Raise the following question: "Why didn't the littlest ant tell the other ants to get into three lines?" Have the children figure out how many ants would be in each line and how many extras there would be. Talking with the children about how they would write the answer gives you another opportunity to talk about representing remainders: $100 \div 3 = 33$ R1.

5. Tell the students they are to work individually on the two parts of the activity: First, students figure out what would happen if twenty ants tried to group themselves into one line, two lines, three lines, and so on up to ten lines. Second, the students choose any other number they'd like and repeat the activity. Having children choose their own numbers gives you an idea of their numerical comfort levels.

6. After all students have had a chance to complete the activity, initiate a class discussion. Ask volunteers to present their work and explain how they figured the answers.

Teaching Notes

In the story *One Hundred Hungry Ants*, by Elinor J. Pinczes, one enterprising ant decides that marching to the picnic single file is too slow. The littlest ant suggests that the ants regroup into two lines of fifty, then into four lines of twenty-five, five lines of twenty, and finally into ten lines of ten. However, by the time the ants arrive at the picnic, all the food is gone. The other ninety-nine ants chase the littlest ant, who quickly turns to go, declaring, "It's not my fault you know!"

In the story, the ants are marching in arrays. Pointing this out to students provides another opportunity for students to make connections between multiplication and division. Arrays are useful for helping students think about multiplication as well as division problems. Consider the following illustration.

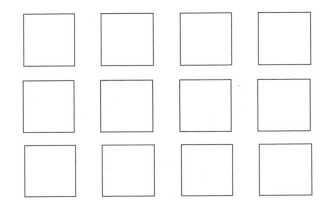

A multiplication problem is *There are three rows of squares with four squares in each row. How many squares are there in all?*

A division problem is *There are twelve squares arranged in three equal rows. How many squares are in each row?*

This lesson gives students experience finding the factors of one hundred as the students consider the various arrangements of the marching ants.

The Lesson

▲▲

I asked the students to sit on the floor where they would be able to see the book I was holding up, *One Hundred Hungry Ants*, by Elinor J. Pinczes. When the children were settled, I began to read the story aloud, showing them the illustrations as we went. The children were fascinated and delighted by the story.

"He's really in trouble now!" Marco said.

"They're going to get him," Cindy said, "but I don't think that's fair. They would've been late anyway."

"They didn't even see the animals taking food!" Robby exclaimed. He had noticed the illustrations of other animals carrying food.

"He's really in big trouble," Marco repeated.

"How did the ants start out?" I asked to focus the children on the rectangular arrays in the story.

"In one line of one hundred," Breanna answered. I wrote on the board:

1 line of 100

"What did the littlest ant do first?" I asked.

"He put them in two lines," William answered.

"There were fifty in each line," Taylor added.

I wrote on the board:

2 lines of 50

Ely raised his hand to report what came next. "Then they went into four lines of twenty-five," he said. I recorded:

4 lines of 25

About a third of the students raised a hand to report what happened next. I called on Annie.

"Next came five lines with . . . ," she faltered and began to count out loud by fives. That didn't seem to help her. "Can I call on somebody to help?" she asked. I nodded and Annie called on Afton.

"It's twenty," Afton said.

"I agree," I confirmed and wrote on the board:

5 lines of 20

"Let's count by twenties to one hundred," I said. The children counted aloud with me as I wrote on the board. "So there are five twenties in one hundred," I said.

I then took the time to draw Xs on the board in five lines of twenty each.

x x x x x x x x x x x x x x x x x x x x

x x x x x x x x x x x x x x x x x x x x

x x x x x x x x x x x x x x x x x x x x

x x x x x x x x x x x x x x x x x x x x

x x x x x x x x x x x x x x x x x x x x

Even though this was time-consuming, I thought it would help children who might be confused. I counted aloud by twenties again, this time pointing to each line of twenty Xs as I counted. Then I said to Annie, "If we count by fives, then you'll get to one hundred also, but you'll have to count each column of ants. Let's try it." As the children counted by fives, I pointed.

"What's the last way the ants reorganized?" I asked. Irina reported and I recorded:

10 lines of 10

"Let me show you how else to record each way the ants lined up," I said, and I recorded on the board:

$100 \div 2 = 50$ $2\overline{)100}^{\,50}$ $\frac{100}{2} = 50$

$100 \div 4 = 25$ $4\overline{)100}^{\,25}$ $\frac{100}{4} = 25$

$100 \div 5 = 20$ $5\overline{)100}^{\,20}$ $\frac{100}{5} = 20$

$100 \div 10 = 10$ $10\overline{)100}^{\,10}$ $\frac{100}{10} = 10$

I then posed a problem. "Why didn't the littlest ant put them into three lines?" Some children raised a hand, immediately knowing that putting the ants in three lines would leave one left over; others, however, didn't know this. "Talk to your neighbor," I said, "and compare what you think."

After a few minutes, I asked the children for their attention. I called on Janie.

"It doesn't work," Janie said. "There would be three lines with thirty-three in each and an extra ant." I wrote on the board:

3 lines of 33 R1

Robby reported what he and Kendall had discussed. "We thought that the extra ant could be like the leader," he said.

"Yeah, it could be the littlest ant," Beth added.

I then introduced a problem to the class. I said, "Now you'll pretend that twenty ants were going to the picnic in one long line. Then figure out what would happen if the ants reorganized into two lines, then three, four, and so on up to ten." I wrote on the board:

20	Hungry Ants
1	line of 20
2	lines
3	lines
4	lines
5	lines
6	lines
7	lines
8	lines
9	lines
10	lines

"Set up your paper as I've shown you on the board," I said. "For some lines, there will be extra ants, so you can record the answer the way I did for one hundred ants in three lines." I pointed to the board where I'd written the answer for one hundred ants in three lines.

I continued, "When you've done this for twenty ants, then do it again, but this time for any number of ants that you choose. Set up your paper the same way, but change the twenty in the title to the number you chose."

There were no questions, so I let the children go to work.

OBSERVING THE CHILDREN

The children worked in different ways. After setting up their papers as I showed on the board, some students worked on the examples in order. Others skipped around, doing what they knew first. Some children drew diagrams to see what happened when the ants got into different numbers of rows; some used materials such as beans or tiles; others figured in their heads or calculated on paper.

Marco was using a calculator. "How does the calculator help you?" I asked him.

"I've got this system," Marco said. "See, I do division, and if I get a weird number, then I do times."

"Show me what you mean," I said. Several other children overheard and gathered around.

"See, with six lines, I pressed twenty divided by six." Marco pushed the buttons and showed me the answer: 3.3333333. "So, I know it doesn't work, but I know they can go in three lines, so I do times, like this." He pressed 3 × 6 and got eighteen. "So there are two extras."

"Neat!" Afton said, appreciating Marco's reasoning.

"I'm going to do that," Ely said.

"I don't get it," Cody complained. "I like to draw better."

Cami came to show me her work in progress. "Look," she said, "I filled in one, two, four, and five. I know those work." She had put a star next to each. Her finished paper showed that she had also found that putting the ants into ten lines came out even.

"How did you figure these out?" I asked.

"You mean the ones I didn't already know?" Cami asked. I nodded.

"I used tiles," she explained. (See Figure 14–1.)

"Our paper's different," Irina said, showing the paper she was working on with Carol. "Is this OK?" In the corner of their paper, they had drawn a picnic tablecloth. They made diagrams, found six ways for the ants to line up, and used multiplication to record them: *1 × 20, 2 × 10, 4 × 5, 20 × 1, 10 × 2, 5 × 4.* Then they wrote: *Here are the ways that the hungry ants can't go to the picnic evenly.* They used division sentences,

such as 20 ÷ 6 = 3 R2, to record them. Even though they hadn't worked individually or set up their paper in the way I had requested, their work was thoughtful and correct. (See Figure 14–2.)

"It's fine," I said. "But when you do the second part, each of you should do your own paper and set it up the way I did."

"OK," the girls said and then returned to their seats. For the second part of the task, Carol used fifteen and Irina chose forty.

The students' choices of numbers for the second part of the activity ranged from ten to eighty. Gabby chose the eighty ants. I noticed that her answers for putting eighty ants in three, six, and seven lines were incorrect. For these numbers, Gabby had recorded:

3 lines of 20 R20

10 lines of 6 R20

7 lines of 10 R10

"Show me how you figured this out," I said to her, pointing to her answer for three lines.

"I know twenty times three is sixty, so that leaves twenty," Gabby answered.

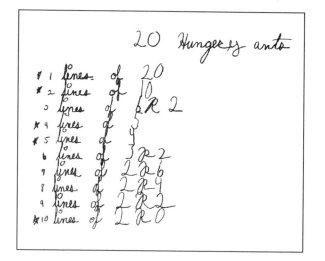

▲▲▲▲▲▲Figure 14–1 *Cami drew stars to indicate lines that had no leftovers.*

▲▲▲▲▲▲Figure 14–2 *Irina and Carol used multiplication and division symbolism to explain their answers.*

"Can you draw a picture of ants in three lines with twenty in each?" I asked.

"Sure," Gabby said, and drew three rows of circles with twenty in each.

"And the extras?" I asked.

"OK," Gabby said, and began to draw twenty more circles.

"Wait a minute," I interrupted her after she had drawn about ten circles. "How come those ants aren't getting in line with the others?"

Gabby was silent for a minute. Then she said, "Oh no, my R number is too many." She went back to work and corrected the answers, making drawings to check herself. At the bottom of her paper, she wrote: *When my R is too many I just make another line.* (See Figure 14–3.)

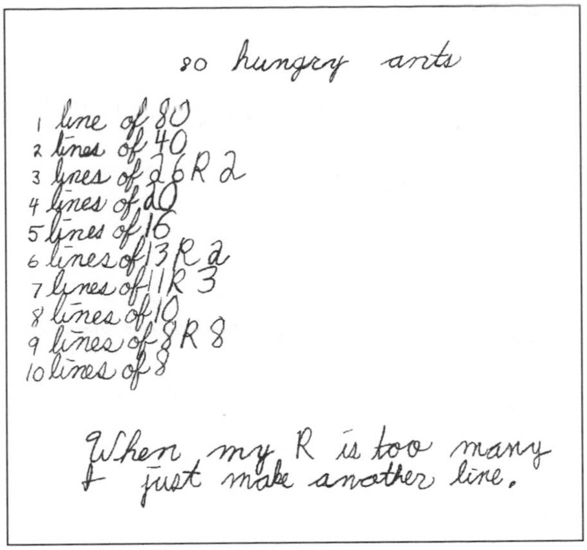

A CLASS DISCUSSION

I initiated a class discussion. First I asked the students to explain how they solved the problem of grouping twenty ants. Next I had volunteers present the work they had done for the second part of the activity.

William explained how he analyzed eighteen. He had carefully drawn a row of

▲▲▲▲▲▲Figure 14–3 *Gabby made a discovery about the size of remainders.*

eighteen ants to illustrate his first answer. "It took too long," he explained, "so I just did circles." (See Figure 14–4.)

"I did eighteen, too," Valerie volunteered next, "but my drawings look different." She showed her work. "And I only drew when I couldn't figure it out in my head," she added. (See Figure 14–5.)

Cindy had chosen forty-two. She showed her paper and explained how she

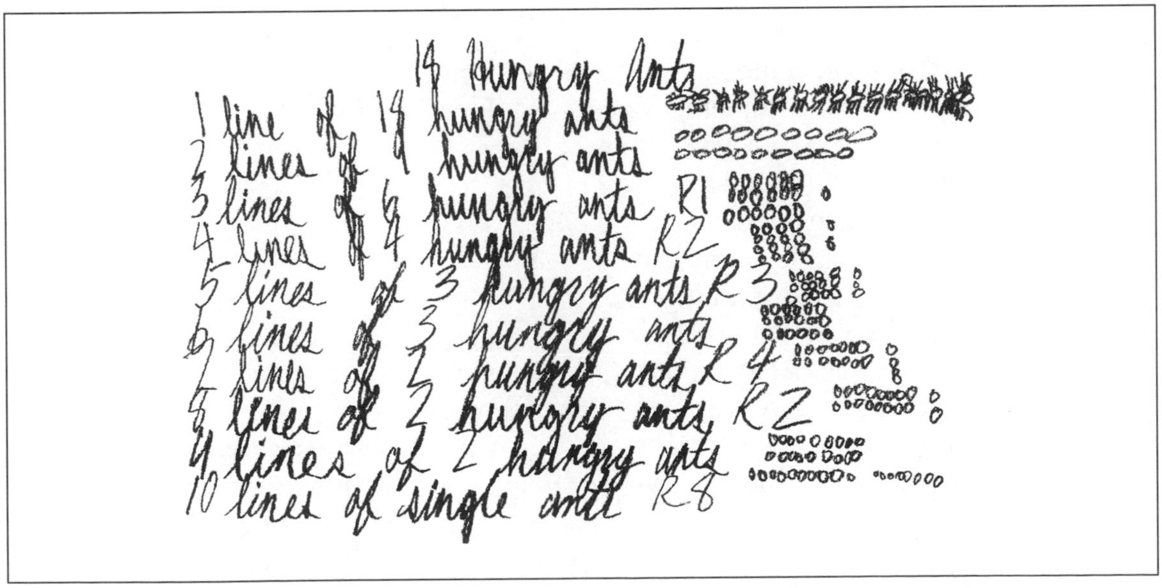

▲▲▲▲▲▲Figure 14–4 *William chose eighteen ants and illustrated each arrangement.*

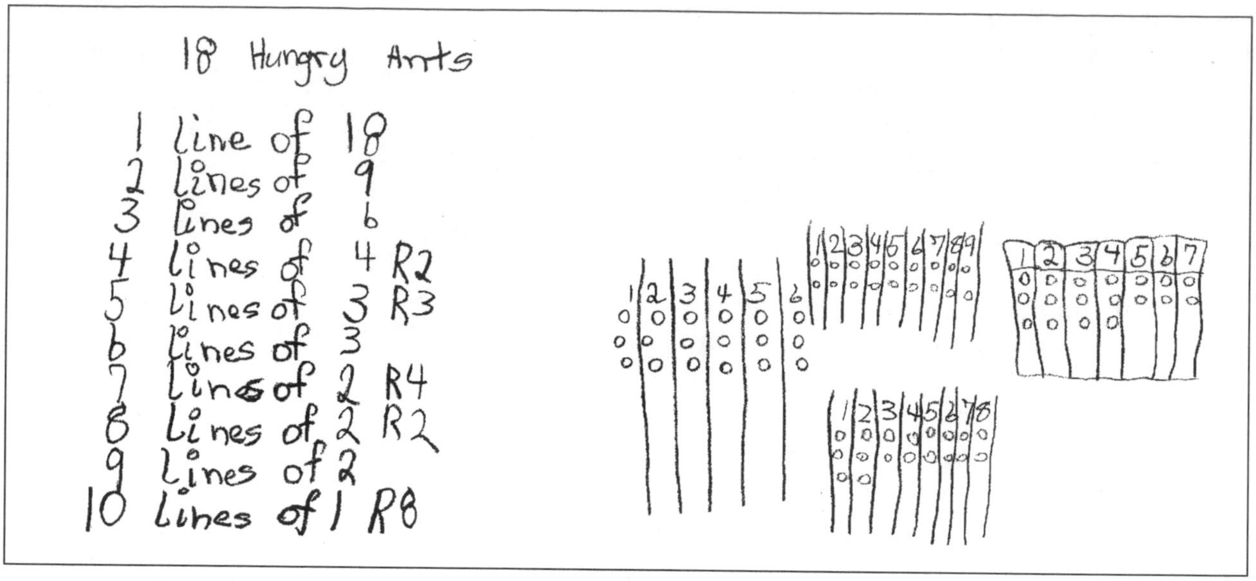

▲▲▲▲▲▲Figure 14–5 *Valerie used diagrams only when she couldn't figure out the answer in her head.*

figured her answers. "I counted up in my head, like five, ten, fifteen, twenty, twenty-five, thirty, thirty-five, forty," she said. She kept track with her fingers as she counted. "When I got to forty, there were two left over, so I knew it was eight remainder two. Sometimes, I wrote the numbers down." (See Figure 14–6.)

Ely had chosen twenty-five and explained that it was easy to do. "I used my basic facts," he said. (See Figure 14–7.)

"I had a hard one to do," Shayna said when it was her turn. "I did seventeen."

"That's not so big," Marco commented.

"But it never came out even," Shayna retorted, "except for one line." The others were interested, and Shayna showed her paper. She was one of only four children who had used this standard method for dividing, and I took the opportunity to show the class how it connected to the problem. I wrote one of Shayna's examples on the board and pointed to each number, explaining how it made sense in the context of ants lining up.

$$3\overline{)17}{}^{5R2}$$
$$\phantom{3\overline{)}}\underline{15}$$
$$\phantom{3\overline{)1}}2$$

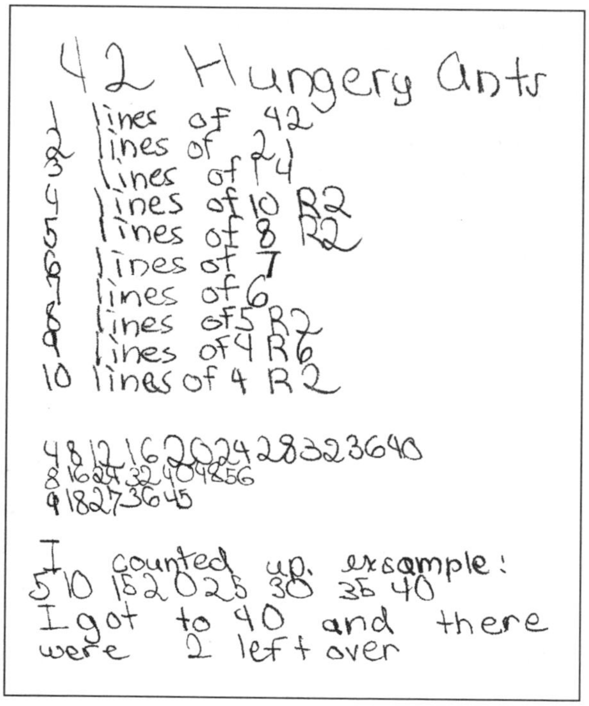

▲▲▲▲▲▲Figure 14–6 *Cindy wrote the multiples for numbers she didn't automatically know.*

"If you divide seventeen ants into three lines," I said, "then there are five ants in each line, and that uses up fifteen ants. If you subtract fifteen from seventeen, you learn that there are two ants left over, so the remainder is two."

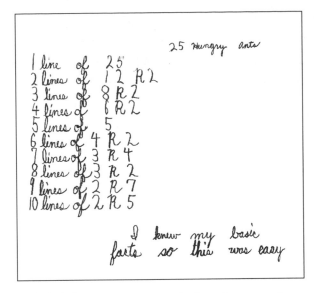

▲▲▲▲▲▲Figure 14–7 *Ely found twenty-five easy to do because he knew the multiplication facts.*

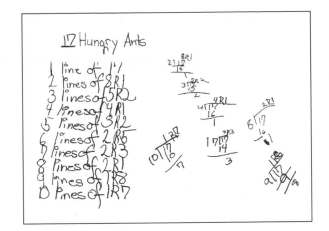

▲▲▲▲▲▲Figure 14–8 *Shayna chose a prime number and had remainders for all but the first answer.*

"Look, they all have remainders," Janie said.

"When a number can't be divided evenly by anything except by one and itself, it's called *prime*," I said. "Did anyone else pick a prime number?" No one else had. (See Figure 14–8.)

"Does anyone have an idea about other numbers that might work like Shayna's did, with all remainders?" I asked.

"Maybe like a million or something," Kareem said. "Something big."

"But one million ants could get into two lines," I said, "with half a million in each." The class was quiet. Some were thinking about my question, but others weren't interested in the challenge. I didn't push it. It seemed like a good time to end the class discussion.

A little while later, Afton came to me. "It would have to be odd," he said.

"What would have to be odd?" I asked, not clear about what Afton was referring to.

"Well, with an even number of ants, they could always go in two lines," he said. He wandered off, still thinking.

Questions and Discussion

▲▲

▲ *Is it really necessary to draw all the Xs for one hundred ants? It took time and I'm not really sure of the advantage. Aren't the illustrations in the book sufficient?*

This visual representation is useful, especially to children who don't see numerical relationships easily. Some of the illustrations in the book show the lines as curved, which can make it more difficult for children to see important relationships. Also, taking the time to draw the Xs gives children think time and a way for all children to think about the meaning of one hundred, a quantity that is large enough to be difficult to grasp.

▲ *There were children who didn't participate in the discussion while others, like Afton, thought about it after the class had gone on to other things. Was the discussion time useful for those who didn't participate?*

It's difficult to know when to push a discussion and when to stop. Generally, if the mathematics is important and if at least half the class is participating, I continue. Even when children aren't sharing ideas, they may still be paying attention and picking up ideas and ways of thinking about the mathematics. Also, as children gain experience with class discussions and recognize that discussions are a part of the classroom culture, more and more children participate on a regular basis, increasing their own learning and confidence.

CHAPTER FIFTEEN
CANDY BOX FAMILY GUIDES

Overview

Working individually or in pairs, students create Candy Box Family Guides to help families decide what size boxes of candy to buy so they can share the candy equally among family members with no leftovers. Creating guides gives students experience thinking about how multiples of numbers relate to division. Some students may explore by focusing on the numbers generated, while other students take a geometric approach and build rectangles.

Materials

▲ chart paper, 1 sheet
▲ centimeter-squared grid paper, 1–2 per student (see Blackline Masters)
▲ optional: 1-inch color tiles, 30–40 per pair of students

Time

▲ two class periods

Teaching Directions

1. Post a chart titled Family Sizes in Our Class and list the numbers from *1* to *10*. (You may have to number further if children have larger families.)

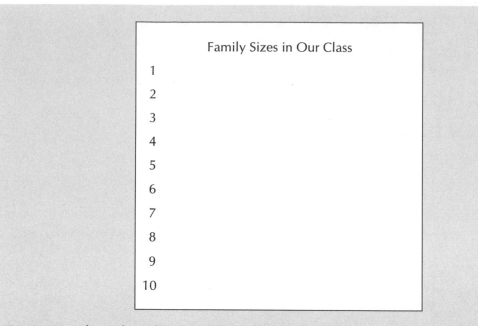

Family Sizes in Our Class

1

2

3

4

5

6

7

8

9

10

2. Have each student draw a tally mark on the chart to indicate the size of his or her family. Define the size of a family as the number of people who live in a student's house.

3. Explain the following: People generally like to buy candy that they can share equally among everyone at their house. For example, if someone buys a box of six candies for a family with five people, there will be one extra candy, and this can cause a squabble.

4. Present the assignment: *Write a guide for families who want to buy candy that they can share equally among all family members. The guide should provide choices for each size family in the class.*

5. Encourage children to make their guides informative and interesting. Children may present the information using numbers, pictures, rectangles, number sentences, or in whatever way makes sense to them and can be understood by others.

6. In a later class discussion, have students report the different numbers of candy possible for each size family and write the numbers on the board. Tell the children that these numbers are "multiples" of the family size and are "divisible" by the number in the family. Rewrite the numbers in ascending order (for example: *Divisible by 4: 4, 8, 12, 16, 20, 24, 28, 32*) and have children add numbers to continue the list.

Teaching Notes

This lesson offers children the opportunity to explore the relationship of multiples to division. This understanding helps children to think about division in terms of how many groups of a certain size, for example five candies, can be made. Children also learn that multiples of a number result with zero as a remainder.

Students generally approach this lesson in one of two ways. Some take a geometric approach and build rectangles to represent candy boxes. They cut them out of centimeter-squared paper to show the sizes of the boxes of candy that would work for a particular size family. The students in the following vignette had previous experience with arranging tiles into rectangles. (See Marilyn Burns's *Teaching Arithmetic: Lessons for Introducing Multiplication, Grade 3*, Math Solutions Publications: 2001.) In addition, the students in the vignette had explored how rectangles relate to both multiplication and division.

Some students approach the activity numerically, by using multiples to count and listing them on their paper. So even if your students haven't had previous experience with rectangular arrays, they will still have access to and benefit from the lesson.

The Lesson

▲▲

DAY 1

I began the lesson by focusing the students' attention on the chart I'd posted before class, titled Family Sizes in Our Class. On the chart I had listed the numbers from 1 to 10. The students talked among themselves about their families. I asked for their attention.

"Does anyone have a family larger than ten?" I asked.

"If I include my cousins and grandma and grandpa I do," Luke said.

"You remind me of an important point, Luke," I replied. "I live with my husband and my daughter, but my son lives in Los Angeles. He no longer lives with us in our house. For today, to figure out the size of your family, count all the people that live at your house. I would say my family has three in it because only three people live in my house. Do your cousins and grandma and grandpa live with you?" I asked Luke.

Luke shook his head, then explained, "Some of my cousins live with me but that's all."

"If you count as your family the people that live at your house, are there more than ten?" I asked. Again Luke shook his head. If

there had been a family with more than ten, I would have extended the numbers on the chart. A note of caution: Discussing families can be a sensitive issue for students, especially those from broken homes or in foster care.

I explained, "In a moment I will ask you to come up by table group and quickly draw a tally mark on the chart to show how many people are in your family. To show my family size, I draw a tally mark by the three." To model for the students, I drew a tally mark by the 3. As a reminder, I drew four tally marks on the board and asked, "How would I mark the fifth tally mark?"

"You make it go sideways," Kayla said.

"That's correct," I said. "When we make the fifth tally mark going sideways, or horizontally, we make groups of five, and it's easier for us to count quickly and accurately."

The students were seated in groups of four. I handed David a marker and said, "I'd like you and your group to come to the chart. Each of you needs to draw your tally mark in the appropriate place, hand the marker to the next person, then go back to your seat." David's group did as instructed. As the last student was drawing a tally mark, I called the next group to the front. In just a few minutes the entire class had marked the chart.

"What do you notice about the information?" I asked.

"The one with the most tally marks is four," Carlos shared.

"We call that the *mode*," I said.

"The smallest family is two and the largest is seven," Kelsey noticed.

"I agree," I responded. "The sizes of our families range from two to seven. There is a range of five." I used the context of the lesson to meaningfully use vocabulary associated with statistics.

"No one has a family of one," Jenny added.

"I don't think a kid could live by himself," Anthony shared. "I'm the only one still alive in my real family, but I live with six other people."

"But an adult could be a family of one," Nicki said.

There were no other comments.

"When people buy candies for their families," I said, "they have to decide how many to buy. One way for them to decide is to choose a number of candies that they can share equally among all the members of their family."

To help the students understand, I gave them several problems to think about. First, I said, "What if there were five people in a family, and someone bought a box with ten candies in it? Could they share them equally?"

"Yes," the children chorused.

"They'd each get two," Catalina added. "Two, four, six, eight, ten." Catalina used her fingers to keep track of the groups of twos as she counted.

"Or you could think of it as two five times and that would be ten," Skip said.

"You could use division," Seth said. "Ten candies is the total. The ten candies have to be divided among five people. So the question is how many candies for

each. The answer is two candies for each person."

"What if the person bought a box with twelve candies for a family of five?" I asked next.

"It wouldn't work," Joaquin said.

"There would be two extras," Jael said.

"The parents could have them," Luke added.

"But kids like candy better," Lindsey offered.

"There might be three kids," Anthony said. "Then there would be trouble."

"So it would be better if people bought the right number of candies so that everyone could have the same amount," I concluded. "How many candies could we buy for a family of five? Talk with your partner about this and see what numbers would work."

After a minute, I asked the children what they thought.

"We thought five or ten," Brenna reported for her and Kelsey.

"I think fifteen works, too," Silas added.

"All the fives would work," Keilani said, "like five, ten, fifteen, twenty, twenty-five, like that. None of those numbers have leftovers."

"So there are many suggestions you could make for a family of five," I said.

I explained the task. "Today, you may work by yourself or with your partner. Your task will be to create a guide for families and give them several choices to help them decide which sizes of boxes would be good ones, so everyone in the family will get the same number of candies. Include all the family sizes on our chart in your guide. Make your guide interesting and informative. Use a different sheet of paper for each family size. When you have finished, put your papers into a book like this," I said as I held up several sheets of paper stapled together in a booklet, "and make a cover. If there is time left, you may add an extra page and solve an extra problem. The extra problem is to see if you can find one size box of candy that would work for families with two, three, four, five, and six people."

"Can we use tiles and grid paper to help us?" Kelsey asked. I nodded.

"Can we do it with numbers?" Seth wanted to know.

"You may do what makes sense to you, but it's important that others can understand your work and know how you thought about the problem," I responded.

There were no more questions. I wrote the following directions and the extra problem on the board as the students got their materials and began working.

1. Create a guide that tells what size boxes of candy to buy so that all family members get the same number of candies. Give several choices. Your guide must be interesting and informative.

2. Use one sheet for each family size.

3. Put your sheets into a booklet.

4. Make a cover.

5. Solve the extra problem: What size box of candies would work for a family of two, three, four, five, and six people?

Observing the Children

As I circulated through the class, I noticed that many of the children used rectangles as a way of displaying their thinking. This is because when studying about multiplication, we had used the context of candy boxes to study rectangular arrays. Jianna's work showed boxes of candy for four. She explained, "I knew a box of four candies would work for a family of four. Each person would get one candy. I used the tiles and made one column of four. Then I made another column of four, counted the tiles, and found out that there were eight tiles. That means eight candies would be shared with four people. That's two candies for each one. Eight divided by four is two. Then I realized I could think in my head, four times what number is eight. The number is two, so I showed it with multiplication, too.

So far I know four, eight, twelve, and sixteen work. I'm going to try twenty next. "

"Why are you going to try twenty?" I asked.

"Because sixteen and four more is twenty. If I just keep counting by fours, the numbers I land on will work for a family of four." Jianna's explanation showed she was developing an understanding of the multiples of four and their relationship to division. (See Figure 15–1.)

Anthony and Carlos took a more commercial approach to their work. They worked on a family guide for families of four. They offered free boxes of candy in a best-for-less campaign. They wrote: *Buy 100 and get two for free.*

Brenna and Lindsey called me over. They were working on a family guide for families of two. Brenna explained, "Lindsey has a cool idea. She wrote 'If you're on a diet, use our two times three box. Having a party? Use our three times six box.'" Brenna's paper offered eleven suggestions for families of two. (See Figure 15–2.)

Other children enjoyed linking the numbers to social realities. Karina and Joclyn designed six possible candy boxes for a family of three, including a 1-by-3 "low-fat" box. Their guide said that the 3-by-2 box was nice for desserts.

Skip and Joaquin, concerned with marketing ploys as they worked on their guide, offered free 4-by-7 boxes to families of four.

I studied their work and then asked, "Who else could get this four-by-seven box without argument? Could a family of two?"

Joaquin carefully counted squares on graph paper and said, "Yes, fourteen pieces each."

"Could a family of three share it?"

"No." Anthony figured the answer in his head, while Joaquin counted squares. "There would be a remainder."

"Six people?" I asked.

Joaquin replied, "Well, six plus six equals twelve, and six more equals eigh-

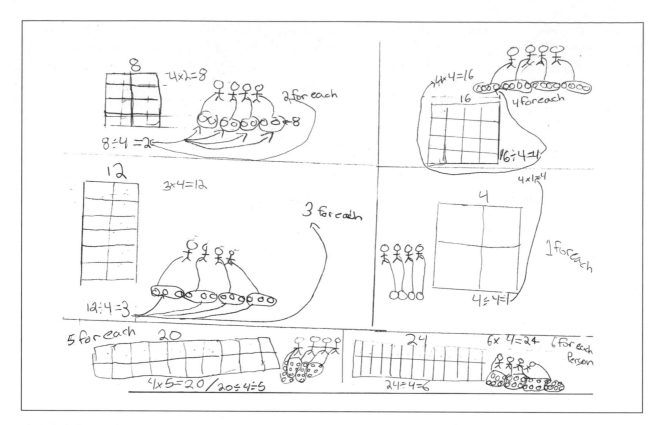

▲▲▲▲▲▲Figure 15–1 *Jianna used rectangles and pictures to show her thinking. She checked her work with multiplication, showing her understanding of the connection between multiplication and division.*

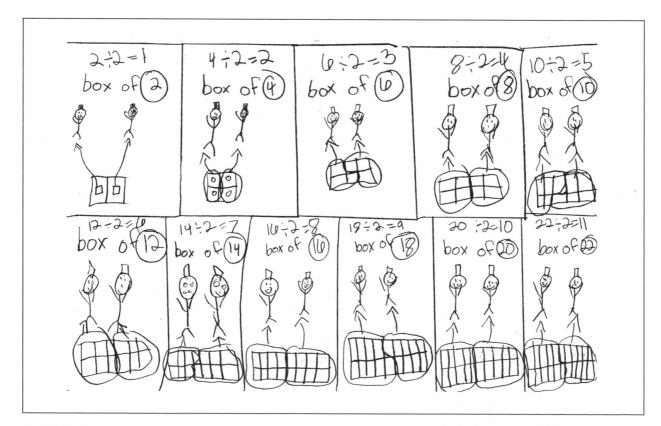

▲▲▲▲▲▲Figure 15–2 *Brenna showed eleven suggestions for candy box sizes for a family of two.*

teen, plus six more is twenty-four, plus six equals thirty." He shook his head. "No, a family of six can't use it."

"So, which size families couldn't share a four-by-seven box?" I asked.

Joaquin and Anthony pondered this and then replied, "Families of three, five, and six couldn't get it."

Kelsey took a different approach than many of the students. Across the bottom of her paper, she listed multiples of four beginning with 4 and ending with 88. Kelsey explained, "I knew for a family of four all I had to do was count by fours to know what size candy boxes would work. The first thing I did was to list those numbers on the bottom of my paper. Then I chose some and checked to make sure." She pointed to the work she had done for sixty-four, fifty-two, sixteen, and thirty-six. (See Figure 15–3.)

When Brenna finished, she raised her hand. "Can I make up my own extra problem?" she asked.

Brenna was a student who always pushed herself to do well. I wanted to encourage her independent thinking and curiosity. I asked, "What did you have in mind?"

"Could I investigate candy boxes that would work for our class?" Brenna wondered. "I counted and we have twenty-two children in the room. I think a box of twenty-two would work and I'd like to figure out what other boxes would work, too." I encouraged Brenna to explore candy boxes for twenty-two people. (See Figure 15–4.)

Jianna was one of seven children who solved the extra problem. Her last page read: *New! buy our new 60 piece candy box! It works for familys of 3, 4, 5, and 6!* (See Figure 15–5.)

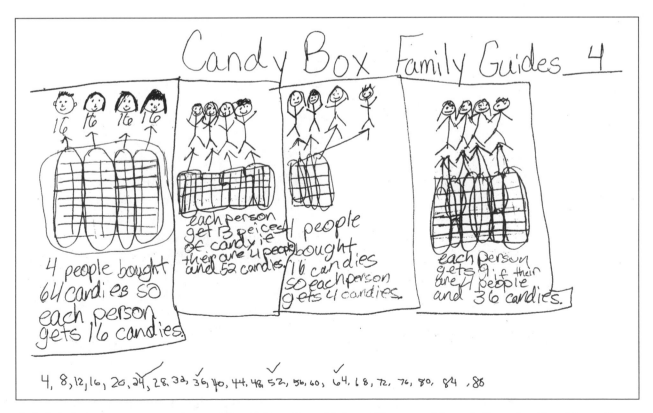

▲▲▲▲▲▲Figure 15–3 *Kelsey realized that all multiples of four would work for a family of four. She listed some multiples across the bottom of her paper and chose a few that were interesting to her to explore.*

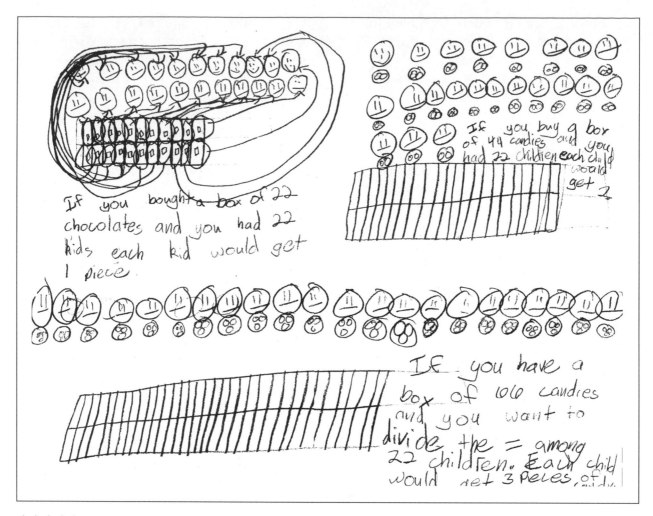

If you bought a box of 22 chocolates and you had 22 kids each kid would get 1 piece.

If you buy a box of 44 candies and you had 22 children each child would get 2

If you have a box of 66 candies and you want to divide the = among 22 children. Each child would get 3 peces of candy.

▲▲▲▲▲▲▲Figure 15–4 *Brenna investigated candy box sizes for the twenty-two students present in class that day.*

DAY 2

I gathered the class for a discussion. I wanted to focus on the mathematics and help the children connect their work to the ideas of multiples and divisibility.

However, Luke was eager to show the class what he had done. Luke held up the guide's cover, on which he had proclaimed: *Delicious and expensive Quality candy. Buy 500 guides, 1 free trip to Bermuda Triangle swim there! No money back guarantee!* The students giggled at the idea of a trip to the Bermuda Triangle, then laughed harder at the idea of being able to swim there for free. They thought the idea of a no-money-back guarantee was uproariously funny. Then Luke wanted to read his price list to the class. He announced that he was selling 1-by-1 candy boxes for one hundred dollars each. The class booed. Then Luke said that a 1-by-3 candy box sold for two hundred dollars. Again, the children booed.

Karina asked, "Who would buy Luke's candy?"

Silas announced, "I'll buy it!"

"Silas is a millionaire," Skip said.

Luke continued to read from his guide: "You touch it, you buy it." (Later, I asked

▲▲▲▲▲▲**Figure 15–5** *Jianna solved the extra problem of a candy box that worked for families of three, four, five, and six.*

Luke to figure out the cost per piece in his two hundred-dollar box. "That's your new job," I said. "Figure out how much each piece of your candy costs. The family needs to know.")

I then asked the children to refer to their guides and report how many candies they recommended for a family of four. I gave them a moment to find the right page and then called on children for their suggestions. "Don't tell your amount if someone else has already offered it," I told them. I wrote children's suggestions on the board as they offered them:

16, 20, 8, 4, 12, 28

"Help me write these numbers in order from smallest to largest," I said, after all children who wanted to had reported. I wrote the list again:

4, 8, 12, 16, 20, 28

"I think there's one number smaller than twenty-eight that would work, but it's missing from the list," I said.

Several students raised a hand. I called on Seth. "It's twenty-four," he said. I added

it, changing the 28 to 24, and then writing *28* again.

"Ooooh, we had that one," Jenny said.

"What would be the next larger size box that would also work?" I asked.

"You keep adding four more," Kayla said, "so it would be . . . let's see . . . thirty-one—no, thirty-two."

"Then comes thirty-six, and then forty," Carlos added. I added these to the list:

4, 8, 12, 16, 20, 24, 28, 32, 36, 40

"These numbers are all multiples of four," I said. "That's why they work. We say that they are divisible by four because when you divide them by four, there aren't any leftovers." I wrote in front of the list:

Divisible by 4: 4, 8, 12, 16, 20, 24, 28, 32, 36, 40

"Let's look at what's possible for families of five," I then said. "What's the smallest size box?"

"Five," several children answered in unison.

"And next?" I asked, knowing that counting by fives was easy for most of the children. I continued writing as children reported:

Divisible by 5: 5, 10, 15, 20, 25, 30, 35, 40, 45, 50

I did the same for twos, knowing that this sequence was also easy for the children:

Divisible by 2: 2, 4, 6, 8, 10, 12, 14, 16, 18, 20

"They're all the even numbers!" Catalina exclaimed, excited by her discovery.

I continued listing the numbers divisible by three and six, and then ended the discussion.

EXTENSION

Give students a candy box size, for example, a box with forty candies. Pose three questions:

1. What size families should buy the box?
2. For each size family, how many candies would each family member get?
3. How many family members could share forty candies if each got two candies? Three? Four? Five?

Change the problem by changing the size of the candy box.

Questions and Discussion

▲▲▲

▲ *You posted a challenge problem on the board, but you let Brenna make up her own problem. Why?*

I posted the challenge problem to give students who were ready a possible idea to explore. However, I allowed Brenna to explore her question because it was of interest to her. When children have an idea that relates to the mathematics at hand, I encourage them to explore their own ideas. They are connecting the mathematics to something of interest to them and use the mathematics as a tool to answer a question they've generated.

▲ *When you use vocabulary words in a lesson, such as* **range** *and* **mode**, *how do you help children remember them?*

Initially, I use the word in context and discuss its meaning as it relates to the activity. I write the word on the board as it's introduced and discussed. After class, the word is added to a vocabulary list that's posted in the room at all times. I often include a picture or key word beside the vocabulary word to help children remember the meaning. During class discussions and writing assignments, children refer to the list frequently.

ASSESSMENTS

Overview

This section contains nine assessments that are useful for evaluating what students are learning as they study division. The first assessment, *What Is Division?*, is helpful for collecting information about students' prior knowledge. Three lessons are linked directly with lessons in the book, making them appropriate to use soon after students experience each of the lessons. *Dividing with Two People* assesses students' understanding of the sharing model of division after they experience the *The Doorbell Rang*. *A Giant's Handful of Pennies* is appropriate after *Pennies and Dimes* and asks students to explain the number of dimes and pennies in a giant's handful of pennies, assessing their understanding of the grouping model of division. *More Division Stories* follows *Division Stories* and gives students another opportunity to write and solve division story problems.

The remaining assessments can be used periodically throughout the students' study of division. In *What Is 20 ÷ 4?* students explain division to an imaginary classmate, revealing how well they understand the basic idea and symbolism of division. *Four Ways to Solve 21 ÷ 4* asks students to solve the same numerical division problem in four different contexts, presenting the problem of looking at remainders in different ways, depending on the context. *Explaining 13 ÷ 4 = 3 R1* is similar to *What Is 20 ÷ 4?* and provides the opportunity to compare student growth using similar problems. In *How Are Division and Multiplication Alike?* students explain their understanding of how division and multiplication relate to each other. The last assessment, *What Is Division? (Revisited)*, is similar to the first assessment, *What Is Division?*, and allows you to examine students' growth in their understanding of division.

Teaching Notes

Assessing children's understanding about what they're learning is an ongoing process. Teachers learn about what students understand from listening to what they say during class discussions, observing and listening as students work on independent activities, conversing with individual students, and reading students' written work. From these observations and interactions, teachers gain insights into their students' thinking and reasoning processes and learn about their students' mathematical interests and abilities. But, not all students contribute to class discussions regularly and during many of the activities, students work with partners. A student's understanding, or lack of it, may not be apparent. Therefore, it's important to assess students periodically on assignments they complete independently and in writing.

Class discussions can play an important role in supporting the writing process for all students. A discussion before writing provides students with ideas to consider and include in their writing. This can be especially helpful when children's learning is new and fragile. Leading a discussion after students write gives them the chance to share their own thinking while considering the ideas of others. These discussions help students become flexible thinkers.

For students, writing assignments provide opportunities to reflect on their learning, solidify their thinking, raise questions, reinforce new ideas, and review older ideas. I typically give students writing assignments at least once per week.

Students sometimes need help knowing what to write. When students ask for help, I begin by asking them to explain what they know about the problem, or I ask questions to spark their thinking. After I listen to students' explanations, I suggest that they begin by writing down the exact words they spoke. Sometimes after students explain their thinking to me, I ask them to send their thoughts back up to their brain and then down again, this time passing their mouth, going down their arm, and out their pencil onto paper. I want students to understand that what they record on paper should represent the thinking they do in their heads.

Typically, division instruction focuses on facts and computation, and assessment is concerned with whether children can "do" division. Teachers test students on their knowledge of division facts and their ability to compute and ask them to solve mostly one-step word problems. The assessments in this section are different.

While it's important that students gain fluency with computation, enabling them to be accurate and efficient, the purpose of these lessons is introductory. Students gain experience with division in several mathematical contexts. These experiences support the development of their conceptual understanding, ultimately leading to accurate, efficient computation. Therefore, these assessments are essentially no different from other activities in this book. Children are asked to solve problems or relate division to real-world situations. Organizing ideas so they can be written down requires thinking and supports the continued learning of students while giving you valuable information about their learning. Individual papers provide valuable information about each child, while a class set provides important insights about the effectiveness of the instruction being provided.

What Is Division?

PROMPT

What is division? What does it mean and what kinds of things can be divided?

Many children have some familiarity with division before they receive formal instruction in the classroom. They have heard about division from parents, from older brothers and sisters, or at day care. Even with prior experience, however, most children do not have a comprehensive understanding of what division is or how to use it.

Begin an initial assessment with a class discussion. Tell the children that you're interested in hearing what they know about division. Hear from all volunteers, accepting their thoughts without judgment or correction. You may want to ask children to clarify their ideas, but don't push too hard. This is not a time to teach but, rather, to collect information about the range of understanding and experience in the class.

After all interested students have responded, ask the students to talk in small groups about what they know about division. Then have them collaborate to write down their ideas about what division means and the kinds of things that can be divided. The students' writing will give you further information about their perceptions.

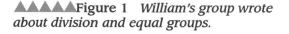

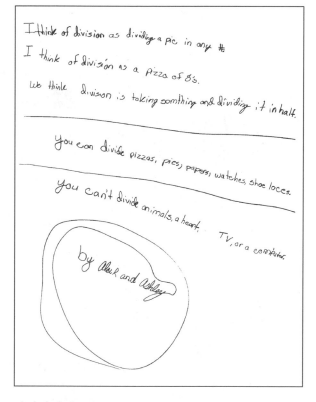

▲▲▲▲▲▲**Figure 1** *William's group wrote about division and equal groups.*

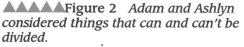

▲▲▲▲▲▲**Figure 2** *Adam and Ashlyn considered things that can and can't be divided.*

Dividing with Two People

PROMPT

1. *Share 25 cents between two people.*
2. *Share 38 balloons between two people.*
3. *Share 5 cookies between two people.*
4. *Share 1 sandwich between two people.*
5. *Share 13 marbles between two people.*

Use words, pictures, and numbers to show your thinking. (See Blackline Masters.)

This assessment provides students the opportunity to show their understanding of the sharing model of division. It's appropriate to use after students have experienced the lesson *The Doorbell Rang.* Students must share equally in each of the above situations and deal with remainders in ways that make sense in the context of each situation.

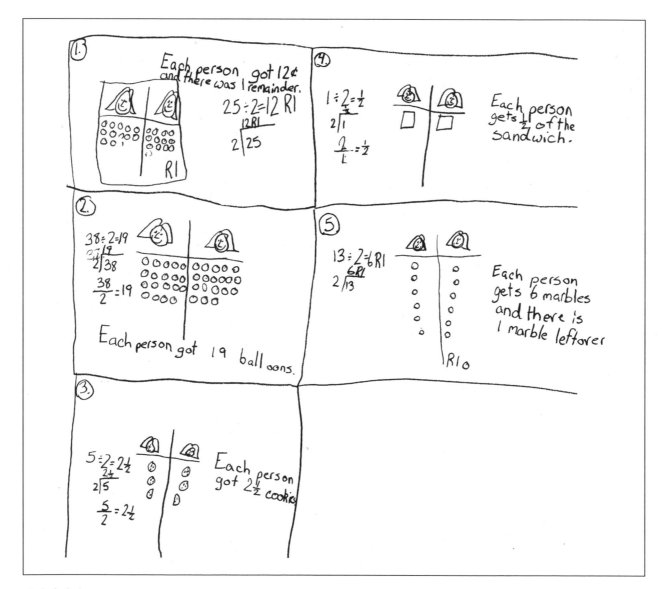

▲▲▲▲▲▲Figure 3   *Briana showed a clear understanding of the concept of division. She incorrectly used fractional notation to show the division of a sandwich between two people.*

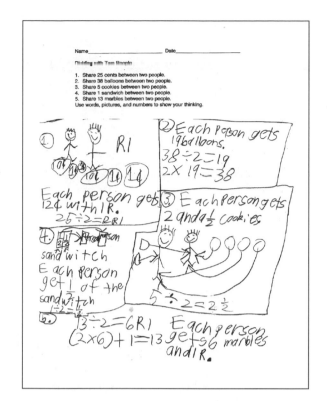

Name_____ Date_____

Dividing with Two People

1. Share 25 cents between two people.
2. Share 38 balloons between two people.
3. Share 5 cookies between two people.
4. Share 1 sandwich between two people.
5. Share 13 marbles between two people.
Use words, pictures, and numbers to show your thinking.

① RI

② Each Person gets 19 balloons.
38÷2=19
2×19=38

Each person gets 12¢ with 1R.
25÷2=12R1

③ Each person gets 2 and a ½ cookies

④ Each person sandwitch
Each person get 1 of the sandwitch
1÷2=1/2

5÷2=2½

⑤ 13÷2=6R1 Each person
(2×6)+1=13 gets 6 marbles and 1 R.

▲▲▲▲▲▲**Figure 4** *Anthony showed strong understanding that division involves equal groups. He used division notation correctly and checked his work on some problems with multiplication.*

Name_____ Date_____

Dividing with Two People

1. Share 25 cents between two people.
2. Share 38 balloons between two people.
3. Share 5 cookies between two people.
4. Share 1 sandwich between two people.
5. Share 13 marbles between two people.

② 12+12=24.
I know that each person would get 19 ballons.

⑩ I know that half of 30 is 15 and half of 8 is 4 so 15+4=19 so is 19.

I know that each person would 25÷2=12 R1 get 12 cents and

④ I know that it is a half becuse two halfs equal 1
1÷2=1/2.
I know that each person will get a half

③ I know that 5 is odd so it will have R1 so if I subtract 1 from 5 it 4 and 4÷2=2. so it will 5 R1
I know that each R1 person will get 2 cookies with R1.

⑤ I know that each person will get 6 Marbles because you can't split 13 so you have R1 marbles. 13÷2=6 R1 so each person gets 6

▲▲▲▲▲▲**Figure 6** *Seth connected his understanding of odd and even numbers and place value to help him solve these problems.*

Name_____ Date_____

Dividing with Two People

1. Share 25 cents between two people.
2. Share 38 balloons between two people.
3. Share 5 cookies between two people.
4. Share 1 sandwich between two people.
5. Share 13 marbles between two people.
Use words, pictures, and numbers to show your thinking.

1. Each person would get 12 cents because 12+12=24 and there is 1 cent remainder.
25÷2=12 R1

2. Each person would get 19 ballons because 19+19 equals exactly 38. So each person would get 19 ballons.
38÷2=19 R0

3. Each person would get 2 and a half cookies because you don't need remainders because you can split a cookie into parts 1/2+1/2=1 and 2 wholes+2 wholes= 4 wholes and 4 wholes+1 whole= 5 wholes.
1÷2=1/2

4. Each person would get a half of the sandwich because 1/2+1/2=1 whole.

5. Each person would get 6 marbles with R1 because 6+6=12 and you have one remainder because you can't split a marble in half.
13÷2=6 R1

▲▲▲▲▲▲**Figure 5** *Jordan's explanation of remainders indicated strong understanding. Jordan relied on addition of equal groups to verify his division.*

A Giant's Handful of Pennies

PROMPT

James the Giant came upon a magic penny pot that allowed him to take one handful of pennies. James reached into the pot and pulled out 137 pennies. The pot told him he could keep the pennies if he could correctly answer two questions:

1. *What is the greatest number of dimes he could get for his pennies?*

2. *How many pennies would be left over after he exchanged his pennies for the greatest number of dimes possible?*

If you were James and wanted to keep the pennies, how would you solve the problem? Use words, pictures, and numbers to help you explain. (See Blackline Masters.)

This assessment examines students' ability to use the grouping model of division to solve a problem. The total number of pennies is known—137 pennies; the group size is 10; and students must figure out the number of groups of 10, or dimes, in 137 pennies.

Ten is a landmark number in our number system. It's important that students understand this idea and develop their ability to apply their understanding to solve division problems. This assessment allows you to monitor their division progress as well as their understanding of ten and its usefulness.

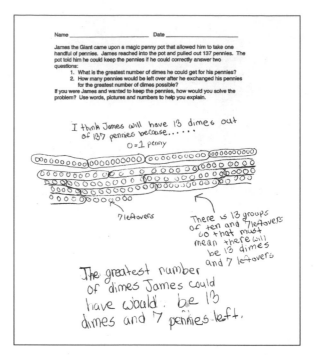

▲▲▲▲▲▲**Figure 7** *Amanda used pictures to help her figure out the number of dimes in 137 pennies.*

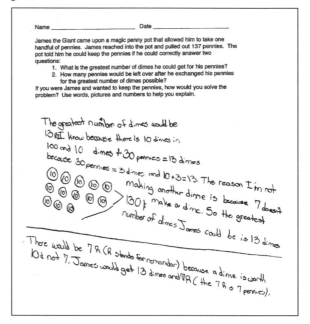

▲▲▲▲▲▲**Figure 8** *Ashlyn's explanation indicated her understanding of remainders.*

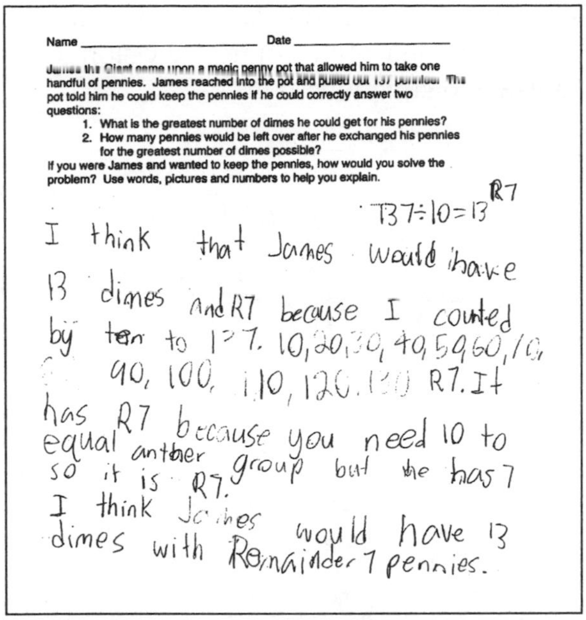

James the Giant came upon a magic penny pot that allowed him to take one handful of pennies. James reached into the pot and pulled out 137 pennies. The pot told him he could keep the pennies if he could correctly answer two questions:

1. What is the greatest number of dimes he could get for his pennies?
2. How many pennies would be left over after he exchanged his pennies for the greatest number of dimes possible?

If you were James and wanted to keep the pennies, how would you solve the problem? Use words, pictures and numbers to help you explain.

$137 \div 10 = 13\ R7$

I think that James would have 13 dimes and R7 because I counted by ten to 137. 10,20,30,40,50,60,70, 90, 100, 110, 120, 130 R7. It has R7 because you need 10 to equal another group but he has 7 so it is R7.
I think James would have 13 dimes with Remainder 7 pennies.

▲▲▲▲▲▲**Figure 9** *Seth counted by tens to find the number of dimes. He also showed why there was a remainder.*

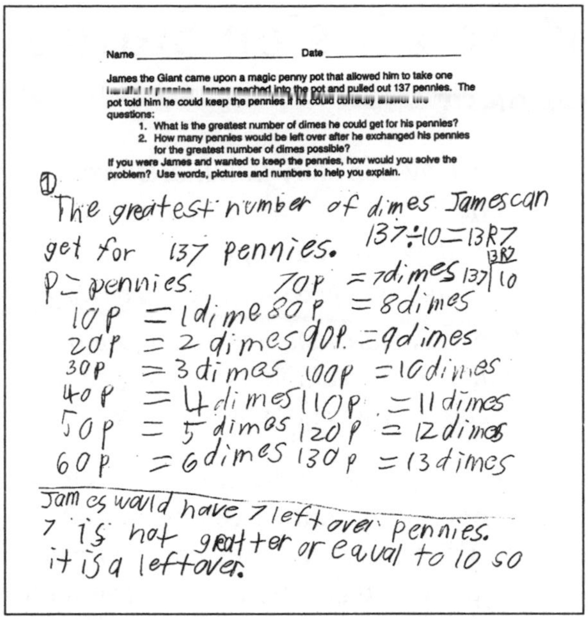

James the Giant came upon a magic penny pot that allowed him to take one handful of pennies. James reached into the pot and pulled out 137 pennies. The pot told him he could keep the pennies if he could correctly answer two questions:

1. What is the greatest number of dimes he could get for his pennies?
2. How many pennies would be left over after he exchanged his pennies for the greatest number of dimes possible?

If you were James and wanted to keep the pennies, how would you solve the problem? Use words, pictures and numbers to help you explain.

① The greatest number of dimes James can get for 137 pennies. $137 \div 10 = 13\ R7$
P = pennies.   70P = 7 dimes   13R2 / 137|10
10 P = 1 dime 80 P = 8 dimes
20 P = 2 dimes 90 P = 9 dimes
30 P = 3 dimes 100P = 10 dimes
40 P = 4 dimes 110 P = 11 dimes
50 P = 5 dimes 120 P = 12 dimes
60 P = 6 dimes 130 P = 13 dimes

James would have 7 leftover pennies. 7 is not greater or equal to 10 so it is a leftover.

▲▲▲▲▲▲**Figure 10** *Anthony made a list to help him figure out the most dimes the giant could get for his pennies.*

More Division Stories

PROMPT

1. Write a division story that meets two conditions:

   a. The story ends with a question.

   b. The question can be answered by dividing.

2. Write a division sentence and figure out the answer. Explain in as many ways as you can how you got your answer.

Having children write division stories tells you if they can describe a situation that involves division and if they can relate division to the world around them. Present this assessment after students have experienced *Division Stories*, learned to use the mathematical symbols for division, and solved problems that connect division to real-world situations.

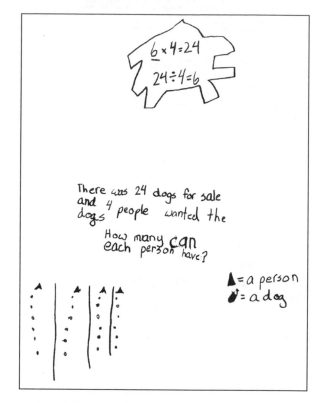

▲▲▲▲▲▲**Figure 13** *Briana's picture showed she understood that division involves equal groups, but her story problem doesn't indicate this understanding.*

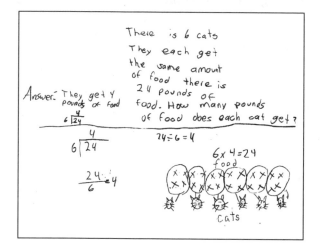

▲▲▲▲▲▲**Figure 11** *Luke wrote a story about cats. His story showed that he understood division is about finding equal groups.*

▲▲▲▲▲▲**Figure 12** *Krystin indicated the importance of equal groups in her story problem.*

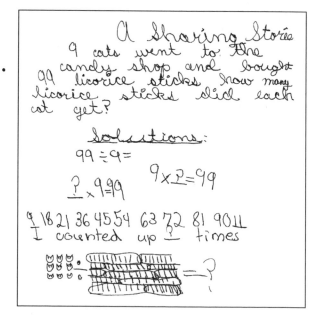

▲▲▲▲▲▲**Figure 14** *Cindy's solution explained her thinking process.*

What Is $20 \div 4$?

PROMPT

What is $20 \div 4$?

1. *What does each part of the equation mean?*
2. *How would you explain $20 \div 4$ to someone who doesn't know about division?*

This assessment checks whether students can interpret the symbolism of division and explain how to find an answer to a division problem. Introduce the assignment by writing on the board: *What is $20 \div 4$?* Tell the children that you'd like them to describe each part of the mathematical symbolism, then explain the problem and how someone could find the answer. Tell them that they can use pictures or diagrams to illustrate their explanations.

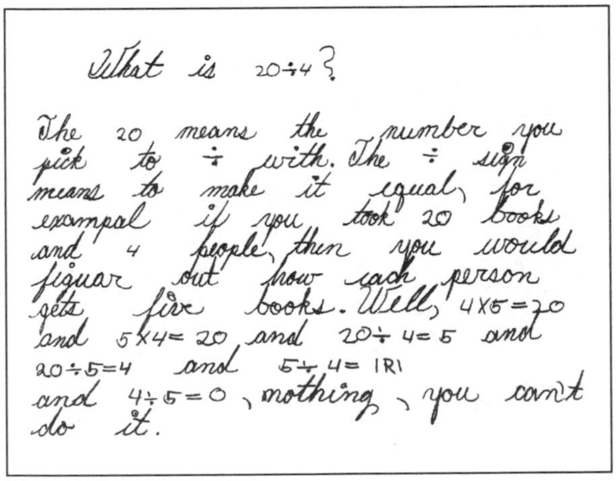
What is 20÷4?

The 20 means the number you pick to ÷ with. The ÷ sign means to make it equal, for exampal if you took 20 books and 4 people, then you would figuar out how each person gets five books. Well, 4x5=20 and 5x4=20 and 20÷4=5 and 20÷5=4 and 5÷4=1R1 and 4÷5=0, nothing, you can't do it.

Figure 15 ***Shayna understood the need for equal groups when dividing.***

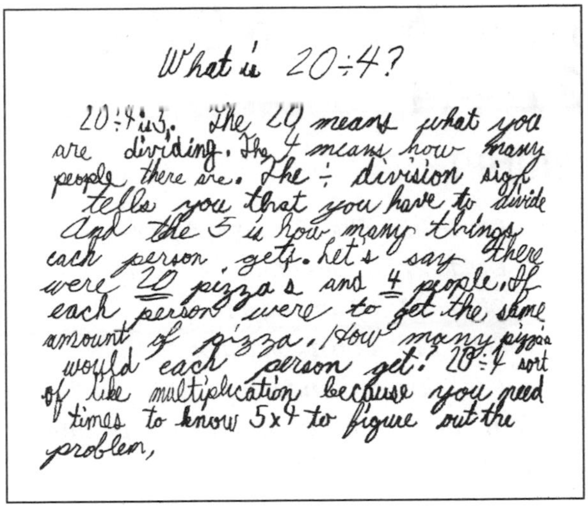
What is 20÷4?

20÷4 is 5. The 20 means what you are dividing. The 4 means how many people there are. The ÷ division sign tells you that you have to divide And the 5 is how many things each person gets. Let's say there were 20 pizza s and 4 people. If each person were to get the same amount of pizza, How many pizza would each person get? 20÷4 sort of like multiplication because you need times to know 5x4 to figure out the problem,

Figure 16 ***Derryl used sharing pizzas to explain $20 \div 4$.***

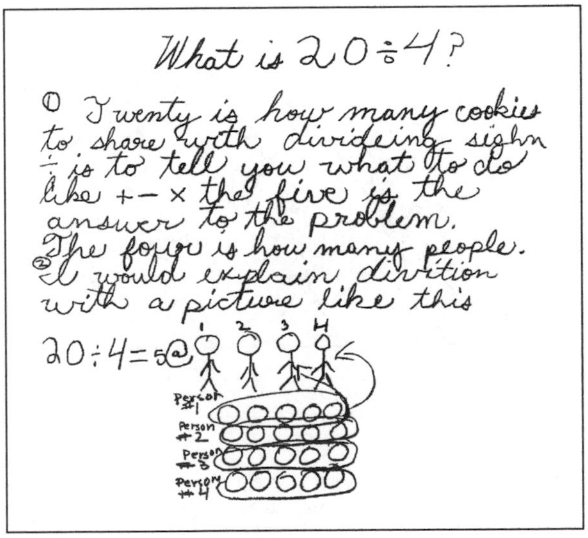
What is 20÷4?

① Twenty is how many cookies to share with divideing sighn ÷ is to tell you what to do like +−x the five is the answer to the problem. The foour is how many people.
② I would explain divition with a picture like this

20÷4=5

Figure 17 ***Maria used sharing cookies to explain $20 \div 4$.***

Four Ways to Solve 21 ÷ 4

PROMPT

1. *Divide 21 balloons among 4 people.*
2. *Divide 21 cookies among 4 people.*
3. *Divide $21.00 among 4 people.*
4. *Solve 21 ÷ 4 on a calculator.*

Write a division sentence that shows each problem and its answer and draw a picture that explains how you figured it out.

Throughout the lessons in this book, children confront division problems with remainders and learn to represent the remainders in ways that relate to the contexts of the situations. In this assessment, children are asked to solve one numerical problem, 21 ÷ 4, in different contexts. In each case, they record their answers symbolically and draw pictures to show how they figured.

To present this assessment, write on the board the numerical problem in two ways:

$$21 \div 4 = 4\overline{)21}$$

Tell the students that they will solve the same problem in four different ways. Write the problems on the board as they appear above. Also, tell the students they are to write a division sentence that shows each problem and its answer and draw a picture that explains how they figured it out.

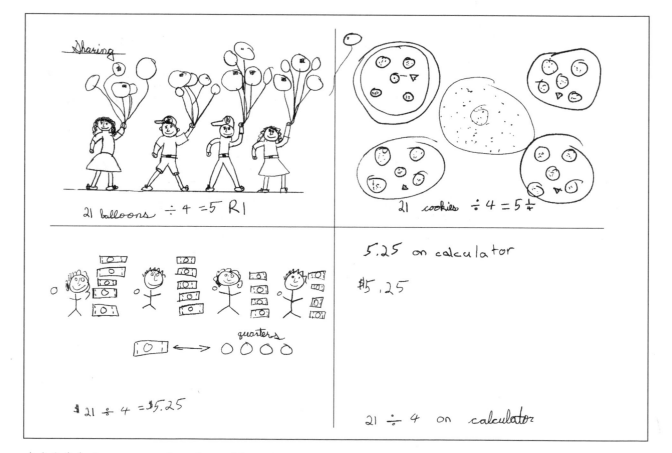

▲▲▲▲▲▲**Figure 18** *Irina showed her ability to represent division problems pictorially and numerically.*

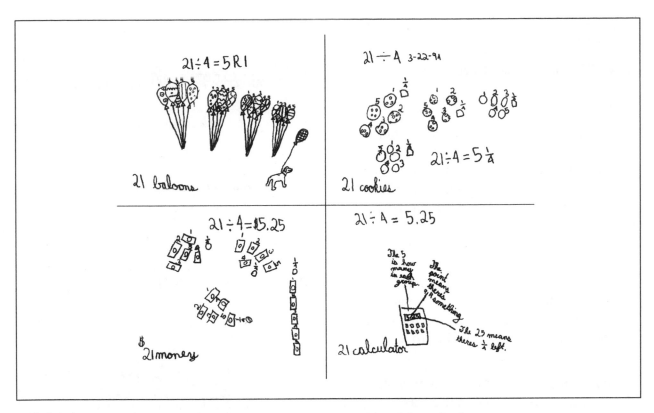

▲▲▲▲▲▲Figure 19   *Cindy was explicit in her interpretation of the calculator answer.*

▲▲▲▲▲▲Figure 20   *Kareem didn't demonstrate an ability to use division notation.*

Explaining
13 ÷ 4 = 3 R1

PROMPT

Imagine that Sammy is a new child in our class who hasn't learned about division yet. Think about how you could help Sammy understand 13 ÷ 4 = 3 R1. What would you tell Sammy to help him? Write about what you might say to help Sammy understand what the problem and the answer mean.

This assessment is similar to *What is 20 ÷ 4?* but asks students to explain a division problem that has a remainder. To introduce the assignment, write on the board:

13 ÷ 4 = 3 R1

Tell the students to imagine a new student, Sammy, has enrolled in the class. He hasn't yet learned about division. Ask the students to think about how they would explain 13 ÷ 4 = 3 R1 to Sammy. (**Note:** Be sure *not* to choose the name of a student in your class.)

Write on the board:

What would you tell Sammy to help him understand what the problem and the answer mean?

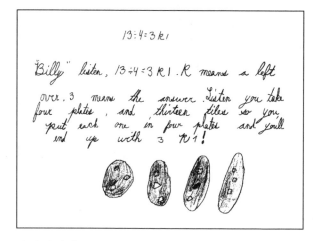

▲▲▲▲▲▲**Figure 21** *Annie referred to the game of* **Leftovers.**

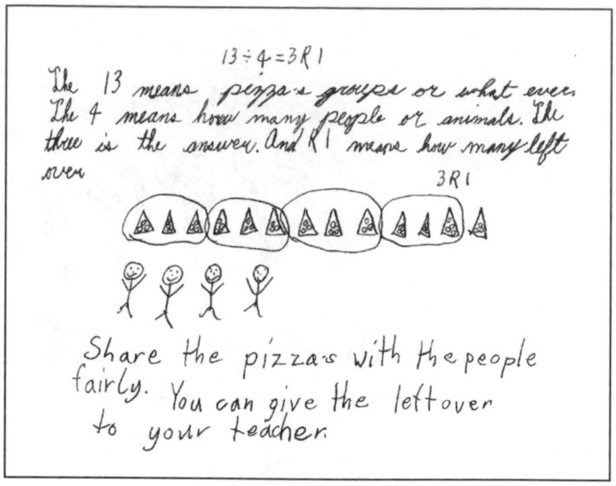

The 13 means pizza's groups or what ever. The 4 means how many people or animals. The three is the answer. And R1 means how many left over.

3 R1

Share the pizzas with the people fairly. You can give the leftover to your teacher.

▲▲▲▲▲**Figure 22** *Janie shared thirteen pizza slices among four people.*

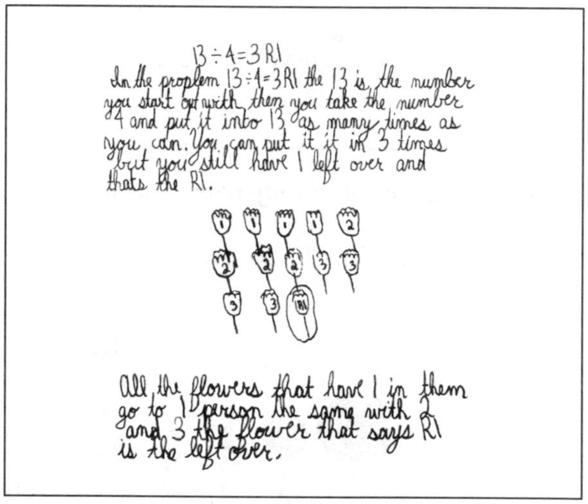

13 ÷ 4 = 3 R1
In the problem 13÷4=3R1 the 13 is the number you start out with, then you take the number 4 and put it into 13 as many times as you can. You can put it it in 3 times but you still have 1 left over and thats the R1.

All the flowers that have 1 in them go to 1 person the same with 2 and 3 the flower that says R1 is the left over.

▲▲▲▲▲**Figure 23** *Beth used flowers to explain how to divide thirteen by four.*

How Are Division and Multiplication Alike?

PROMPT

Someone told Sammy that division and multiplication are alike. Someone else told him that division and multiplication aren't alike. What would you tell Sammy?

The primary focus of this assessment is to find out if children understand how division and multiplication relate to each other. This assessment draws on the same context used for explaining 13 ÷ 4 = 3 R1, in which children explained their understanding to "Sammy," an imaginary student. For this assignment the children again explain what they understand to Sammy. Tell them, "Someone told Sammy that division and multiplication are alike, and someone else told him that division and multiplication aren't alike. Sammy wants to know which statement is true or if both of them are true." Ask the children to write about what they would tell Sammy. (Again, be sure not to choose the name of someone in your class.)

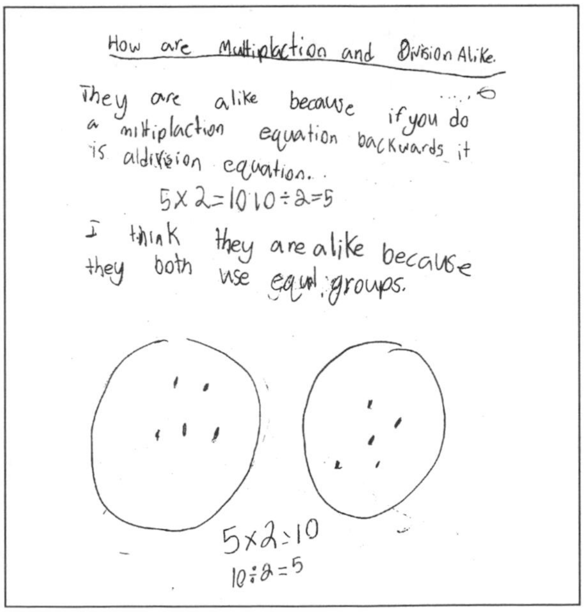

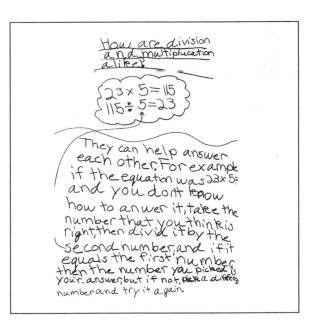

▲▲▲▲▲▲**Figure 25** *Casey was clear in her understanding about how multiplication and division relate to each other.*

▲▲▲▲▲▲**Figure 24** *Seth showed the relationship between 5 × 2 = 10 and 10 ÷ 2 = 5.*

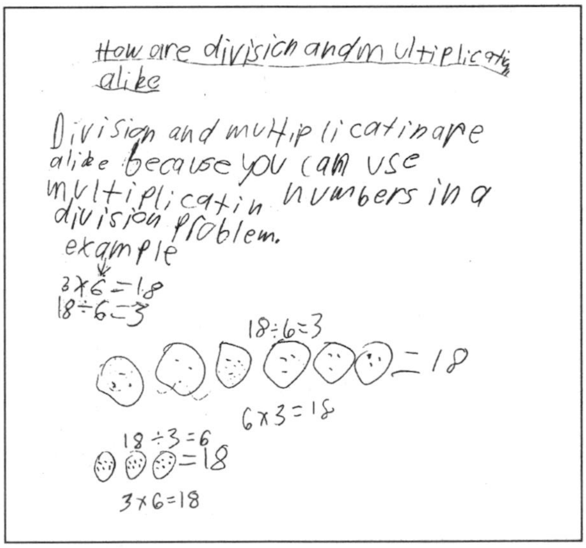

▲▲▲▲▲▲**Figure 26** *Anthony used numbers and pictures to show the relationship between multiplication and division.*

What Is Division? (Revisited)

PROMPT

What is division?

The primary focus of this assessment is not children's numerical proficiency, but their overall understanding of division. What do they understand both about division and the mathematical notation used to represent division situations? Do they understand that division involves equal groups? What is their understanding of remainders? What are their misconceptions? How does their current knowledge differ from when they started their study of division?

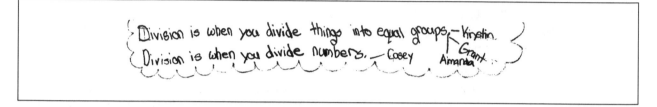

▲▲▲▲▲▲**Figure 27** *Krystin, Grant, Amanda, and Casey shared their prior knowledge of division.*

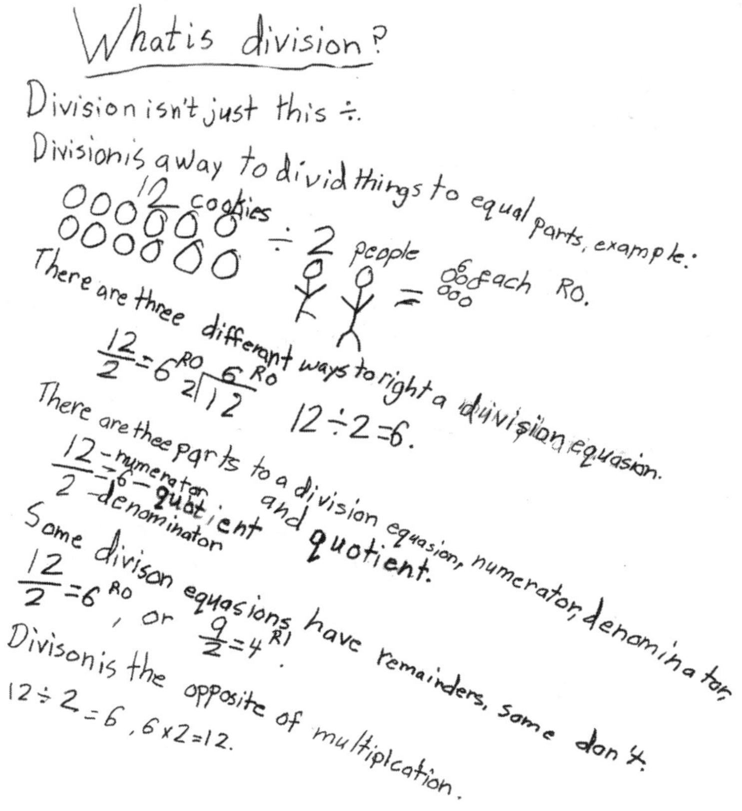

▲▲▲▲▲▲**Figure 28** *Krystin's understanding of division showed growth.*

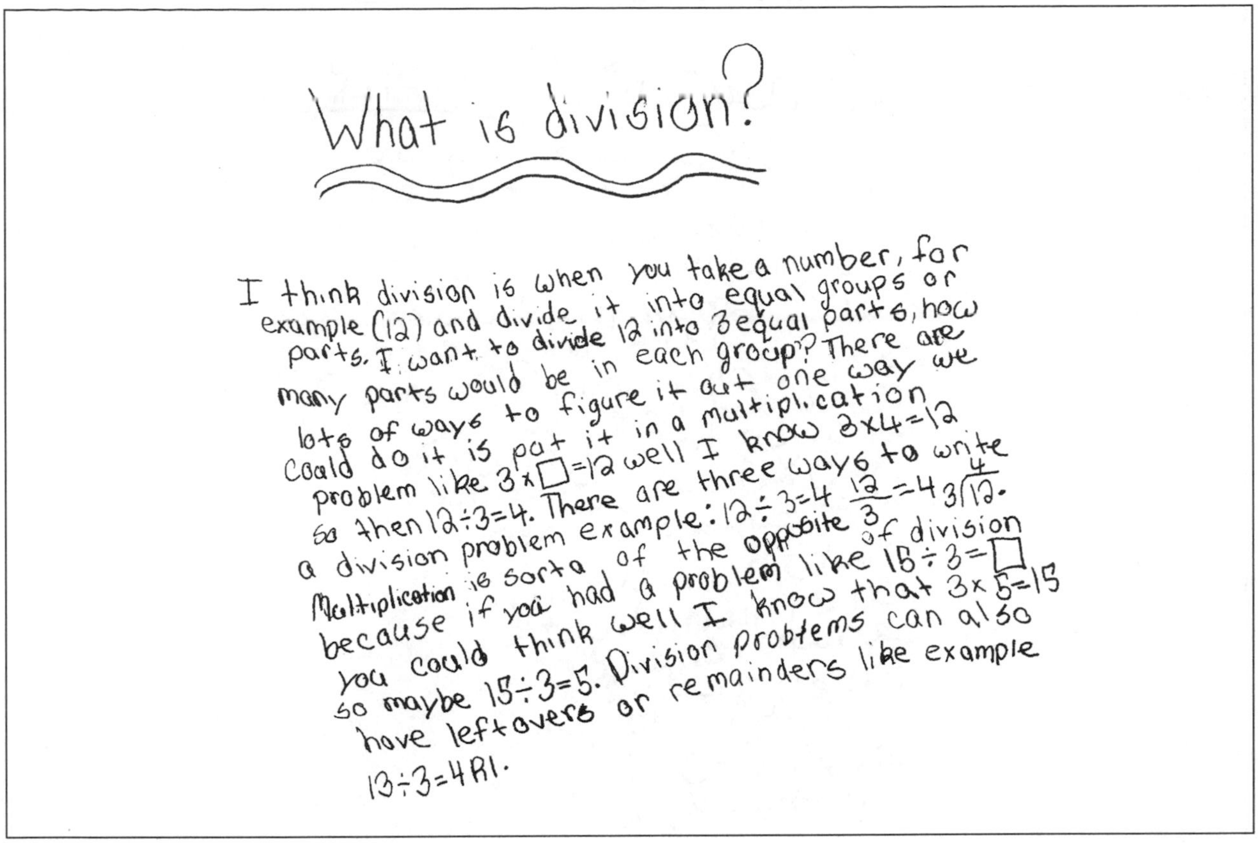

What is division?

I think division is when you take a number, for example (12) and divide it into equal groups or parts. I want to divide 12 into 3 equal parts, how many parts would be in each group? There are lots of ways to figure it out one way we could do it is put it in a multiplication problem like $3 \times \square = 12$ well I know $3 \times 4 = 12$ so then $12 \div 3 = 4$. There are three ways to write a division problem example: $12 \div 3 = 4$ $\frac{12}{3} = 4$ $3\overline{)12}$. Multiplication is sorta of the opposite of division because if you had a problem like $18 \div 3 = \square$ you could think well I know that $3 \times 5 = 15$ so maybe $15 \div 3 = 5$. Division problems can also have leftovers or remainders like example $13 \div 3 = 4R1$.

▲▲▲▲▲▲**Figure 29** *Amanda gave a strong written description of her understanding of division and its relationship to multiplication.*

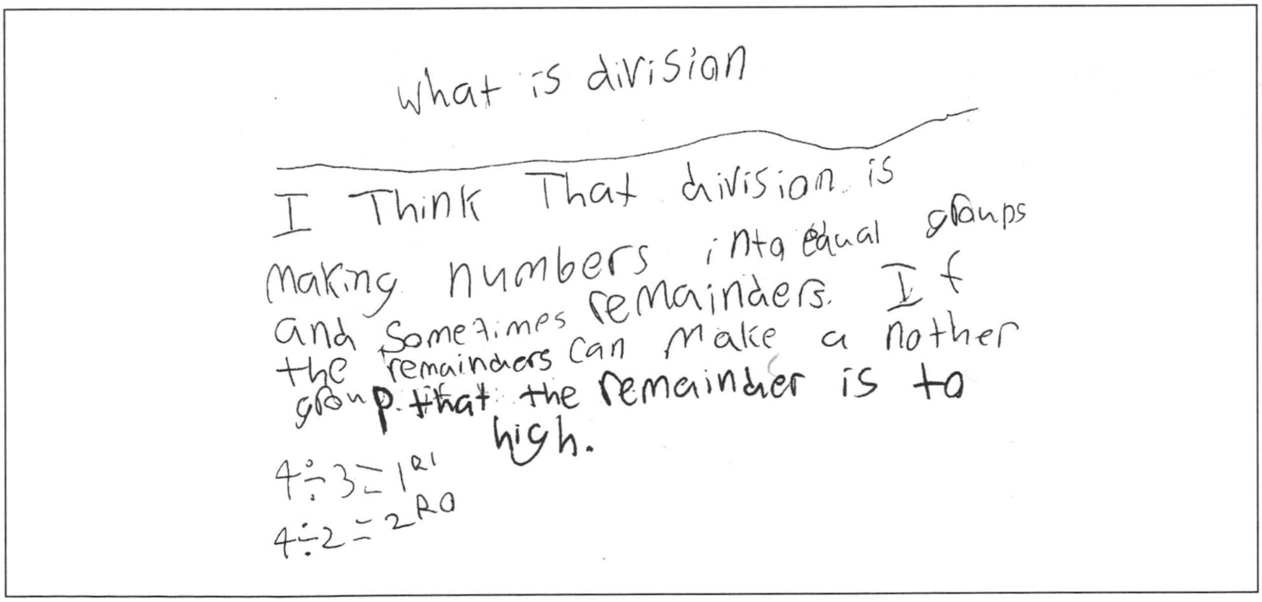

what is division

I Think That division is making numbers into equal groups and sometimes remainders. If the remainders can make a nother group. that the remainder is to high.

$4 \div 3 = 1R1$

$4 \div 2 = 2R0$

▲▲▲▲▲▲**Figure 30** *Grant wrote about his understanding of remainders.*

What is division?

Division is a way of subtraction. There are three different ways of writing a division problem. You can use ÷, /, or ___ to write a division problem. Division is related to multiplication. For example if you didn't know the answer to 9÷3 then try 3×3 and then see if it equals 9. Then that's how division and multiplication can answer each other. How division is subtraction problem is easy. 9÷3=3 and 3 is less than 9. So it's like your subtracting 3 groups of 3 from 9.

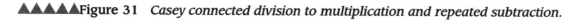Figure 31   *Casey connected division to multiplication and repeated subtraction.*

BLACKLINE MASTERS

Dividing Cookies

Names _____ _____

_____ _____

Share _____ cookies equally among 4 people. Paste each person's share in a box.

How much did each person get?

From *Lessons for Introducing Division, Grades 3–4* by Maryann Wickett, Susan Ohanian, and Marilyn Burns. © 2002 Math Solutions Publications

Cookies

 From *Lessons for Introducing Division, Grades 3–4* by Maryann Wickett, Susan Ohanian, and Marilyn Burns. © 2002 Math Solutions Publications

Leftovers

You need:
    a partner
    1 die
    15 color tiles
    1 cup to hold the tiles
    6 3-inch paper squares ("plates")

1. Take turns. On your turn, roll the die, take that number of paper plates or squares, and divide the tiles among them. Keep any leftover tiles.

2. Both players record the math sentence that describes what happened.

    For example: $15 \div 4 = 3$ R3

    In front of each sentence, write the initial of the person who rolled the die.

3. Return the tiles on the plates to the cup before the next player takes a turn.

From *Lessons for Introducing Division, Grades 3–4* by Maryann Wickett, Susan Ohanian, and Marilyn Burns. © 2002 Math Solutions Publications

Leftovers, continued

4. Play until all the tiles are gone. Then figure your scores by counting how many tiles each of you has. The winner is the player with the most leftovers. Add your scores to make sure that they total the 15 tiles you started with.

5. When you finish a game, look at each of your sentences with a remainder of zero (R0). Write on the class chart each sentence with R0 that isn't already posted.

 From *Lessons for Introducing Division, Grades 3–4* by Maryann Wickett, Susan Ohanian, and Marilyn Burns. © 2002 Math Solutions Publications

Candy Bars

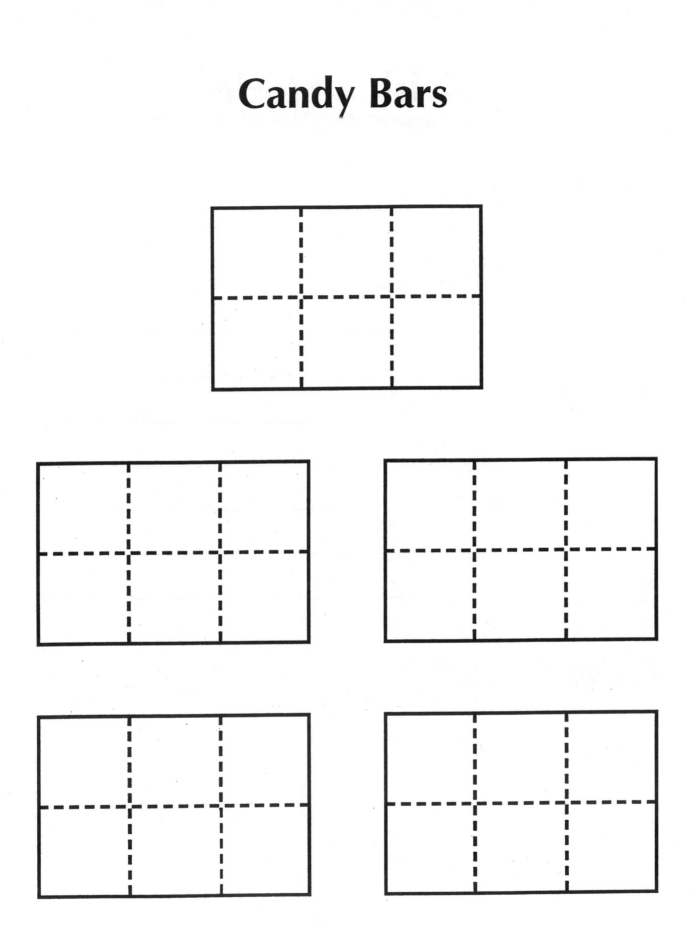

Division Stories

Estimate   Equation   _____

    Problem   _____

_____

_____

_____

_____

_____

_____

Figuring

 From *Lessons for Introducing Division, Grades 3–4* by Maryann Wickett, Susan Ohanian, and Marilyn Burns. © 2002 Math Solutions Publications

From *Lessons for Introducing Division, Grades 3–4* by Maryann Wickett, Susan Ohanian, and Marilyn Burns. © 2002 Math Solutions Publications

Dividing with Two People

Name _____ Date _____

1. Share 25 cents between two people.

2. Share 38 balloons between two people.

3. Share 5 cookies between two people.

4. Share 1 sancwich between two people.

5. Share 13 marbles between two people.

Use words, pictures, and numbers to show your thinking.

From *Lessons for Introducing Division, Grades 3–4* by Maryann Wickett, Susan Ohanian, and Marilyn Burns. © 2002 Math Solutions Publications

A Giant's Handful of Pennies

Name _____ Date _____

James the Giant came upon a magic penny pot that allowed him to take one handful of pennies. James reached into the pot and pulled out 137 pennies. The pot told him he could keep the pennies if he could correctly answer two questions:

1. What is the greatest number of dimes he could get for his pennies?

2. How many pennies would be left over after he exchanged his pennies for the greatest number of dimes possible?

If you were James and wanted to keep the pennies, how would you solve the problem? Use words, pictures, and numbers to help you explain.

From *Lessons for Introducing Division, Grades 3–4* by Maryann Wickett, Susan Ohanian, and Marilyn Burns. © 2002 Math Solutions Publications

INDEX